# Soviet and Post-Soviet Politics and Soc

ISSN 1614-3515

**General Editor:** Andreas Umland,
*Institute for Euro-Atlantic Cooperation, Kyiv,* umland@stanfordalumni.org

Con
Lond

CW00555661

# Soviet and Post-Soviet Politics and Society (SPPS)

ISSN 1614-3515

Founded in 2004 and refereed since 2007, SPPS makes available affordable English-, German-, and Russian-language studies on the history of the countries of the former Soviet bloc from the late Tsarist period to today. It publishes between 5 and 20 volumes per year and focuses on issues in transitions to and from democracy such as economic crisis, identity formation, civil society development, and constitutional reform in CEE and the NIS. SPPS also aims to highlight so far understudied themes in East European studies such as right-wing radicalism, religious life, higher education, or human rights protection. The authors and titles of all previously published volumes are listed at the end of this book. For a full description of the series and reviews of its books, see www.ibidem-verlag.de/red/spps.

**Editorial correspondence & manuscripts** should be sent to: Dr. Andreas Umland, Institute for Euro-Atlantic Cooperation, vul. Volodymyrska 42, off. 21, UA-01030 Kyiv, Ukraine

**Business correspondence & review copy requests** should be sent to: **ibidem** Press, Leuschnerstr. 40, 30457 Hannover, Germany; tel.: +49 511 2622200; fax: +49 511 2622201; spps@ibidem.eu.

**Authors, reviewers, referees, and editors** for (as well as all other persons sympathetic to) SPPS are invited to join its networks at www.facebook.com/group.php?gid=52638198614 www.linkedin.com/groups?about=&gid=103012 www.xing.com/net/spps-ibidem-verlag/

## Recent Volumes

211    *Li Bennich-Björkman, Sergiy Kurbatov (Eds.)*
When the Future Came
The Collapse of the USSR and the Emergence of National Memory in Post-Soviet History Textbooks
ISBN 978-3-8382-1335-4

212    *Olga R. Gulina*
Migration as a (Geo-)Political Challenge in the Post-Soviet Space
Border Regimes, Policy Choices, Visa Agendas
With a foreword by Nils Muižnieks
ISBN 978-3-8382-1338-5

213    *Sanna Turoma, Kaarina Aitamurto, Slobodanka Vladiv-Glover (Eds.)*
Religion, Expression, and Patriotism in Russia
Essays on Post-Soviet Society and the State
ISBN 978-3-8382-1346-0

214    *Vasif Huseynov*
Geopolitical Rivalries in the "Common Neighborhood"
Russia's Conflict with the West, Soft Power, and Neoclassical Realism
With a foreword by Nicholas Ross Smith
ISBN 978-3-8382-1277-7

215    *Mikhail Suslov*
Russia's Ideology of Authenticity
Varieties of Conservatism in Russian History from the Late 19th Century to the Present
With a foreword by Mark Bassin
ISBN 978-3-8382-1361-3

216    *Alexander Etkind, Mikhail Minakov (Eds.)*
Ideology after Union
Political Doctrines, Discourses, and Debates in Post-Soviet Societies
ISBN 978-3-8382-1388-0

218    *Oksana Huss*
How Corruption and Anti-Corruption Policies Sustain Hybrid Regimes
Strategies of Political Domination under Ukraine's Presidents in 1994-2014
With a foreword by Tobias Debiel and Andrea Gawrich
ISBN 978-3-8382-1430-6

219    *Dmitry Travin, Vladimir Gel'man, Otar Marganiya*
The Russian Path
Ideas, Interests, Institutions, Illusions
With a foreword by Vladimir Ryzhkov
ISBN 978-3-8382-1421-4

Dmitry Travin, Vladimir Gel'man, Otar Marganiya

# THE RUSSIAN PATH

Ideas, Interests, Institutions, Illusions

With a foreword by Vladimir Ryzhkov

*ibidem*
Verlag

**Bibliografische Information der Deutschen Nationalbibliothek**

Die Deutsche Nationalbibliothek verzeichnet diese Publikation in der Deutschen Nationalbibliografie; detaillierte bibliografische Daten sind im Internet über http://dnb.d-nb.de abrufbar.

Bibliographic information published by the Deutsche Nationalbibliothek

Die Deutsche Nationalbibliothek lists this publication in the Deutsche Nationalbibliografie; detailed bibliographic data are available in the Internet at http://dnb.d-nb.de.

ISBN-13: 978-3-8382-1421-4

© *ibidem*-Verlag, Stuttgart 2020

Alle Rechte vorbehalten

Printed in the EU

# Contents

# Foreword:
## *The Russian Path –*
## *From Enigma to an Understanding*

As Winston Churchill once stated, "I cannot forecast to you the action of Russia. It is a riddle wrapped in a mystery inside an enigma. But perhaps there is a key. That key is Russian national interest." This statement by a great British politician reflects one of the major global myths about Russia, which asserted Russia's incompatibility with other states and nations and Russia's genetic irrationality and unknowability. Churchill's statement, made in October 1939, was relevant for Stalin's Russia, tightly isolated from the outside world and almost inscrutable to international scholarship and diplomacy at that time. Soviet social sciences, in turn, could do little to achieve a better understanding of state and society in their own country, being hostages of the dogmatic doctrines of Marxism-Leninism. All other schools and approaches were prohibited and systematically suppressed by the Soviet authorities. This is why Communist Russia became an enigma not only for Western observers but also for domestic scholars, who faced censorship and state repressions.

Today, the situation has changed completely when it comes to understanding Russia. The country has become open and the social sciences have been liberated from official state doctrines. The intellectual "Iron Curtain" fell during Gorbachev's perestroika, and Russian social scientists were able to read any books and to choose their own scholarly approaches. Joint seminars and research projects by Russian and international scholars soon became routine, and Russia became an open space not only in terms of the ability to cross its borders in both directions but also in terms of availability of information about politics, economy, and societal processes. For the first time since 1917, new opportunities became available for the study of Russia through contemporary scholarship, making it possible to unwrap Churchill's "enigma", uncover its mystery, and explain to experts and to the mass public what is so special and unique about Russia vis-à-vis global trends and developments.

However, a scholarly understanding of Russia is still a difficult task even in a more open environment. The main obstacles result from numerous myths, which developed and accumulated during Russia's long decades of isolation. Stereotypes stemming from the Cold War are also still alive and inhibit unbiased research. The ideational vacuum that emerged after the collapse of the Soviet utopian project has been filled by old romantic stories from the nineteenth century about Russia's "special path" and reincarnations of "Orthodoxy-autocracy-nationality" reactionary doctrines, fueled by aggressive anti-Westernism and driven by official state propaganda. In addition, many Russian scholars are barely aware of major advancements in the modern social sciences, remain impeded by a language barrier, and are faced with a shortage of funding, as well as with difficulties in everyday life in a depressive society against the general background of unsuccessful reforms.

This is why the efforts and key achievements of Russian scholars who quickly and solidly fit their research into the broader context of international social sciences are so valuable. These scholars become an indispensable and visible part of the international scholarly community of experts on Russia and other post-Communist countries who focus on analyses of their political and economic transitions. These scholars and research centers have, for the first time in many decades, set research on Russia on the solid foundation of modern social sciences, with their rationalism, academic rigor of concepts and argumentations, use of broad empirical evidence, and in-depth theoretical reasoning. With every new book, their studies leave less room to perceive Russia as an "enigma", and open new horizons for understanding Russia as it truly is, with all its contemporary problems and different possibilities for development.

The major hub for research on contemporary Russia emerged in St. Petersburg at the European University at St. Petersburg (EUSP), one of the best non-state academic and educational institutions in present-day Russia. The EUSP brought together a large

8

group of extraordinary scholars whose research is conducted in various fields of the humanities and social sciences. One of the leading EUSP research centers, the Center of Modernization Studies, led by Dmitry Travin and Vladimir Gel'man, alongside center president Otar Marganiya (who is also the dean of the economics department of St. Petersburg State University), prepared this book based on the center's numerous research projects, and addressed it to an international audience.

The authors of this book consistently and convincingly analyze how and why Russia, after three decades of post-Communist transformations, finds itself on a path far from the common European space of free democratic, market, legal and constitutional states. They explain why twenty-first century Russia has experienced the entrenchment of a political regime of electoral authoritarianism and highly corrupt monopolistic state capitalism, an overall politico-economic order of bad governance with a very low quality of institutions, and ruling elites oriented exclusively around preserving their political monopoly and the extraction and redistribution of rents in their own favor. These developments in Russia and in a number of other post-Communist states contradict classical theories of democratic and market transition, and so such tendencies have to be understood and explained from scholarly perspectives. The authors pay very detailed attention to the combination of factors which affect post-Soviet economic, political, and social processes: ideas widespread in Russian society, interests of key elite groups, cultural and historical legacies of Soviet and pre-Soviet Russia, institutions of the late Soviet Union, and Russian citizens' illusions or myths and their effects on public perception. Only such a comprehensive approach, focused on a broad set of factors, allows scholars to explain the consequences of transformation for a large post-Communist region.

The predominance of market-capitalist ideas among reformers who belong to the generation of the "Seventiers" contributed to the orientation of their 1990s reforms around the development of markets and privatization, but not around creation of major democratic institutions and the rule of law. In Russia, against the background of a weak civil society, the dominant post-Soviet interest groups were able to make the reforms serve their private and group interests at the expense of society at large. Elite-driven pressure groups were much stronger than an atomized post-Soviet society, and formed mechanisms of vertically integrated favoritism and systemic corruption based upon state- or quasi-state monopolies. As a result, former Soviet assets have been isolated from strategic foreign investors and come under the control of representatives of the former Soviet nomenklatura. The main negative effect of the legacy of Soviet history on post-Soviet reforms was the lack of legitimacy of private property, which was largely considered unacceptable, in the eyes of Russians. As a result, brutal practices of state control over private businesses, merging of state apparatus and companies, and regular redistribution of market assets by state bureaucrats were perceived by many Russians as a normal and legitimate mechanism of governance. The "power vertical", a mechanism of comprehensive state paternalism, facilitates control and redistribution of wealth, and state officials, business people and ordinary citizens are heavily dependent upon it. Finally, illusions serve as an instrument for preservation of social and political stability under conditions of ubiquitous corruption, ineffectiveness of the state and enormous socio-economic inequality. These widespread mass perceptions enabled Russian citizens to not only close their eyes to the systemic vices of the existing societal order, but also accept and even justify it. In the 2000s, the complex of national-patriotic and imperial perceptions became predominant among these illusions, and reached its peak after the annexation of Crimea in 2014. The imperialist ideas which had been of little importance during the period of the Soviet collapse now became major sources of illusion for frustrated and impoverished Russians after a series of unsuccessful and unpopular reforms.

Bad governance is also a logical outcome of multi-dimensional changes in Russia over the last thirty years. Its major features are the lack (or perversion) of the rule of law, a very high level of corruption, poor quality of state regulations, and low effectiveness of government. Bad governance in Russia emerged as a side effect of a long chain of short-sighted decisions by selfish ruling elites, and closed windows of opportunity for modernizing Russia. However, it provides a stable low-level equilibrium, which cannot be overthrown overnight. The Russian politico-economic order presents a dual nature, which often gives wrong impressions to foreign observers. It preserves all the formal constitutional structures of a "normal" legal and democratic state. However, the "core" of bad governance exists in parallel to these constitutional structures, which is why the latter function more or less as an empty shell: the "core" of bad governance is the real driver of politics and policymaking in Russia. This dual nature of the politico-economic order enables the capture of the Russian state from within by rent-seekers in the state apparatus and their business cronies.

The politico-economic order of bad governance has made systemic reforms of the Russian political system and economic policy practically impossible. Reforms are conducted by the state bureaucracy, which sabotages these reforms or perverts their substance. Some attempts by liberal technocrats to initiate major improvements have faced a regime-driven veto on key policy changes. Even though some changes have brought certain successes, these are often short-lived, do not extend beyond narrow boundaries, and have limited impact on the broader spectrum of socioeconomic issues. In essence, the development of bad governance in Russia has turned into a "vicious circle" of unsuccessful partial reforms, while the country is faced with stagnation and even degradation.

This book by Dmitry Travin, Vladimir Gel'man, and Otar Marganiya convincingly demonstrates many problems for economic and political reforms in post-Communist countries. It clarifies for international readers many issues and processes which took place over recent decades not only in Russia but also in the East European flank of the European Union, ranging from Poland and Hungary to East Germany, as well as in post-Soviet Eurasia. One might find many parallels in these countries with recent developments in Russia.

Are Russia and other post-Communist neighbors doomed to eternal crooked paths within the "vicious circle" of bad governance? Far from it. Several important factors give us hope for Russia moving further towards democracy, rule of law, good governance, and a modern market economy. First, the generational shift will open doors for the Russian youth, who share different values from their parents and grandparents and are more inclined to support ideas of human rights, political pluralism, democracy, and justice. Second is the gradual rise of an autonomous civil society in Russia, which persists despite all attempts by the state to place it under strict control. Third, the worsening of Russia's prospects under conditions of increasing global competitiveness will push the country towards conducting broad rather than narrow modernization programs. Fourth, the politico-economic model of bad governance is weak overall because of its low legitimacy in the eyes of Russian citizens. Over time, all of this can move the balance of forces in Russia in the direction of major changes and systemic economic and political reforms.

If the Russian "enigma" can now be unwrapped by scholars, then we can more clearly understand all the vices and weaknesses of the Russian politico-economic order of bad governance, and thus we can contemplate another future for Russia and other post-Communist countries. Now is the time for action by Russian civil society and responsible and patriotic segments of the Russian elites. Europe, in turn, should also put forth its best possible efforts for the sake of the future. The deep and systemic changes in Russia may forever break the "vicious circle" of lawlessness, corruption, militarism, and ineffectiveness.

**Vladimir Ryzhkov,**
Russian liberal politician, member (1993–2007) and first deputy chair (1996–1999) of the Russian State Duma, professor of the National Research University – Higher School of Economics

Moscow, October 2019

# Introduction

The Russian economy is in a difficult situation. Following a period of rapid economic growth (1999–2007), it entered a deep but brief recession (2008–2009), after which the economy recovered slightly, but was unable to regain its former dynamic. In 2010–2013, the economic growth rate in Russia was significantly lower than in the pre-crisis period, and after a new crisis in 2014–2015, the economy has been growing very slowly.[1] Many analysts do not expect economic growth in Russia to accelerate in the foreseeable future,[2] and are skeptical about the country's further prospects for development.

The ongoing economic problems of Russia are no accident. It cannot be said that they are only linked with the tensions in the international arena since the Russian annexation of Crimea in March 2014. Although the sanctions imposed by Western countries in response to Russia's actions influenced its economic development to a certain degree, they only served as an additional factor, as serious problems in Russia's development had manifested themselves long before this crisis arose. Understanding the causes and mechanisms of these serious problems requires an objective and professional analysis. In our opinion, this analysis should not only concern the economic policy pursued by the Russian government, which deserves only limited attention, but mostly address the fundamental causes and mechanisms, which affect Russia's long-term development within a broad comparative and historical perspective. This analytical framework[3] will make it possible to understand the pattern of economic, political and societal changes in Russia during recent decades without falling into either determin-

---

[1]    For a detailed overview, see Chris Miller, *Putinomics: Power and Money in Resurgent Russia* (Chapel Hill: University of North Carolina Press, 2018).

[2]    See Keith Grane, Shanthi Natharaj, Patrick B. Johnston, Gursel Rafig oglu Aliyev, *Russia's Mid-Term Economic Prospects* (Santa Monica, CA: Rand Corporation, 2016); Marek Dabrowski, Antoine Mathieu Collin, 'Russia's Growth Problem', *Bruegel Policy Contribution*, N 4 (February 2019).

[3]    See Yegor Gaidar, *Russia: A Long View* (Cambridge, MA: MIT Press, 2012).

ism, as manifested by some scholars,[4] or voluntarism, which is widespread among numerous journalistic publications and many political analysts.

In scholarly literature as well as Russian public opinion, there are two extreme approaches, which do not take into account the complexity of modern-day Russia's transformation, a fact that reflects long-term modernization controversies. On the one hand, the dominant opinion among many observers is based on the assumption that the economic reforms and the process of market transition were intentionally carried out ineffectively, giving rise to a considerable decline in economic output, impoverishment of the Russian population, institutional distortions and, ultimately, the problems connected with Russia's long-term development.[5] On the other hand, in recent years the focus of criticism of Russia's transformation has shifted from discussing the troubles of the Russian economy (which was at the center of discussions of the 1990s) to the current authoritarian political regime, the lack of political and economic freedoms, and the destructive foreign policy.[6] Whatever the causes of Russia's ongoing problems, most critics argue that its negative economic and political tendencies will inevitably lead to the complete collapse of the economic system and to a large-scale political crisis.

Both of these views on the problems of Russia's transformation seem to be one-sided and excessively politicized. Naturally, one cannot deny that many serious issues went unresolved in

---

[4]  See Stefan Hedlund, *Russian Path Dependence: A People with a Troubled History* (London: Routledge, 2005).

[5]  See Peter Reddaway, Dmitry Glinsky, *The Tragedy of Russia's Reforms: Market Bolshevism against Democracy* (Washington, DC: United States Institute of Peace, 2001); *The New Russia: Transition Gone Awry*, Lawrence R. Klein, Marshall Pomer (eds.) (Stanford: Stanford University Press, 2001).

[6]  See Sergey Aleksashenko, *Putin's Counterrevolution* (Washington, DC: Brookings Institution Press, 2018); Anders Åslund, *Russia's Crony Capitalism: The Path from Market Economy to Kleptocracy* (New Haven: Yale University Press, 2019).

the wake of the complex and contradictory reforms of the 1990s.[7] Nor can one deny that many features of the current Russian political regime[8] have a strong negative impact on the investment climate, and give rise to numerous problems, which were not observed in Russia in the early 2000s, when the country had overcome the consequences of the transformational recession. However, both of these extreme views often do not serve the goals of an objective scholarly analysis, but act as means of opposing political leaders and their policies – namely, Boris Yeltsin and Yegor Gaidar in the first case, and Vladimir Putin and Dmitry Medvedev in the second. These opposing views are also shared by certain segments of the Russian public. Many Russian citizens whose standards of living fell drastically in the 1990s do not accept the complex nature of the troubles which the country faced in that period, and believe that Yeltsin and Gaidar did everything wrong. And many Russian citizens who would like to see true democratization of the country often believe that all the socio-economic problems of modern Russia are caused solely by Putin's authoritarian aspirations.

However, scholarship should go beyond blaming leaders and their policies. In our opinion, the causes of Russia's ongoing problems lie much deeper, and the nature of changes in Russia comes not only from the particulars of the recent domestic and international developments or from certain steps taken by politicians. Economic transformation in Russia is a complex process of comprehensive economic, political, and societal changes, just as with modernization processes and major reforms in many other countries at different historical periods. They include both steps forward on the path of modernization and development, and temporary steps backward (although sometimes these steps can be

---

[7]    See Andrei Shleifer, Daniel Treisman, *Without a Map: Political Tactics and Economic Reforms in Russia* (Cambridge, MIT Press, 2000); Marshall Goldman, *The Piratization of Russia: Russian Reform Goes Awry* (London: Routledge, 2003).

[8]    See Vladimir Gel'man, *Authoritarian Russia: Analyzing Post-Soviet Regime Changes* (Pittsburgh: University of Pittsburgh Press, 2015); Brian Taylor, *The Code of Putinism* (Oxford: Oxford University Press, 2018).

profound and protracted).[9] These backward steps are not only connected with the conservative beliefs of certain political leaders, but also with objective conditions, including the very fact that societies at large are not always willing to accept all the changes which are necessary for economic development. During these reforms, the transformation process results from complex and often contradictory interactions between new radical ideas, which are promoted by intellectual and political elites, economic interests that are defended by various influential groups, and institutions ("rules of the game") established under the influence of these ideas and interests. The key interest groups, in turn, do not emerge arbitrarily, but under the strong influence of the nature of the historical path of each country. And finally, illusions also influence the pathways of transformation, especially given the fact that society at large is often dissatisfied with economic development and with the dynamics of real incomes. Thus, a serious analysis of large-scale economic, political, and societal transformations should include a study of four I's – ideas, interests, institutions and illusions – against the background of a detailed and nuanced understanding of the historical path taken by the country in question. The process of change followed by Russia over the last few decades and discussed in our book is no exception: the trajectory of Russia's transformation was also affected by the alignments of these four I's and Russia's historical path.

In this book, we attempt to examine the mutual connections between:

- *Ideas*, which gave rise to the economic and political reforms of the second half of the 1980s–early 1990s;
- *Interests*, which affected the transformation of ideas in the process of their practical implementation;
- Ineffective *Institutions*, which were created under the influence of the ideas and interests of various groups;

---

[9]    See Dmitry Travin, Otar Marganiya, *Evropeiskaya modernizatsiya*, 2 vols. (Moscow: AST, 2004)

- *Illusions*, which deeply affected Russian society and played an important role in overcoming the economic and political consequences of the use of inefficient institutions;
- and Russia's *historical path*, which contributed to the formation of certain configurations of interest groups from the beginning of perestroika up until the 2020s.

This approach continues the logic of some of our previous publications.[10] Overall, we argue that each of the elements of these four I's is not a ready-made parameter setting, but represents changes in the process of transformation, including as a result of mutual impact. Some ideas lose their relevance over numerous stages of political and economic change and are replaced by others; some interest groups become winners in the wake of reforms, while others lose their influence; some institutions consolidate and survive over time, while others are short-lived; some illusions vanish over time, while others survive for generations. Finally, changes in all four of these I's in the process of reforms add new sections to the historical path travelled by the country. This is especially true for Russia, whose trajectory of ongoing changes has been increasingly affected not only by the influence of its Soviet (or pre-Soviet) past, but also by changes in the recent decades since 1985.

Although this book discusses highly contested ongoing processes, which give rise to heated political discussions, we strive to explain the trajectory of Russian changes of the late twentieth and early twenty-first century through the lenses of scholarly analysis. Our task is not to involve ourselves in a politicized discussion of Russia's current problems, and place the blame for these problems on particular personalities over and over again, or, on the contrary, deem these problems inevitable and fundamentally unsolvable. Offering yet another "guilty" verdict will do little to help with an understanding of Russia's potential directions of development. We believe, however, that a proper understanding of the logic of development and changes in present-day Russia, of the causes be-

---

[10]   See Vladimir Gel'man, Otar Marganiya, Dmitry Travin, *Reexamining Economic and Political Reforms in Russia, 1985-2000: Generations, Ideas, and Changes* (Lanham, MD: Lexington Books, 2014).

hind the current complexities and difficulties faced by the country, of the environment in which key actors are operating, and of the factors, which affect their actions, is essential. This framework for analysis may form an appropriate basis for consideration of further economic, political, and societal changes in Russia and beyond, and also help with policy-related conclusions and recommendations, and other actions, which may be in demand during new rounds of Russia's ongoing transformation.

The structure of our book is as follows. The first five chapters present an overview of the interactions between these I's within the context of the historical path of Russia during the Soviet and post-Soviet periods of Russian history. The following two chapters show that present-day Russia's inefficient institutions did not merely emerge by default from the ruins of the Soviet collapse, but were purposely created by powerful interest groups throughout the entire post-Soviet period. Owing to these processes, institutions in Russia do not serve ideas of development, but the interests of actors who pursue the goal of rent-seeking. In the short conclusion to this book, we summarize the analysis and discuss possible prospects for further changes in Russia.

The authors of the book work at the Center of Modernization Studies at the European University at St. Petersburg (EUSP) and thank EUSP rectors Nikolay Vakhtin, Oleg Kharkhordin, and Vadim Volkov, as well as EUSP founding rector Boris Firsov, for their ongoing support. Our colleagues, with whom we have discussed the ideas in this book during our seminars over the last decade – Nikolay Dobronravin, Dmitry Lanko, Maria Matskevich, Andrey Scherbak, Andrey Starodubtsev, Anna Tarasenko, Pavel Usanov and Andrey Zaostrovtsev – deserve special credit for stimulating and thought-provoking interactions and intellectual exchanges. We would also like to thank Tatiana Khruleva for effective administrative support of our collective work, Simon Patterson for translation of the book manuscript into English, and Alexei Stephenson for excellent proofreading. Vladimir Gel'man's research has been supported by the Aleksanteri Institute, University of Helsinki as part of the Finnish Center of Excellence "Choices of Russian Modernization" (Academy of Finland grant №

284664). The authors also thank Andreas Umland, the editor of the "Soviet and Post-Soviet Politics and Society" series, and Ibidem Verlag for interest in our work and the opportunity to publish this book in English.

# Chapter 1.
# The Major Ideas of Russian Reforms

The era of major ideational changes in the Soviet Union (in Russia in particular) began during the second half of the 1980s, when the most diverse ideas began to compete with each other. In this decade, Leonid Brezhnev died in 1982 after leading the country for 18 years. In 1985, Mikhail Gorbachev came to power and launched a real transformation of the Soviet Union, known as perestroika. During Gorbachev's reign, the first wave of economic reforms began in 1987. These transformations influenced the Soviet system in very strong and contradictory ways, and paved the way for the collapse of the Soviet Union in December 1991.

The events that took place over this short period came as a great shock for the country and its population. The Soviet citizens who faced these changes were forced to develop opinions and perceptions of the rapid and dramatic economic, political, and societal changes, as well as their understanding of how the country could and should live in the future. These opinions, perceptions, and understanding emerged in Soviet (and Russian) society on the basis of four major blocks of ideas, which had formed by that moment in the Soviet Union: (1) orthodox-Communist (2) reformist-socialist, (3) market-capitalist and (4) national-patriotic and imperialist ideas. We will examine each of these blocks of ideas in more detail.

## Orthodox-Communist Ideas

The essence of this complex of ideas was the following. The socialist system that existed in the Soviet Union was considered to be only the first phase in the making of a Communist society. Through the development of productive forces, over time the Soviet Union was to become able to form the material and technological basis for Communism. The people would live much better lives, and would transition to a Communist system of labor and distribution of goods: "from everyone according to their ability –

to everyone according to their needs". The development of productive forces capable of ensuring the realization of such an ambitious goal was to be carried out on the basis of a centrally planned (administrative) economy, which would lack the common vices of capitalism (overproduction crises, unemployment, inflation, high income differentiation, etc.). Socialism would manage resources much more efficiently than capitalism, and so economically socialist countries would close the gap and then overtake capitalist ones.[11]

This set of ideas was attractive for many Soviet citizens throughout the period from the 1920s until the 1950s. The generations growing up soon after the 1917 Bolshevik revolution, and in the decades following it, wanted to believe in a better future. They believed that heroic efforts to build a new socialist society would enable a radical transformation of the entire social system in a short historical period (but of course, not immediately). Furthermore, in the wake of the revolution and Stalinist industrialization, certain social lifts were created, and these lifts greatly contributed to major improvements in standards of living for some segments of the population, at the expense of many others. At the same time, millions of peasants moved from the half-starving countryside to the towns, became factory workers and thus guaranteed their own survival, if nothing else.[12] Some of them found administrative jobs in cities, which gave them stable rations and decent housing. The mass repressions "cleared a place" for skillful careerists and allowed a small percentage of urban residents to become members of the Soviet nomenklatura – a new elite which enjoyed all the benefits of the Soviet system.

However, by the beginning of the 1980s, those who had become the immediate beneficiaries of the formation of the Soviet system had either died or retired, and had increasingly less influ-

---

11    For example, see Politicheskaya ekonomiya. *Uchebnik dlya ekonomicheskikh vuzov i fakul'tetov*, vol.2, Sotsializm – pervaya faza kommunisticheskogo sposoba proizviodstva, Alexei Rumyantsev (ed.) (Moscow: Politizdat, 1977).

12    See Maxim Trudolyubov, *Lyudi za zaborom: chastnoe prostranstvo, vlast' i sobstvennost' v Rossii* (Moscow: Novoe izdatel'stvo, 2015), 16–17.

ence on political and social life. Members of Brezhnev's Politburo, who were mainly representatives of the revolutionary and Stalinist generations,[13] passed away one after another, making way for their successors, who, in turn, had no serious grounds to look at the prospects of building Communism with any optimism. There were several reasons for this.

First, for the new generations of the Soviet people, the Stalinist social lifts had ceased to work. Mass repressions stopped after the death of Stalin in 1953. The Soviet nomenklatura felt more at ease since no one purposefully sought to destroy its ranks, as had happened during the period of the Great Terror in the 1930s. The nomenklatura grew old in office, and thus delayed the promotion and upward mobility of the next echelon of Soviet careerists. Migration from the countryside to the urban centers continued, but its scope decreased over time. Former peasants could still find work in major industrial hubs, and feel themselves to be truly successful people, but for urban residents in the second and third generations, this feeling of advancement was no longer possible. Even if they were provided with primary material goods (food, clothing, housing, furniture, and the like), they understood that by the age of retirement they would have approximately the same modest standards of living that they had at the early stages of their lives. Prospects for a bright future, both for individuals and for the country as a whole, vanished by the early 1980s.

Second, by the 1980s, it had become clear to everyone that the Communism with its principle "from everyone according to their ability – to everyone according to their needs" would never be built. Educated people forgot about such illusions and switched to short-term individual goals, preferring a "bird in the hand to two in the bush". Hardly anyone took the 1960s slogan "The current generation of the Soviet people will live under Communism" seriously anymore, as it was all too obvious that the country's numerous problems could not be resolved any time soon even in the best-case scenario.

---

[13]    See Jerry F. Hough, *Soviet Leadership in Transition* (Washington, D.C.: The Brookings Institution, 1980).

Third, the increase in scope of these problems clearly demonstrated that the existing Soviet model for running the economy
was imperfect and required major changes. Ordinary people, of
course, did not and could not know exactly which changes needed
to be proposed and implemented, but the daily experience of go-
ing to shops to buy groceries and consumer goods suggested to
millions of people that they should not have positive expectations
for the future (at any rate, not under Brezhnev and rulers like
him). There was an acute shortage of goods throughout almost the
entire country, and the situation was particularly grave in many
provinces. Consumers were often unable to buy the most necessary items, including meat, sausage, dairy products, fresh fruit
and vegetables, and so on.[14]

Fourth, high-ranking officials and members of the Soviet
nomenklatura, who should have been the most interested in preserving the old system and its ideology, in practice strove to turn
the privileges they had already possessed for a long time into capital available for inheritance by their children and grandchildren.[15]
But this was impossible to achieve without fundamentally changing the Soviet institutions, and without rehabilitating private
property. Thus, over time, the Soviet elite became even more anti-
Soviet in its hearts and minds than the millions of ordinary citizens who did not have any privileges.

The combination of all of these factors made orthodox-
Communist ideas unattractive for Soviet citizens by the early
1980s. Formally, the old dogma of building Communism in the future was continuously supported by the Soviet propaganda machine. This doctrine was not officially rejected, even though it was
obvious that the ideas it declared would never become reality. No

---

[14]    For evidence and descriptions, see, for example: Igor Dedkov, *Dnevniki, 1953–
1994* (Moscow: Progress-Pleyada, 2005); Anatoly Chernyaev, *Dnevnik dvukh
epokh: sovmestnyi iskhod, 1972–1991* (Moscow: ROSSPEN, 2008); Yuri Chur-
banov, *Moi test' Leonid Brezhnev* (Moscow: Algoritm, 2007); Dmitry Travin,
*Ocherki noveishei istorii Rossii, vol.1, 1985–1999* (St. Petersburg: Norma, 2010),
16–37; Galina Vishnevskaya, *Galina: istoriya zhizni* (St. Petersburg, Bibliopolis,
1994).

[15]    See Michael Voslensky, *Nomenklatura: The Soviet Ruling Class* (New York:
Doubleday, 1984).

one in the party leadership was prepared to take on responsibility for ideological changes. And in reality, by all appearances no one was even interested in doing so. The Soviet system seemed quite stable, and it was difficult to imagine it collapsing. It was impossible even to imagine a mass uprising of people who had lost faith in future Communism, or a military coup inspired from abroad, or protest voting at non-competitive elections to Soviets. The regime easily reproduced itself without paying attention to the increasing challenges to the country. Thus, the ruling gerontocracy minimized personal effort and attempted nothing beyond patching the most gaping holes. And ideology, unlike the economy, was the field in which one could easily do nothing.

As a result, young Soviet people continued to be exposed to the Communist system of brainwashing from childhood. Everywhere they were informed of the greatness of the ideas proclaimed by the Bolshevik revolution of 1917, that we would swiftly close the gap with capitalist countries economically, and that life in the Soviet Union was much better now than the life of ordinary workers of Western Europe and America. However, the propagandists themselves usually did not believe the dogmas they attempted to impose on the minds of the common Soviet people. History teachers, Soviet party propagandists, university lecturers of Marxism-Leninism and journalists from the media were completely indifferent as to whether the Soviet citizens believed their words. It is not surprising that, under these conditions, the effectiveness of the Soviet propaganda system was very low. On paper, the Communist ideas were very much alive, but in reality, they were already dead and beginning to rot.

Thus, despite the formal preservation of the strategy for building Communism, in reality the set of orthodox-Communist ideas was less than popular in late Soviet society. Intellectuals sought to find some alternative to orthodox-Communist worldviews. Poorly educated people were indifferent to everything, but were internally prepared to accept alternative viewpoints, as they suffered greatly from a shortage of goods. And only a relatively tiny strata of Communist true believers (usually elderly people and/or great admirers of Stalin) did not wish to abandon their outdated preferences.

## Reformist-Socialist Ideas

The growing skepticism towards the command administrative economy and orthodox-Communist ideology did not mean that Soviet society was in principle prepared to reject socialist ideas. On the contrary, ideas of justice and equality still continued to attract a large number of Soviet people. By the 1980s, many of them still believed that serious mistakes had been made in building socialism (above all by Stalin and his entourage), resulting in the formation of an inefficient Soviet economic model, but that the good ideas proposed by Marx, Engels and Lenin should not be rejected because of individual failures. To understand this phenomenon, we should remember that although various ideas about how to develop socialism were expressed in the Soviet Union after Stalin's death, any "bourgeois" capitalist propaganda was strictly prohibited. Tourist and even business trips rarely gave Soviet people an opportunity to visit the West, and books and media, which revealed the truth about everyday life beyond the Iron Curtain, were virtually unavailable.

Accordingly, thoughtful people could accept and discuss various options for building socialism (if only in secret, in the kitchens of their apartments), while capitalism, with its crises, unemployment, inflation and high income differentiation between rich and poor, often seemed like a stage Russia had long since left behind, even to educated people. The Soviet people, who were poorly informed about the modern Western welfare states, did not want to "return to the past". They believed that it was possible to combine the advantages of socialism with the advantages of the market economy, thus creating an optimal model of development, with nothing but positive features, and without any embedded defects.

In particular, the ideas of reforming socialism were widespread among the generation of the "Sixtiers" (the so-called *shesti-*

*desyatniki)*.[16] The most notable representatives of this generation were those who came of age after the death of Stalin, and especially after the Twentieth Congress of the Communist Party (1956), where Nikita Khrushchev denounced Stalinism. Unlike their older comrades, the Sixtiers did not associate themselves firmly with Stalinism. They had not made their careers during the era of mass repressions, and did not hold leadership positions that were previously held by people murdered by Stalin. In their childhood, the Sixtiers may naturally have adhered to the practices of Stalinist propaganda forced on society, but under the impact of the ideas of Khrushchev's Thaw, it was not difficult for this generation to reject the old ideological baggage. Many Sixtiers said that they cried genuine tears on the day of Stalin's funeral, but just a few years later despised him as a tyrant and murderer.

The idea of reforming socialism was easily spread among the Sixtiers, among other things because it was thought that Stalin had fundamentally revised Lenin's ideas, distorted and even perverted them. As long as the figure of Lenin remained the main symbol of the Soviet Union and the most respected figure in the pantheon of Soviet leaders, the idea of renewing socialism was fully legitimized. Millions of people could say in the 1960s that they were for Lenin and against Stalin, and this viewpoint was not considered anti-Soviet. The mythologization of Lenin, against the background of the demonization of Stalin, formed the dream of a socialism "with a human face" during the years of the Khrushchev Thaw. For a broader Soviet public, which had a poor grasp of economics, this socialism meant an end to mass repressions, with mass enthusiasm (for example, the enthusiasm for the development of the Virgin Lands of Kazakhstan), a certain democratization of party

---

[16]  See Petr Vail', Alexander Genis, *60-e: mir sovetskogo cheloveka* (Moscow: Novoe literaturnoe obozrenie, 1996); Boris Firsov, *Raznomyslie v SSSR, 1940-60-e gody: istoriya, teoriya, i praktiki* (St. Petersburg: European University at St. Petersburg Press, 2008); Vladislav Zubok, *Zhivago's Children: The Last Soviet Intelligentsia* (Cambridge, MA: Harvard University Press, 2009); Vladimir Gel'man, Dmitry Travin, 'Fathers versus Sons: Generation Changes and the Ideational Agenda of Reforms in Late-Twentieth Century Russia', in *Authoritarian Modernization in Russia: Ideas, Institutions, and Policies*, Vladimir Gel'man (ed.) (Abingdon: Routledge, 2017), 22–39.

life, and a liberalization of culture, an area which attracted a number of young talents during the Thaw. For Soviet people with a professional understanding of economics, socialism "with a human face" not only meant de-Stalinization in political and cultural fields, but also serious reforms of the Soviet economic system.

Here, Sixties often mentioned Lenin's New Economic Policy (NEP), which they saw as an alternative to the harsh Stalinist industrialization, which had laid the foundations of the Soviet administrative economy. Under the NEP, not only were peasants free, but industrial state enterprises also had a higher degree of autonomy, to say nothing of private entrepreneurship in small business. As the NEP was protected by the sacred name of Lenin, it was permissible to mention it even in the most official and orthodox Marxist circles,[17] and thus in the minds of Sixties, the idea of the autonomy of state enterprises could oppose the idea of directive planning imposed from above. How could this autonomy be organized in concrete terms, would it be effective given the lack of private property and market competition, and could such ideas, borrowed from the distant past, be relevant in the new situation? To these and many other important questions, the Sixties usually did not have a precise answer. But on the whole, the idea of a new NEP seemed attractive, and was perceived as an alternative to the status quo. In general, there was no doubt in reform-minded circles that it was necessary for socialist enterprises to receive considerably greater autonomy in the new economic situation than under the old administrative (Stalinist) economy. In the wake of the so-called "Kosygin's reform" launched in the 1960s, an attempt was made to provide a certain (very slight) degree of autonomy to enterprises, though it was soon curtailed.[18] It became

---

17    See Gennadii Bogomazov, *Formirovanie osnov sotsialisticheskogo khozyaistven-nogo mekhanizma v 20-30-e gody* (Leningrad: izdatel'stvo LGU, 1983).

18    See *Prem'er izvestnyi i neizvestnyi: Vospominaniya o A.N.Kosygine*, Tom Fetisov (ed.) (Moscow: Respublika, 1997), 118; Viktor Andiyanov, *Kosygin* (Moscow: Molodaya gvardiya, 2003); Leonid Mlechin, *Brezhnev* (Moscow: Prospekt, 2005), 347–390; Travin, *Ocherki noveishei istorii Rossii*, 63–67; Dmitry Travin, Otar Marganiya, *Modernizatsiya: ot Elizavety Tudor do Egora Gaidara* (Moscow, AST: 2011), 531–544.

more difficult to imagine how market mechanisms could be implemented in the Soviet economy and how they could function under socialism.

By the 1960s, market socialism was already operating in Yugoslavia, allowing shops to fill with goods, but also resulting in "unacceptable features of capitalism" such as inflation and unemployment. In Czechoslovakia, a movement towards market socialism was also announced on the wave of reforms declared in the Prague Spring (1968), although we do not know now how it would have ended, as the changes were interrupted by the invasion of Soviet tanks. In Hungary, certain market elements were introduced after 1968 as part of the strategy of so-called "Goulash socialism", but they were very limited, as reformers were afraid of provoking the Soviet leadership and sharing the miserable fate of Czechoslovakia. Finally, one should note that in Communist Poland, a large agrarian private sector had been preserved since pre-WWII times, although it did not have a significant impact on overall economic patterns.[19]

In the Soviet Union, after the suppression of the Prague Spring in 1968, any attempts at economic (let alone political) reforms ceased for almost twenty years. But the Sixtiers' generation, formed during the Thaw, did not disappear. The idea of the need to give socialism a human face remained in the hearts and minds of Soviet intellectuals. However, until the beginning of perestroika, they could not publicly discuss the need for market elements in the Soviet economy, could not write academic articles about these issues, and could not tell their students about the Yugoslavian or Hungarian experiences of economic self-management during lectures. But in kitchen conversations and at certain unofficial ("underground") scholarly seminars, the ideas of socialism "with a human face" continued to be discussed.

Furthermore, the enthusiasm of youth, which so vividly emerged during the Thaw period (later curtailed and weakened by the conservatism of the Brezhnev decades), made a strong impact on many intellectuals among the Sixtiers. In fact, this genera-

---

[19]    See Travin, Marganiya, *Evropeiskaya modernizatsiya*, vol.2.

tion as a whole proved more susceptible to the ideas of reformist socialism than to the ideas of building a capitalist market economy. Owing to censorship and information barriers, Sixtiers could not effectively analyze the experience of self-management in the Yugoslavian economy (which, in reality, was not very successful), and so they mythologized it. They wanted to establish, sooner or later, an optimal social system in the Soviet Union that would combine the advantages of socialism with the advantages of the market, but they did not seek a full restoration of capitalism.

By the mid-1980s, reform-minded Sixtiers were highly influential in the Soviet Union. They held prominent positions in scholarship, as the Stalinist academic bosses of older generation were now dead or very old. The Sixtiers dominated in culture (literature, theater, cinema), as their books, articles, plays, films, and the like became popular among millions of readers and viewers. They comprised the majority of Soviet economic advisers, who were very fond of the idea of autonomy and self-management of socialist enterprises. Finally, the Sixtiers gradually reached the very highest levels of the party leadership. Gorbachev himself was undoubtedly a notable representative of this generation.[20] By the beginning of perestroika, he was one of several people among the party leadership who were interested in reforming socialism. Naturally, Gorbachev strengthened the positions of this group of his allies, and greatly weakened the position of conservatives of the orthodox-Communist type. Furthermore, by announcing perestroika, Gorbachev received the broad support of the intellectuals who belonged to the Sixtiers. Thus, for a while Gorbachev was able to create new opportunities for ideas of reformist socialism in the USSR. This ideological stream was much more popular in the second half of the 1980s than the orthodox-Communist one, and seemed as if it might become dominant.

---

[20]   See Mikhail Gorbachev, *Memoirs* (New York: Doubleday, 1996); Archie Brown, *The Gorbachev Factor* (Oxford: Oxford University Press, 1996); Andrei Grachev, *Gorbachev's Gamble: Soviet Foreign Policy and the End of the Cold War* (Cambridge: Polity, 2013); William Taubman, *Gorbachev: His Life and Times* (New York: W.W.Norton, 2018).

## Market-Capitalist Ideas

It was forbidden to promote capitalism in the Soviet Union in any form; even during the years of Khrushchev's Thaw, there were no official supporters of this socio-economic system. Furthermore, contact between the Soviet Union and Western countries beyond the Iron Curtain was very limited. The vast majority of citizens did not have the opportunity to see with their own eyes how capitalist countries lived and whether the horrors that Soviet propaganda constantly spoke of truly existed – even the vast majority of Soviet intellectuals could not visit these countries. Not only a lack of money for long-distance trips, but more importantly the harsh system of administrative restrictions on contact with foreigners and crossing the country's borders barred the Soviet people from first-hand experience of capitalism. The regime often prevented "undesirable" visits to the West with special commissions that checked the reliability of potential travelers abroad in order to avoid the spread of unwanted information, and, even worse, there were incidents where visitors to the Soviet Union were unable to return to their native country. Even scholars conducting professional research on foreign states and nations were often prohibited from leaving the Soviet Union altogether because of their presumed unreliability.[21]

Very rarely were serious scholarly books about the market economy translated into Russian and put on sale. Foreign-language books were held in large libraries in Moscow and Leningrad, but they were in low demand, and furthermore were often kept in special storage sections to which ordinary readers had no access without special permission. Nevertheless, by the early 1980s, a certain number of Soviet citizens were prepared to accept

[21]    See, for example, Iren Andreeva, *Chastnaya zhizn' pri sotsializme: otchet sovetskogo obyvatelya* (Moscow: Novoe literaturnoe obozrenie, 2009), Mikhail German, *Slozhnoe proshedshee* (St. Petersburg: Iskusstvo, 2000); Georgii Mirskii, *Zhizn' v trekh epokhakh* (Moscow and St. Petersburg: Letnii sad, 2001); Yakov Penzner, *Vtoraya zhizn'* (Moscow: Mar'ina roshcha, 1995); Boris Fedorov, *10 bezumnykh let: pochemu v Rossii ne sostoyalis' reformy* (Moscow: Sovershenno sekretno, 1999); Thomas C. Wolfe, *Governing Soviet Journalism: the Press and the Socialist Person after Stalin* (Bloomington: Indiana University Press, 2005).

capitalism and the market in their "pure" form. This shift was linked to the process of generational change, and also to the fact that the outdated Soviet ideology could no longer prevent the informal spread of new ideas.

A new generation proved particularly receptive to new ideas – the generation of the "Seventiers".[22] Unlike the long-standing concept of the Sixtiers, the notion of the Seventiers has not fully established itself in the scholarly literature. However, we have found such a term valid and useful, as today, representatives of this generation hold key positions in politics, business, media and culture in Russia. By "Seventiers", we refer to the generation who became adolescent after the suppression of the Prague Spring, during the period when conservative ideas dominated Brezhnev's Soviet Union, and near the beginning of perestroika. Khrushchev's Thaw was mere history to the Seventiers, and they learned about hopes for socialism "with a human face" not from their own life experience, but merely from the stories of their parents and teachers.

The Seventiers emerged as a generation throughout the 1970s and the first half of the 1980s. The distinguishing feature of the Seventiers was their perception that Brezhnev's system would continue for a long time, if not forever,[23] and so one should not believe too strongly in the transformation of socialism, or in the improvement of living conditions and of life in society at large. Therefore, one needed to adjust to the current socio-economic and political system and forget about hopes for a better future. With the coming of perestroika, young people naturally no longer had such pessimistic perceptions, and for this reason, we do not classify those who came of age after 1985 as Seventiers.

For this generation, capitalism was something neutral. The pre-1917 era was very distant. Even the parents of the Seventiers

---

[22]   See Gel'man, Marganiya, Travin, *Reexamining Economic and Political Reforms;* Gel'man, Travin, 'Fathers versus Sons'.

[23]   For an in-depth analysis, see Alexei Yurchak, *Everything Was Forever, Until It Was No More: The Last Soviet Generation* (Princeton: Princeton University Press, 2005).

had not lived under capitalism. At best, they could learn about it from their grandparents' stories, but they were more likely to learn about it solely from books and historical movies. For these reasons, young Seventiers did not interpret what Soviet propaganda said about capitalism (crises, unemployment, inflation, income differentiation) as relevant to them. And as Soviet propaganda was primitive and of poor quality, the grown-up Seventiers often believed that the horrors of the market economy were greatly exaggerated by Marxism. At the same time, the Seventiers had a good personal understanding of the shortage of goods in the Soviet shops, the low quality of Soviet production and the Soviet Union's serious technological lag in relation to the West. Against the background of the obvious weaknesses of the Soviet system, both in terms of the economy and of propaganda, capitalism was heavily mythologized. Many people regarded it as a world where everything was very well organized, while socialism in general was seen as a world where everything was organized imperfectly.

Western consumer goods, which entered the USSR from behind the Iron Curtain, amazed the young Seventiers with their convenience and design. They were seen as coming from a different, brighter and more exciting world. Jeans, chewing gum, vinyl records and even such little things as the contoured Coca-Cola bottle "with a waist", or bright candy wrappers formed sympathy to capitalism, where such things were in abundance.[24] Furthermore, the Seventiers had the opportunity to become aware to some extent (if sometimes in a distorted way) of the features of everyday life in capitalist countries, even despite the Iron Curtain and lack of readily available serious literature about how the market economy and democratic political systems functioned. In the 1970s, many foreign films were released in the Soviet Union. This kind of entertainment was not heavily censored by the Soviet propaganda, and the Seventiers practically all grew up on French

---

[24]  For vivid and detailed descriptions of the experience of the late-Soviet youth, see Sergei I. Zhuk, *Rock n Roll in the Rocket City: The West, Identity, and Ideology in the Soviet Dniepropetrovsk, 1960-1985* (Baltimore: Johns Hopkins University Press, 2016).

and American movies. The Sixtiers had also often been interested in foreign cinema, but it had not been as widely available in their youth as it was in the 1970s. In addition, the popular movies of the 1950s and 1960s had painted a rather contradictory picture of capitalist society. Along with the attractive models shown, for example, by the French movies *The Umbrellas* of *Cherbourg* or *A Man and a Woman*, the Soviet viewer watched examples of Italian neo-realism, where the West was portrayed as a monochrome world of injustice and poverty. By the 1970s, neo-realism had practically left the screens, and the new generation received a bright, colorful high-quality picture that portrayed France or the USA almost entirely from a positive angle, with few flaws, if any. Soviet censors attempted to control the import of Western movies, but did so very clumsily. Erotic scenes were cut from films, but everything that formed the perceptions of the growing Seventiers about the socio-economic system of Western countries remained on-screen. Viewers saw how the streets of modern Western cities looked: an abundance of cars, bright neon ads, and well-dressed, smiling people. If the action took place in a shop, viewers could see that the shelves were overflowing with goods. If the houses and apartments of the characters were shown in the movies, viewers saw how freely and spaciously their characters lived. They did not have to be crowded in small rooms like the average Soviet person. Viewers who watched the latest Western movies involuntarily compared everything: the abundance of goods in "their world" with the permanent shortages in ours, the atmosphere of permanent celebration in "their world" with the need to toil in a dreary, gray atmosphere at Soviet factories and plants.

Of course, the world on the other side of the Iron Curtain was not as wonderful in reality as it was depicted in movies. If the Italian neo-realism of the 1950s and 1960s emphasized the difficulties of the life of an ordinary person in the capitalist world, the American and French filmmakers of the 1970s–1980s, on the contrary, rarely showed urban districts inhabited by the poor, blacks and immigrants. The critical Soviet viewer, of course, understood that just as Communist propaganda did not tell the whole truth about capitalism, Western films were made for mass entertainment did not tell the whole truth about capitalism. But the majority of Soviet people, willingly or not, mythologized concepts of the West. And the worse life became in the Soviet Union of the Brezhnev era, the more viewers wanted to discover a different world somewhere else – a world that they aspired to with all their hearts.

Western movies had the greatest influence on the Seventiers' generation. Young people grew up and came of age watching dozens of American and French films. For them there was practically no real alternative to the "cinematographic" capitalism as the most attractive world. Or rather, while the Soviet system was considered the only possible one in the Soviet Union, the Seventiers had obediently existed according to the conditions imposed on them. But when radical changes took place in the years of perestroika, and young people began to think seriously about which social system most attracted them, the temptations of capitalism won without contest. Neither the old Soviet system, nor the world of socialism "with a human face", which the Seventiers barely understood, could be attractive compared to the bright and tempting picture of the West. However, one should remember that, since during the perestroika years the country was mainly run by Sixtiers, the ideas of market capitalism were more popular with the masses than with the ruling elite. The Seventiers initially took a back seat, yielding the dominant places in politics, economy, media and culture to their fathers and senior comrades. Only by the 1990s, and especially by the 2000s, had a generation emerged in Russia which had never wanted any socialist alternative, and which aspired to the greatest possible degree to build a society of mass consumption and business opportunities. This generation was prone to the temptation to possess a multitude of goods far more than to the desire to live in a fair society.

## National-Patriotic and Imperial Ideas

So far, we have mainly examined the evolution of ideas in the late Soviet Union from the socio-economic perspective. Their variety, between orthodox-Communist, reformist-socialist and market-capitalist viewpoints, was based on different perceptions and rational positive assessments of the existing situation, and resulted in choices of the preferred normative models of the country's development. However, there was also a fundamentally different approach, in which irrational aspects were predominant. Soviet people not only strove to optimize their lives in material terms, but also wished to establish a psychologically comfortable habitat. Many of them had no understanding of economics, and were incapable of making a competent judgement about economic models, whether ones based on a planned or on a market economy. Rather, they wished to be proud of their country and identify themselves as a great power, capable of defeating any enemy and determining the fate of the world.

From the school history curriculum, Soviet people knew that prior to the revolution of 1917, the Russian Empire was one of the largest powers in the world. Communist propaganda over several decades was able to successfully discredit Tsarism and persuade ordinary people that the empire was nothing more than a jail that bound nations in place. Meanwhile, as a result of the world revolution, a true brotherhood of all peoples from Japan to England would soon arise, as one enthusiastic poet of the Stalinist era wrote. But the world Communist revolution did not take place. Instead, the world fragmented into hostile groups during the period of Hitler's ascendance to power, which emerged as a real threat to the very existence of the Soviet Union. Stalin feared threats both from the capitalist democratic nations and from Nazism. In any event, the old Leninist idea that the workers' international of different countries should battle against the bourgeoisie proved unworkable. Foreign workers could become soldiers of armies fighting against the Soviet Union, rather than partners in the battle against the world bourgeoisie. In this situation, Stalin gradually began to change the old Soviet ideology. Without formally rejecting orthodox-Communist ideas, he launched a revival of the imperial idea. Stalin began to cultivate the Soviet people's pride in their country, and on this basis to develop Soviet patriotism, which was intended to become an important tool for mobilizing the mass public in case of potential future wars with Western countries. At the same time, proletarian internationalism was given a smaller and smaller role.

Soviet ideology underwent a major transformation quickly during World War II, when the cult of old Russian heroes – colonels, generals and admirals – was revived. Even the Russian Orthodox Church was partially rehabilitated in a country of "triumphant atheism", as many people, despite the dominance of Marxism, continued to secretly believe in God.[25] It was suddenly revealed that Tsarist Russia was not merely a jail of nations, but also the homeland for which the finest people of the country had fought heroically. The successful heroization of the past in the Stalinist era and victory in the Great Patriotic War in many ways ensured the subsequent formation of the cult of old heroes that existed in the Soviet Union until the beginning of perestroika.

In fact, after the death of Stalin, it was possible that his legacy might be rejected in this field as well. The mood of the Sixtiers, which was expressed in the famous phrase "Lenin is good, Stalin is bad", could have revived proletarian internationalism, and buried the revived imperial elements as one of the manifestations of Stalin's cult of personality. But Stalin's successors did not reject patriotism as an important tool for mobilizing the masses, as it had shown its positive side. However, under Khrushchev and Brezhnev it was not given as much importance as during the war.

Thus, the transformation of orthodox-Communist ideology into national-patriotic and imperial ideology paradoxically took place under Stalin, i.e. before reformist-socialist and market-capitalist ideologies became widespread. For a long time, this ideology was a synthesis of Communist and imperial ideas: they were not distinguished from each other. In the Soviet Union, the official dogma declared that the entire Soviet people, from Russians and Ukrainians to Estonians and Tajiks, were a single "new historical community", the unified Soviet nation. The regime left the Soviet intellectuals who tried to cultivate this strange ideological mixture mostly untouched, unlike those intellectuals who

---

[25]  See Jeffrey Hosking, *Rulers and Victims – the Russians in the Soviet Union* (Cambridge, MA: Harvard University Press, 2005).

spoke out for the democratization of society in the spirit of the Prague Spring, let alone for a return to capitalism.

In practice, national-patriotic and imperial ideas were not distinguished from each other (at least in Russia) until the collapse of the Soviet Union and the rise of acute inter-ethnic conflicts, which had been invisible over the preceding decades, but developed in latent forms and acquired more and more supporters during perestroika. In this type of ideology, as strange as it may seem, the socio-economic component was relegated to the background and played a minimal role (if any). Leading proponents of national-patriotic views usually associated themselves with particular major characters of the Soviet cultural milieu: they were interested in various topics surrounding these ideas, but gave little thought to how the economy should function.

One important aspect of this ideology was glorifying the victory of the Soviet people in the Great Patriotic War. More state funds were allocated to this type of propaganda than to promotion of the old Leninist ideas of the proletarian international. Gradually, many books and films were released about the war, and numerous monuments were built. The people who specialized in this glorification did not, by all appearances, have any socio-economic views that differed even slightly from the official ones. In their minds, a kind of synthesis took place between great Russian patriotism and the Soviet administrative economic system. Perhaps for many, the victory of the Soviet Union in World War II appeared to be proof of the superiority of the Soviet system. Private property and the market, which had existed in the Russian Empire before the revolution, were forced to make way for state property and the planned system as mechanisms capable of ensuring mobilization and funneling of resources into the military-industrial complex (MIC).

This approach was not at odds with several important tendencies that had formed in the West after World War II. The state was actively attacking the market. Everywhere in the West, the system of social welfare was expanded. The tax burden grew. In some countries, the share of state ownership drastically increased. Influential intellectuals discussed the need for indicative planning. Some thinkers even raised the idea of convergence of the two systems, i.e. that the East could replicate the best elements of the West, and the West of the East.[26] Soviet state officials may have believed that the Soviet economy was developing in more or less the right direction, without delving into details on a professional level or understanding the essence of the process in the first place. If so, then after the potential fall of the Communist regime, only some minor elements of the Soviet system would need to be adjusted for normal development of the country, while the main tool for restoring the imperial nation would be the revival not of the economy, but of religion.

Another side of the national-patriotic movement was the glorification of old Russian culture (particularly in the provinces and rural areas) and old Russian history. Among the cultural figures who supported this ideology, doubts may have arisen about the legitimacy of the Soviet system, together with a desire to restore pre-revolutionary Russia with all its distinctive features. But hostility towards the West, from which Marxism and the revolutionary movement had first emerged, dissuaded these people from developing a serious understanding of modern democracy and modern market economy. They cultivated their own myth of the past rather than forming real plans for transforming the Soviet Union.

Finally, among the national-patriots and enthusiasts of the empire, there was an influential anti-Semitic movement, whose members believed that Holy Russia had been destroyed by the Jews, who had been numerous among the 1917 revolutionaries, and whom Stalin had mostly repressed. Representatives of this ideological stream supported Stalinism in all its manifestations, and had negative feelings towards modern democratic capitalism, which cultivated tolerance in issues of nationality. Obviously, for this segment of the national-patriotic movement, market institutions were highly unpopular, as they symbolized capitalism while being unrelated to the Stalinism they respected so greatly. Nation-

---

[26]   See, in particular, John Kenneth Galbraith, *The New Industrial State* (Boston: Houghton Mifflin, 1972).

al patriots with far-right leanings had absolute loyalty to the Soviet system and were against a possible softening of the political regime, behind which they saw a conspiracy involving international Zionism.

The national-patriotic and imperial direction in Soviet ideology seemed as if it was likely to emerge triumphant after the final discrediting of orthodox-Communist ideology, as it was the most deeply embedded in Soviet soil. But when perestroika began, many people were primarily concerned with their material situation. National-patriotic ideology, lacking any serious economic program, could not realistically compete with reformist-socialist and market-capitalist ideologies. During perestroika, only a negligible section of society was concerned by nationalists' stories about a Jewish conspiracy, while the majority of those interested in resolving social problems focused more on the rational (if not always realistic) advice from scholars, experts, and pundits on how to reform the inefficient administrative economy. Nevertheless, nationalism did not vanish from the minds of Russian citizens, and made itself known several more times, especially in the wake of numerous ethnic conflicts in the territory of the former Soviet Union, including Russia.

## In Lieu of Conclusions

Thus, by the time when perestroika began, four sets of ideas competed in the minds of Soviet citizens. However, they were not evenly matched.

Practically no one supported the orthodox-Communist ideas any longer, even though they were formally supposed to dominate overall. In practice, these views could only be used to manipulate the minds of the most backward and dogmatic parts of the Soviet people, but even the manipulators who used them skillfully were unable to achieve noticeable success.

Reformist-socialist views dominated among the representatives of the Soviet elites, which belonged to the Sixtiers' generation. These views had better conditions for dominance during the period of perestroika, when the Sixtiers came to power. But international experience demonstrated that it would be difficult to achieve major positive results from reforming the Soviet economy on this ideological basis.

Market-capitalist views dominated primarily in the minds of the Seventiers. By the beginning of perestroika, these ideas had not yet developed to their fullest extent, as they had previously been prohibited. However, their importance and influence grew as the Seventiers matured, gained experience and began to hold positions in the higher echelons of power and business.

National-patriotic and imperial views had been maturing for a long time within the Soviet system with minimal resistance. By the beginning of perestroika, they were influential in certain elite circles and cultural milieus. But Soviet society, preoccupied with major material concerns, could not take on an ideology in which almost no attention was paid to economic issues.

This arrangement of sets of ideas changed dramatically over following decades. Nevertheless, all of them exist in the Russian ideational landscape of today to one degree or another, and exert various forms and levels of influence on Russia's economic and political development.

# Chapter 2.
# The Process of Reforms and the Influence of Interest Groups

Perestroika began in the Soviet Union in 1985, when Mikhail Gorbachev became General Secretary of the Communist Party Central Committee after the death of his predecessor, Konstantin Chernenko. However, no major economic reforms were carried out in the Soviet Union immediately after Gorbachev's ascendance. The new leadership of the country did not regard economic problems as truly complex. They believed that they could be solved by palliative measures, without carrying out radical transformations.

In the first two years of perestroika, the leadership's actions were restricted to attempts to improve the existing order and manage the organization of production. It was believed that Soviet citizens consumed too much alcohol, and that this led to serious violation of labor discipline. As such, the first "reformist" measure of the new leadership led by Gorbachev was an anti-alcohol campaign, launched in May 1985. The second important measure of the early stage of perestroika was providing Soviet plants and factories with new modern and highly efficient equipment. Mechanization of industrial production, combined with promotion of labor discipline, was supposed to provide economic growth via increase of labor productivity. This was presumably supposed to solve the problem of shortage of consumer goods.[27] But after two years or so, it emerged that these measures did not lead to any positive results. Furthermore, their application complicated the financial situation in the country: mechanization of industrial production re-

---

[27] For manifestations of this viewpoint, see Abel Aganbegyan, *Nauchno-tekhnicheskii progress i uskorenie sotsial'no-ekonomicheskogo razvitiya* (Moscow: Ekonomika, 1985); Nikolay Ryzhkov, *Desyat' let velikikh potryasenii* (Moscow: Assotsiatsiya "Kinga. Prosveshchenie. Miloserdie", 1995). For some critical analyses, see Anders Åslund, *Gorbachev's Struggle for Economic Reform* (Ithaca: Cornell University Press, 1991); Travin, *Ocherki noveishei istorii Rossii*, 102–127; Chris Miller, *The Struggle to Save the Soviet Economy: Mikhail Gorbachev and the Collapse of the USSR* (Chapel Hill: University of North Carolina Press, 2016).

quired additional state expenditures for purchasing new equipment, and the anti-alcohol campaign reduced the amount of money received by the budget from excises for alcohol consumption. At the same time, the global price of oil fell significantly on the world market, which further worsened the state of affairs in the Soviet economy, as for over two decades the Soviet Union had imported food and consumer goods using the currency it earned from the sale of energy resources abroad.[28]

## The Economic Reform of Perestroika

All of these problems gave rise to the need to commence serious preparation for real economic reform in 1987, which fundamentally transformed the Soviet economic system that had existed all but unchanged since Stalin's time. The plan for reform was developed by a group of renowned scholars and approved at a plenary session of the Communist Party central committee. Implementation of the new measures was to begin in January 1988.[29] This reform was carried out in the spirit of reformist-socialist ideas typical for the Sixtiers as a generation. None of the reformers cast any doubt on socialism as such. On the contrary, Gorbachev talked emphatically about improving socialism, creating the idea that it was possible to preserve the advantages of the existing Soviet system while merely diminishing its obvious shortcomings.

On the one hand, the reform proposed to reject the administrative foundations of Soviet socialism. This referred in particular to directive top-down planning and comprehensive control, the harsh subordination of factories to sectoral branch ministries, the non-market mechanism of supply of technical equipment, and centralized price-setting carried out without taking into account

---

[28]   For a detailed analysis of the role of energy export in the Soviet economy, see Yegor Gaidar, *Collapse of an Empire: Lessons for Modern Russia* (Washington, DC: Brookings Institution Press, 2007), especially Chapter 5.

[29]   See Travin, *Ocherki noveishei istorii Rossii*, 128-145; Åslund, Gorbachev's *Struggle for Economic Reform*; Vladimir Mau, 'Perestroika: Theoretical and Political Problems of Economic Reforms in the USSR', *Europe-Asia Studies*, vol.47, No.3 (1995), 387–411; Miller, *The Struggle to Save the Soviet Economy*.

supply and demand. It was proposed that the Soviet state enterprises would receive autonomy for economic activity, and themselves form their own plans to determine the volume and content of production. Accordingly, Soviet factories were also supposed to individually acquire the necessary parts and raw materials they needed, entering into direct contact with suppliers without the involvement of central state agencies, and being free from their control. The labor collectives of factories were supposed to elect their director at general assembly meetings, instead of being governed by the top managers appointed by respective ministers.

On the other hand, this transition to autonomy of state enterprises was not accompanied by a transition to a market economy. Even the word "market" was not mentioned in official Soviet documents until 1990. Only fundamental restructuring of state control of the economy, i.e. a major improvement of socialism, was proclaimed as a goal,[30] and all the measures proposed were regarded as socialist. Reform could not allow significant income differentiation among the population. Or rather, income differentiation was accepted only within the framework established by the main socialist principle "from everyone according to their ability – to everyone according to their need". Ordinary Soviet citizens were not supposed to lose their incomes because of circumstances beyond their influence – bankruptcy of factories, unemployment, inflation. Although the state had rejected the administrative Stalinist model of the economy, it still considered itself to be the only guarantor of improvement in the well-being of Soviet citizens. Within these limitations and constraints, reform began to be realized. Formally, all Soviet people were interested in its success, as they all wished for better economic development of the country and improvement of standards of living as a common good. However, the process of implementation of Gorbachev's economic reforms demonstrated that various interest groups were not satisfied with the proposed measures, and strove to change the implementation of the reform policies' conduct to their own advantage.

---

[30] See *O korennoi perestroike upravleniya ekonomikoi: Sbornik dokumentov* (Moscow: Politizdat, 1987).

This issue is worthy of special attention in our analysis. Any attempt to examine the known advantages of the market reforms only in general terms leads to the erroneous conclusion that Soviet (and, later on, Russian) society resisted necessary changes out of either stupidity or ignorance, or because of essential errors made by reformers. Based on these conclusions, we would arrive either at the extremely pessimistic conclusion that the Soviet or Russian society is fundamentally unfit for market reforms, or at the extremely superficial conclusion that the public resistance to economic changes was in itself a sign that the reformers' plans were critically flawed. But if we examine incentives for various interest groups at different stages of economic reforms, we will determine why even very thoughtful and well-educated individuals could oppose sensible and well-prepared reforms. The resistance to reforms from interest groups is hardly a peculiarity of Soviet Union or Russia: in actuality, many countries that passed through difficult reforms in certain periods of history faced similar problems. Initially, various interest groups opposed the changes, and sometimes this created the impression that the country did not accept a transition to a market economy and/or democracy. But over time, it became clear that the nature of interest groups could change, and society became different, adjusting to challenges of modernization. Observers who did not delve deeply into its history began to believe that this country had always been advanced, and undergone transitions in the distant past almost effortlessly.

A similar observation is relevant for the analysis of reforms during the perestroika. Diverse interest groups (management and labor collectives of factories, branch ministries and departments, Communist party organizations, and consumers), exerted major pressure and attempted to distort or even transform the initial reform plans for the sake of their own self-interest.

The first major change was related to the mechanism of state order. A large number of Soviet officials working in state planning and supply agencies, as well as in ministries, would have lost their influence, and ultimately their high-paying positions, in the transition of state enterprises to autonomy. These people naturally did not want to see this happen, and furthermore, most of them believed that the Soviet economy could not exist without central planning and control. The political leaders of the country also feared that autonomy of state enterprises could leave the country without certain important goods, which no one wanted to produce. Thus, the provision for autonomy of state enterprises in their planning of production was supplemented by the right of superior state agencies to introduce mandatory state orders for certain types of production.

In itself, the provision for state orders should not have resulted in major distortions, as these practices existed in many developed market economies: the state acquires a number of goods for its needs, especially in the military-related sectors. But in the Soviet Union during perestroika, state orders became almost ubiquitous. It emerged that many Soviet state enterprises did not aspire to autonomy and had little interest in deciding for themselves what to produce, but wished to receive state orders, as the state was then supposed to provide the suppliers with the appropriate resources. In other words, enterprises capable of producing goods and services that were in demand found it more profitable to remain within the old system of administrative planning (under the guise of state orders). With regard to state orders, the interests of the Soviet officialdom, which did not wish to lose its power, the Soviet political leaders who were afraid of an increase in shortage of goods, and the directors of numerous Soviet factories, which lacked the ability to go beyond the boundaries of state planning, coincided. With this combination of interest groups, state orders began to change the entire direction of economic reforms. In full accordance with Olson's theory of collective actions,[31] special interest pressure groups proved stronger than Soviet society as a whole, and even stronger than the Soviet leaders. Although interested in the implementation of economic reform, it was incapable of influencing it to any great degree.

---

[31]    See Mancur Olson, *The Logic of Collective Actions: Public Goods and the Theory of Groups* (Cambridge, MA: Harvard University Press, 1965); for in-depth analyses of the role of interest groups in economic reforms under Gorbachev, see Gaidar, *Collapse of an Empire*; Miller, *The Struggle to Save the Soviet Economy*.

Nevertheless, the interests of Soviet society at large were also taken into account by Soviet reformers, but not always in the correct way. The other important aspect, which fundamentally influenced the conduct of reforms, was effectively a rejection of a transition to market prices because of fear of inflation (the term "free prices" i.e. unregulated ones, was even not used at the time, to avoid associations with capitalism). The autonomy given to Soviet enterprises in determining the content and quantity of production also implied a shift to market prices. Otherwise, the severely distorted structure of the Soviet economy would also be reproduced under the new conditions, and with much worse consequences for Soviet citizens. Production, which was previously given artificially reduced prices, could only attract manufacturers' attention if they were able to raise prices. But if this did not happen, the shortage could worsen: no one would be interested in manufacturing these goods without orders and instructions from the state. Reformers understood this problem and included a provision in the reform plan for the need to move to unregulated prices. In practice, however, nothing of the kind was done in the late 1980s. The political leadership feared public dissatisfaction with an increase in inflation, and so slowed this element of the reforms.[32] As a result, increasing the autonomy of state enterprises could not help to eliminate the shortage of many goods with artificially low prices, including basic products such as food. Unsurprisingly, the importance of state orders only increased with this approach. The Soviet government was forced to set state orders for many goods that remained unprofitable for enterprises to manufacture.

The third problem caused by the reforms of the second half of the 1980s was that the directors of Soviet enterprises, freed from scrupulous supervision by their branch ministries, pursued their own interests, which did not coincide with the interests of the labor collectives. The directors realized that they had now received not only autonomy, but also a great deal of control over a significant amount of resources, such as state property and the financial flows, which passed through their enterprises. At the same time,

---

[32]    See Åslund, *Gorbachev's Struggle for Economic Reform*; Mau, 'Perestroika'

this reform did not propose any privatization, as private property, capital markets, the stock exchange and other institutions were considered to be manifestations of capitalism. Accordingly, the directors of Soviet enterprises would inevitably start contemplating the desirability of nomenklatura (spontaneous) privatization, with which state assets could effectively be used in their private interests while formally remaining under the guise of state ownership. These interests contributed to the emergence of cooperatives, which were permitted by the Soviet legislation during the years of perestroika. Cooperatives were a kind of substitute for private entrepreneurship, as they formally belonged to a collective (i.e. socialist) form of ownership. They acted practically in market conditions, decided what to produce themselves, set prices themselves, and were supposed to cover expenses with their own revenues. The Soviet regime hoped that cooperatives would improve the economic situation by producing goods and services for mass consumption and compensate for shortages, but in fact they were used a tool of spontaneous privatization, as the interests of cooperatives coincided ideally with the interests of the Soviet enterprise directors. Directors could order various types of products and services for their factories from cooperatives, or rent out their enterprise facilities for cooperative production needs. They could also sell their goods at market prices through cooperatives. In each of these cases, both sides gained a significant advantage. Products and services were ordered by state enterprises, which used state funds, while the rent payment taken from cooperatives by enterprise directors was extremely low. The sale of goods through cooperatives at market prices was in essence legalized speculation. In all of these cases, directors received their kickbacks as part of the profit that the cooperatives received with their help. The result of the joint activity of Soviet enterprise directors and cooperatives was not at all what the reformers had expected.

Ultimately, the reformers of the second half of the 1980s only aggravated the already difficult economic situation in the country. Efficient state enterprises received the opportunity to earn more, and distribute money earned relatively freely within the labor collectives. Workers' incomes increased, they sought to purchase more goods, and in light of shortages, they quickly bought up everything available in the shops even before the start of the reforms. The incomes of directors, and cooperative heads connected with them, grew even more swiftly. Soon, the first commercial banks and factories with foreign capital appeared in the Soviet Union (the so-called joint enterprises). They also actively joined in the spontaneous privatization and made a considerable profit from these activities. However, those Soviet enterprises which were inefficient, and also those that were loss-making within the planned economic system (the MIC, agricultural producers etc.), had to be financed by the state in one way or another. No one intended to close them, as that would allow unemployment and a decline in standards of living of the population. But the old Soviet mechanism of redistribution of funds from profitable to unprofitable enterprises, already dysfunctional, could no longer function in the new conditions. Efficient enterprises aspired to keep their own incomes for themselves.

These changes resulted in two problems. First, instead of stable taxation, Soviet enterprises were set changing norms for distributing their profits. Unprofitable enterprises had little taken from them for the state budget, while their profitable counterparts had almost everything taken from them.[33] This severely undermined the aspiration to improve economic performance. Moreover, some enterprise directors reached individual agreements with central state agencies about special treatment and more advantageous norms of payment to the state budget, and also gave kickbacks to officials responsible for decision-making. Second, as there was a major shortage of money in this financial system for supporting the national economy, the state resorted to escalating monetary emission. In a situation of state-controlled prices, this did not lead to inflation, but to an increasing shortage of goods (this phenomenon is known as hidden inflation or a "monetary overhang"). At the beginning of the 1990s, the situation in the consumer market in the Soviet Union was considerably worse than in

---

[33] See *Perestroika upravleniya ekonomikoi: problemy, perspektivy*, Pavel Bunich (ed.) (Moscow: Ekonomika, 1989), 248.

the Brezhnev era. The aggravation of shortage problems led to people frenetically buying up goods, and shops became even emptier.

Many Soviet citizens, seeing the worsening problems from a consumer position, became increasingly angry with the erroneous actions of the Communist party apparatus, nomenklatura, state officials and other "enemies of perestroika", as they were called at the time. But the same Soviet citizens often found themselves on the "winning" side if they held certain positions related to the production and distribution of goods. Workers in well-functioning Soviet enterprises increased their nominal incomes, and for a time were in a position of "cash illusion" – the feeling that their real incomes were increasing. Workers in loss-making enterprises at least maintained their position, continuing to receive support from the state and cultivating illusions that they were bringing benefits to the Soviet state and society, and held the right to financial assistance. Directors, officials and the emerging class of entrepreneurs were rewarded with very large sums (by Soviet standards) by their involvement in spontaneous privatization. At the same time, as this "privatization" only assisted the expropriation of state property, and not effective market management, privatized funds were also quickly devalued, along with the salaries of ordinary workers.

## Yeltsin and Gaidar's Economic Reforms

The formal boundary between the reforms of Gorbachev's perestroika and the reforms carried out in Russia after the collapse of the Soviet Union was the coup of August 1991, followed by the Belovezha Accords on dissolving the Soviet Union signed in December of that year. But in reality, it is impossible to draw such a strict boundary, as Yegor Gaidar did not begin his economic reforms from zero. It is vitally important to understand that Gaidar and his team inherited a complex legacy from the Soviet Union leaders and their policies, and were forced to resolve a large set of problems. They included:

- Increasing macroeconomic imbalance, manifested in the enormous "monetary overhang";
- Lobbying activity by the management of Soviet enterprises, which were unprofitable but secured major financial support from the state authorities;
- And spontaneous privatization, through which state-owned assets quickly moved into private hands.

On the one hand, this legacy of Gorbachev's determined the balance of forces between various interest groups, which, in turn, affected the conduct of economic reforms. On the other hand, the nature of the reforms was to a great degree determined by the dominant ideas in reformer circles. In the 1990s, these ideas already differed fundamentally from those, which had most influenced the approaches to Gorbachev's perestroika in the second half of the 1980s. The reputation of reformist-socialist ideas was significantly undermined, if not ruined, by unsuccessful changes under Gorbachev. The proponents of these changes all but lost power with the collapse of the Soviet Union, and the scholars and experts who had advised the Soviet leaders and developed proposals for economic reforms found themselves out of favor with Boris Yeltsin. But another, perhaps even more significant factor in the changes was that significant ideational shifts had taken place in the Soviet society during perestroika. Soviet citizens gradually ceased to adhere to formerly popular socialist ideas. The freedom provided to the mass media under Gorbachev and strengthened in the years of Yeltsin's rule assisted the appearance of a series of articles, op-eds and speeches discussing the need for a real market, and not a socialist substitute for it. As early as 1987, the first analytical texts explaining the advantages of capitalism were published in the Soviet media.[34] Soviet intellectuals discussed them with a certain surprise and timidity, even though these discussions were made rather academic by the rapid deterioration of the Soviet economy.[35] But when the first program for market reforms,

---

[34]    See Nikolay Shmelev, 'Avansy i dolgi', *Novyi mir*, no. 6 (1987), 142–158.

[35]    See Åslund, *Gorbachev's Struggle for Economic Reform*; Mau, 'Perestroika'.

the "500 Days", appeared in 1990 with the support of both Gorbachev and Yeltsin, it left nothing of socialism even in its reformed form; the very term was no longer used in this document. When shops became completely empty, socialist ideas no longer seriously concerned anyone. The Russian citizens wanted a well-functioning economy, and the people were uninterested in what label it would be given: "socialism", "capitalism" or something else.

Thus, when Yegor Gaidar, who was appointed in November 1991 to the position of deputy prime minister of the Russian government, and received carte blanche to carry out market reforms, proposed his program of liberalization of consumer prices, financial stabilization, and privatization of enterprises, he did not encounter any obstacles on the ideological level. The ideas of the advantages of capitalism advocated by the Seventiers were widespread, and even the liberalization of prices no longer discouraged the population, as it provided hope that goods would finally appear on sale, if at high prices. However, pressure from various interest groups was very significant, and it increased greatly in the wake of the post-1991 economic reforms, serving as their major economic and political constraint, despite Gaidar's resistance.[36]

The key elements of Gaidar's reform were the following:[37]

- liberalization of 90% of retail prices and 80% of wholesale prices;[38]
- transition to a modern and unified system of taxation instead of the "arbitrary" system of reallocation of profits;
- mass privatization of state property according to universal rules and regulations, terminating late Soviet-era privatization by the nomenklatura;

---

[36] For detailed accounts, see Anders Åslund, *Russia's Capitalist Revolution: Why Market Reform Succeeded and Democracy Failed* (Washington, DC: Peterson Institute for International Economics, 2007); Vladimir Mau, *Russia's Economy in the Epoch of Turbulence: Crises and Lessons* (Abingdon: Routledge, 2018); Shleifer, Treisman, *Without a Map*.

[37] See Travin, *Ocherki noveishei istorii Rossii*, 228–229.

[38] See Evgeny Yasin, *Rossiiskaya ekonomika: istoki i panorama rynochnykh reform* (Moscow: State University – Higher School of Economics, 2003), 194.

- liberalization of foreign trade and economic activity, including legalization of owning foreign currency for Russian citizens and companies.

Ideally, Russia was to become an ordinary country with a market economy, and a part of the world capitalist economy.[39] The ideology of market reform envisaged Russia's development in this direction. But finding themselves faced with influence of various interest groups, reformers were forced to adjust their policy to a great degree, and these adjustments often changed the direction of reforms; such changes ultimately influenced the opinions of experts and masses alike about the failure of the economic reforms in Russia. Some elements of the policy of economic reforms were adjusted with the involvement of Gaidar himself, who strove to make compromises on individual issues in order to preserve the course of reforms in general. Other adjustments were made by other actors (for example, the head of the Central Bank, Viktor Gerashchenko) with the de facto agreement of Gaidar, who was attempting to preserve his political influence. Finally, some elements of market reforms were altered after Gaidar was dismissed (in December 1992), and could not influence the course of events.

In any case, the economic changes of the 1990s proceeded under strong pressure from various interest groups, and were less an implementation of Gaidar and his team's original ideas than a result of numerous formal agreements and informal compromises. While in the beginning, the economic reforms of the 1990s were the quintessence of the Seventiers' market-capitalist ideas, their output was a contradictory and not particularly effective set of policy measures, which were altered or even distorted due to pressure from all kinds of interest groups. But on the whole, the market-capitalist direction of the economic reforms was preserved. This ensured the transformation of the Russian economy, and the shops began to fill with domestic and imported goods,

---

[39]    See Andrei Shleifer, *A Normal Country: Russia After Communism* (Cambridge, MA: Harvard University Press, 2005).

which meant the end of the shortages typical for the Soviet past.[40] Furthermore, Gaidar's economic reforms created the basis for the further rapid development of the Russian economy in the 2000s, when swift economic growth began. But in all key directions, the results of market reforms deviated greatly from the initial plans:

- Price liberalization led to high inflation, devaluing the savings of Russian citizens and resulting in very negative incentives for investment;
- The transition to the modern fiscal system could not prevent large-scale tax evasion, aggravating the already complex problems of the deficit of the Russian state budget due to a protracted and deep transformational recession;
- Privatization of enterprises was carried out in the interests of labor collectives, which in effect meant privatization in the interests of the directorate of these enterprises and certain interest groups connected with them;
- Liberalization of foreign trade and economic activity against the background of high inflation, a severe transformational recession and compromise privatization led to capital flight instead of attracting investments;

All of this unmistakably worsened the transformation recession, which was inevitable in the process of restructuring the Russian economy, but which could have been overcome in a shorter time frame (if one judges by the experience of the market reforms conducted at the same time in countries of Central and Eastern Europe).

In the first months after price liberalization, Gaidar unsuccessfully strove to achieve financial stabilization. Although the "monetary overhang" which remained as a legacy of Gorbachev's economic policies meant that significant inflation immediately after liberalization was inevitable, the Russian government strove to reduce high inflation gradually. It was necessary to reduce the deficit of the state budget, and cease relying on monetary emission

---

[40] See Yegor Gaidar, 'Smuty i instituty', in Yegor Gaidar, *Vlast' i sobstvennost'* (St. Petersburg: Norma, 2009), 139–140, 163–165.

to finance it. In carrying out mass privatization, its key architect
Anatoly Chubais – a friend and colleague of Gaidar – was guided
initially by the importance of selling state assets directly to strategic investors, and not to enterprise directors or representatives of
the labor collectives. This approach would make it possible to attract the capital necessary for the development of the Russian
economy. Unlike strategic investors, workers did not possess capital, but did possess ambitions that interfered with natural development of the economy. The Yugoslavian experience of work collectives controlling enterprises showed that this practice resulted
in economic populism,[41] while privatization via selling of assets,
which can immediately attract investments because of the inflow
of capital (for example, in the United Kingdom under Margaret
Thatcher), was considered to be a successful role model by Russian reformers.

But despite these initial beliefs, neither financial stabilization
nor privatization in the interests of strategic investors was
achieved. The obstacles were not related to a sudden transformation of reformers' ideas and preferences, but to the need to adjust to individual and collective pressure from various interest
groups. Ignoring this pressure, the reformers believed, could have
led them to even worse policy outcomes, specifically freezing
prices (and essentially stopping liberalization) and continuing un-
controlled spontaneous privatization. In fact, an attempt at freezing once-liberalized prices was indeed made in late 1992 or early
1993, immediately after Gaidar's dismissal. But in practice, spontaneous privatization was carried out until change of ownership
of former state enterprises according to the rules prescribed by
Chubais.

---

[41]   See Sergey Vasil'ev, *Khozyaistvennye reformy v Yugoslavii: razvitie i krizis pro-
izvodstvennogo samoupravleniya* (St. Petersburg: St. Petersburg Finanical and
Economic Institute, 1991), 25; Ichak Adižes, *Industrial Democracy: Yugoslav
Style* (London: Adižes Institute, 1971), 130; Ljubo Sirc, *The Yugoslav Economy
under Self-Management* (New York, St. Martin's Press, 1979), 44, 55; Sharon Zu-
kin, 'Self-Management and Socialization', in *Yugoslavia in 1980s*, Sabrina Petra
Ramet (ed.) (Boulder, CO: Westview Press, 1985), 81, 91, 93.

In spring 1992, President Boris Yeltsin faced intense pressure from various interest groups, which had suffered losses as a result of the transition to the market economy, and sought to receive financial support from the state to compensate for them and improve their position.[42] While during an ordinary recession under market conditions, major losses affect relatively small sections of the national economy, and the state often finds the opportunity to help companies without major macro-economic distortions, the transformational recession in Russia in the early 1990s affected the interests of most sectors of the economy against a background of high inflation.

First, the MIC, which was financed by the state via orders, was in critical need of state support. In the Soviet Union, which sought to maintain strategic and military balance with the USA in the arms race, this sector was excessively developed. The military expenditure of the Soviet Union usually exceeded the gross national product by 20% in the post-WWII period. According to some estimates, the share of military production in the volume of the Soviet industrial production exceeded 40%.[43] There were many qualified specialists employed in this sector, so pressure on the state came not only from the directorate, but also from the intelligentsia, who had formed the mass basis for support of democratic and market transformations in the perestroika years. Engineers, scientists, and other employees of the MIC suddenly discovered that the transition to the market economy could leave them without salaries, as the state budget was incapable of supporting the number of orders and defense projects that it had in the past. Ignoring the interests of the intelligentsia employed in this sector also threatened Yeltsin with losing the support of an active group of the electorate which he had until recently relied upon.

Second, many towns in Siberia and the Far North required infrastructural support. Development of these towns was also to a considerable degree connected with the MIC. In the Soviet period,

---

[42]    Gaidar, 'Smuty i instituty', 166–167.

[43]    See Valentin Kudrov, *Ekonomika Rossii v mirovom kontekste* (St. Petersburg: Aleteia, 2007), 386.

some plants and factories' production was transferred to poorly accessible and remote areas of the country in order to maintain secrecy. But the Soviet government did not take into account that maintaining these towns in harsh climate and weather conditions, where no food could be produced, would be very expensive. During the transition to the market economy, this problem became very acute, as areas in the Russian North required additional support to survive. The state was unable to terminate these supplies, as residents of these towns could not relocate because they lacked funds to purchase housing in Central Russia or other more suitable areas.

Third, agriculture also sought state support. In principle, this sector of the economy could have developed more successfully under market conditions, as its production (unlike the production of the military-industrial sector) was necessary for consumers. But the efficiency of agriculture in the Soviet Union was extraordinarily low. The state gave loans to collective farms, and then wrote off unpaid loans. Furthermore, it gave extra support to the countryside, forcibly sending a large number of urban residents (primarily students) to aid in harvesting. Rural residents were accustomed to the fact that they could not fully provide for the production process themselves. Of course, the market economy was supposed to teach agrarian producers to be more efficient, and from this viewpoint, Russia could survive without supporting agrarians, and there was an increase in agricultural import. But the Russian state had a different view: the position of the agrarian economy could be completely undermined by the shift to import, and maintenance of food security and the need to supply domestic food in the case of war was considered an essential goal.

Fourth, a wide range of sectors of industry suffered from the liberalization of foreign trade and economic activity. A large number of products from countries with low wages and relatively well-developed production of consumer goods flooded the Russian market. The food industry in many Russian cities faced major difficulties in competition with products manufactured in various European countries. Light industry visibly lagged behind manufacturers from China and Turkey; the Soviet car industry, which was essentially only represented on the consumer market by the VAZ factory in Togliatti, and had existed for a long time with virtually no competition, now lost the battle to many foreign brands (especially relatively cheap used cars, which were now imported in large quantities). Domestic appliance manufacturers found themselves in approximately the same position.

The problems for the survival of inefficient Russian enterprises also significantly worsened with the intense development of shuttle trading. Many Russian citizens who had lost their jobs, or simply wished to switch to new, more profitable forms of economic activity against the background of wage arrears, began to travel abroad to buy and resell consumer goods on the Russian market. It was difficult to prohibit shuttle trading, as it fed a large number of people, and furthermore was an example of entrepreneurship, which was welcomed by economic reformers. But the importing of consumer goods from abroad without customs duties made these goods even more competitive in comparison with local products. Spontaneous marketplaces began cropping up all over Russia like mushrooms, and shuttle traders and their partners sold imported products at these locations at very low prices.

Thus, representatives of the most diverse sectors of the Russian economy, which suddenly proved uncompetitive, began actively lobbying their interests in the corridors of power. The president and the government could not ignore their demands. Furthermore, not only the losers but also the winners of economic liberalization, representatives of successful businesses, became involved in lobbying. In particular, winners such as commercial banks, which made considerable profits in the early 1990s, could make a profit on high inflation, and accordingly were objectively interested in preservation of this situation, thus opposing targeting inflation and financial stabilization.[44]

---

[44] See Mikhail Dmitriev, Dmitry Travin, *Rossiiskie banki na iskhode zolotogo veka* (St. Petersburg: Norma, 1996), 67–80; Juliet Johnson, *A Fistful of Rubles: The Rise and Fall of the Russian Banking System* (Ithaca, NY: Cornell University Press, 2000).

Lobbyist pressure on the government did not come only from businesspeople, industrialists and agrarians. The military leadership was also a strong lobbyist. Although the Russian army remaining after the Soviet collapse was considerably smaller than the Soviet army had been, the president and government could not completely ignore the military's demands for funding. In a situation of political instability and unpopular reforms, it would be too dangerous to make an enemy of the army. In particular, in September–October 1993, the fierce conflict between President Yeltsin and the Congress of People's Deputies led to a presidential decree on dissolution of the parliament. Then the anti-Yeltsin opposition, a coalition including the militant Union of Officers and led by Vice-President Alexander Rutskoi and Chair of the Supreme Council Ruslan Khasbulatov, attempted to overthrow Yeltsin. In turn, Yeltsin relied on the support of the army to suppress the uprising, and even brought out tanks onto the streets of Moscow. After some hesitation, the military leadership took the president's side: tanks fired shots at the parliament building, which soon forced the insurrectionists to surrender. Naturally, in this situation the state was forced to pay attention to the interests of the military leadership and satisfy its financial demands.[45]

Some lobbyist pressure was also exerted by public sector employees. The media was filled with alarmist articles discussing the grave situation of professors, teachers and doctors, who received extremely low salaries with huge delays in payment. Throughout the 1990s, the living conditions of the Russian intelligentsia became increasingly difficult. Yet this was the very social group that had supported Yeltsin in the late 1980s, and actively supported market reforms from the very beginning. Accordingly, the president and government could not ignore their interests either, especially in advance of election campaigns.

---

[45]    On details of the 1993 conflict and its outcomes, see Lilia Shevtsova, *Yeltsin's Russia: Myths and Realities* (Washington, DC: Carnegie Endowment for International Peace, 1999), 31–78; Michael McFaul, *Russia's Unfinished Revolution: Political Change from Gorbachev to Putin* (Ithaca, NY: Cornell University Press, 2001), 121–204; Travin, *Ocherki noveishei istorii Rossii*, 238–253.

In practice, the situation was more complex, as the various lobbyists were loosely organized, and many pressure groups consisted of a variety of actors who had their own narrow interests: sometimes they formed ad hoc coalitions, but at other times, they competed with each other for the same pool of state resources. This situation gave the Russian government some room to maneuver, but its degree of freedom was limited given the protracted recession amid political conflicts, polarization, and election battles. Of course, one should not take a simplistic view of the situation in the 1990s and reduce the problems involved in choosing a path for post-reform Russia to economic interests alone. While recognizing the pressure of various interest groups as a factor in the economic changes in Russia, and explaining the transformation of the initial reform policy from this viewpoint, one should not fall into the other extreme and claim that material incentives were all that influenced the preferences of Russian citizens. Many people sincerely sought changes and were prepared to endure the considerable difficulties involved. They supported Yeltsin politically even when their lives became much more difficult during the reforms of the 1990s. Such a contradiction could be seen in 1996, when Yeltsin, despite economic problems and his initially low approval rate, was re-elected for a second presidential term after a convincing victory over his main rival, the Communist leader Gennady Zyuganov.

In the first place, for the Russian intelligentsia, the very proposal of a "return to Europe" was extremely important after long decades behind the Iron Curtain. Educated people hoped that the economic difficulties would be short-lived, but that reforms would provide an opportunity to transform Russia into a real European country belonging to the developed world. Second, a considerable section of the Russian population in the post-reform years was inspired by Yeltsin's charisma, trusted the president and was ready to support him as a candidate for re-election, despite the fact that the government's performance was significantly below public expectations. The president's admirers may not even have discussed the pluses and minuses of Gaidar's team, but only supported it because it belonged to Yeltsin. Third, part of the Rus-

sian electorate was ready to support the government simply because it could not imagine any realist alternative, and had no real
way to express its discontent. These people did not take part in
any protests (which were fairly limited and attracted few Russians
in the 1990s), and were prepared to "tick the right box" at elections due to the influence of official propaganda, or pressure from
the local authorities.

This complex set of factors influenced public support for
market reforms. The results of the referendum held in April 1993
demonstrated that Russian society as a whole was inclined to
support Yeltsin and his policies, even in the face of economic difficulties. Nevertheless, the problem of influence of various interest
groups on economic policy should be considered an extremely
important factor for the entire post-reform period.

## Problems of the Post-Reform Economy in Russia

The problem of appeasing numerous special interests in post-
reform Russia gave rise to a special mechanism for adjustment of
financial policy to political conditions. The Russian authorities
slowly abandoned their positions under pressure from lobbyists
but continued their attempts to balance the budget, though without great success. Where the government initially strove to carry
out a more or less responsible financial policy, the parliamentari-
ans who entered a confrontation with Yeltsin attempted to follow
a populist policy to increase their influence among the mass public, and were prepared to adopt budgets with a deficit that went
beyond reasonable limits.[46]

A permanent "monetary overhang" led to a major budget
deficit in the first post-reform years, and the most important way
of covering this deficit was still monetary emission. There was little opportunity to rely on loans from foreign countries and international financial organizations: the money needed by the budget

---

[46]    See McFaul, *Russia's Unfinished Revolution,* Chapters 4–5; Travin, *Ocherki noveishei istorii Rossii,* 238–253.

greatly exceeded the resources they allocated to Russia,[47] and the practice of borrowing money in a domestic financial market emerged only in the mid-1990s. Printing money, in turn, put an end to the policy of financial stabilization that Gaidar had initially tried to implement. While the tasks of the transition to the market economy and liquidation of the shortage of goods were resolved despite all difficulties, the situation with financial stabilization in Russia was clearly worse than in the countries of Central and Eastern Europe, which carried out reforms in the same years. True, Russia was able to avoid the hyperinflation that struck Serbia, Montenegro and Croatia, but until 1997, the overall inflation rate was too high for healthy development of the Russian economy. Inflation made Russia unattractive for serious investments, and instead stimulated various speculative operations.

Thus, post-reform policy was as follows: the state attempted to satisfy the demands of the powerful interest groups, which for political or socio-economic reasons it, found difficult to ignore (not least because of the corruption of the state apparatus). Inflation, in turn, devalued the subsidies and loans that the lobbyists were able to secure from authorities. This approach diverged strongly from the ideas with which the reformers had come to power. No one was deliberately pursuing high inflation; it was quite unlike the attractive capitalist model that had tempted Russian citizens to transform socialism. As a result, shops filled with goods, but Russians faced a rise in consumer prices, which to a considerable degree devalued the meaning of market achievements.

The contradictory nature of reform results also gave rise to a contradictory attitude towards the economic reforms of the 1990s. On the one hand, no one in Russia was interested in returning to

---

[47]    See Anders Åslund, *Building Capitalism: The Transformation of the Former Soviet Bloc* (Cambridge: Cambridge University Press, 2001); Martin Gilman, *No Precedent, No Plan: Inside Russia's 1998 Default* (Cambridge, MA: MIT Press, 2010); for a broader overview of post-Communist market reforms, see *The Great Rebirth: Lessons from the Victory of Capitalism over Communism*, Anders Åslund, Simeon Djankov (eds.). (Washington, DC: Peterson Institute for International Economics, 2014).

the Soviet economic model. Supporters of the administrative economy gradually left big politics because they lacked public support. On the other hand, most citizens came to believe that reforms in Russia had been poorly conducted, and that there must be a different method for reforming the Soviet economic system – a method in which the wolves (the winners of economic reforms) would be fed, and the sheep (the losers of economic reforms) would be safe. In fact, as we can see, the problems that arose in the post-reform period were caused not by the nature of market reforms and not by the personalities of the reformers, but by the influence of numerous interest groups, which distorted the government's plans and made their implementation imperfect at best.[48]

The most serious obstacle in the process of implementation of market reforms was probably the decision taken in the summer of 1992 by Viktor Gerashchenko, head of the Central Bank of Russia, to provide large-scale loans for enterprises in order to end the non-payment crisis. In accordance with this decision, the Central Bank directly injected huge amounts of money into practically all spheres of economic activity. Gerashchenko's aspiration to help everyone at once, instead of slowly "retreating" under pressure from lobbyists, intensely accelerated inflation rates, but naturally did not save the Russian economy. A large number of enterprises which had been severely harmed by the transformation recession because of their uncompetitive production (of goods that could not be sold within the market), were able to survive for a certain time due to Gerashchenko's decision. But sooner or later, they were still forced to cease their previous economic activity. This form of "loans for all" was fundamentally much worse than the individual bargaining for resources that the government had conducted with various interest groups. If Gaidar's ideology was forming a market economy on the basis of an anti-inflation policy (which he was unable to carry out for the reasons given above),

---

[48]    For a systematic overview, see Shleifer and Treisman, *Without a Map*; for an in-depth analysis of the role of "early winners" in inhibition of market reforms, see Joel Hellman, 'Winners Take All: The Politics of Market Reforms in Post-Communist Transitions', *World Politics*, 50, no. 2 (1998), 203–234.

Gerashchenko's ideology was essentially an aspiration to preserve the entire Soviet economy in the hope that it would somehow miraculously avoid the transformational recession. In the end, Gerashchenko himself was a victim of the inflation he had caused. In 1993, Finance Minister Boris Fyodorov achieved a certain improvement of the situation, but after his dismissal in early 1994, the Central Bank once more began vigorously increasing the volume of monetary emission,[49] and in October 1994 (on so-called "Black Tuesday"), the ruble dropped drastically. After this, Gerashchenko was forced to resign.

"Black Tuesday" had another important effect. It marked the beginning of a new stage of anti-inflation policy, managed by Chubais, who became the deputy prime minister responsible for macro-economic policy as a whole. This policy resulted from a series of compromises with major interest groups. Unable to reduce budget expenditures drastically, Chubais began to develop a mechanism for the domestic financial market that would cover the budget deficit without the monetary emissions on which Gerashchenko had relied so much before "Black Tuesday". This mechanism was initially established in 1993 by Fyodorov, but it was Chubais who implemented it in full.

During the period of initial accumulation of capital (the late 1980s–early 1990s), large amounts of money accumulated in Russian business circles, which used little of it for investments in the real sector of the economy for the reasons given above, but instead actively moved it abroad, or used it for currency speculation. Chubais offered high profitability on state bonds so that Russian business would give loans to the state. In other words, the interests of the government in the financing of the budget deficit coincided with the interests of business actors in achieving high profits. This combination led to major progress in combatting inflation, as its rate began to drop, and the currency exchange rate stabilized. Or rather, the ruble no longer fell swiftly, but lost its value

---

49    See *Rossiiskie ekonomicheskie reformy: poteryannyi god*, Andrei Illarionov (ed.) (Moscow: Institute of Economic Analysis, 1994), 27, 31.

relative to the US dollar within previously established limits (the so-called currency corridor policy).[50]

This mechanism effectively merges the collective benefits of major interest groups at a given moment, postponing the need to "pay the bills" for years to come. International experience shows that state bonds become an important tool for solving financial problems in many countries, regardless of the level of development of democracy and a market economy. From a purely economic point of view, this approach merits serious criticism, as (all else being equal) it inhibits private investments. Money loaned by the state can no longer be invested in building factories or roads. But given the weakness of the Russian state, the ongoing fiscal crisis, and the strong pressure from interest groups, it became a more convenient mechanism for solving problems than significantly cutting state expenditures or carrying out monetary emission.

Chubais' efforts to ensure financial stabilization in the mid-1990s were based on the experience he had gained during mass privatization in 1992–1994. Evidently, that was what had taught him to not only build his policy on economic ideas he had adopted beforehand (however correct they may have been), but also to take into account the influence of key interest groups. As the head of the Goskomimushchestvo (State Property Committee), Chubais understood that it would be difficult to carry out privatization with the maximum possible involvement of strategic investors, for a number of reasons.[51]

First, state enterprise directors and labor collectives simply could not allow investors who had acquired a major stake via an

---

[50]   See Daniel Treisman, 'Fighting Inflation in a Transitional Regime: Russia's Anomalous Stabilization', *World Politics*, 50, no.2 (January 1998), 235–265; Travin, *Ocherki noveishei istorii Rossii*, 285–288.

[51]   For an overview of the government's approach to privatization, see Maxim Boycko, Andrei Shleifer, Robert Vishny, *Privatizing Russia* (Cambridge, MA: MIT Press, 1995); see also Alfred Kokh, *The Selling of the Soviet Empire* (New York: S.PI Books, 2000); Shleifer, Treisman, *Without a Map*. For critical analyses, see, for example, Joseph R. Blasi, Maria Kroumova, Douglas Kruse, *Kremlin's Capitalism: Privatizing the Russian Economy* (Ithaca, NY: Cornell University Press, 1997); Andrew Barnes, *Owning Russia: The Struggle over Factories, Farms, and Power* (Ithaca, NY: Cornell University Press, 2006).

auction or in a tender to enter their enterprise, and thus would not allow them to become real owners. Insiders had already long regarded enterprises as their own, and this perception was guided by Soviet ideology, which stated that in the Soviet Union, enterprises and factories had belonged to the workers since the 1917 revolution. Furthermore, in the course of spontaneous privatization, directors had seen that the control they had over the enterprise gave them a genuine opportunity for rent-seeking and receiving major revenues, and they certainly had a great interest in preventing any outsiders from entering their territory.

Second, the Russian state, which had just emerged from the ruins of the Soviet Union and faced a great deal of economic problems, was relatively weak and unable to implement laws if influential interest groups strongly opposed its decisions. With regard to privatization, this meant that in the majority of cases, it was impossible to remove a de facto owner from an enterprise using the assistance of law enforcement agencies. Government decrees could not be implemented as the prosecutor's office, judges and police were more dependent on regional authorities than on the federal center. The regional authorities, in their turn, were in close contact with the directors of major enterprises, and interested in avoiding mass protests by director-controlled labor collectives.

Third, it was impossible to attract strategic investors in the wake of privatization in post-reform Russia because of both financial and political instability.[52] Market reformers risked losing their power, while prospects of a Communist revenge in Russia severely devalued ownership, as in this scenario privatization could soon be replaced by new nationalization and major financial losses for investors. Russia was also unattractive for investment because many of its enterprises were inefficient, and required excessively large-scale restructuring. With the exception of the oil and gas industries, ferrous and non-ferrous metallurgy, forestry, diamond and gold production, construction in large cities, energy in-

---

[52] For details, see Yegor Gaidar, *Days of Defeat and Victory* (Seattle: University of Washington Press, 1999); McFaul, *Russia's Unfinished Revolution*, Chapters 6–9; Shleifer and Treisman, *Without a Map*.

dustry and certain areas of shipbuilding, there were very few enterprises in Russia that would interest potential investors. Thus,
even ignoring the investment climate in the first half of the 1990s,
privatization with the use of strategic investors could likely only
affect a minor share of enterprises, while their bulk would remain
unattractive. In this sense, the conditions in those small countries
of Central and Eastern Europe which had a small number of enterprises attractive for investors were considerably different from
the conditions that had formed in Russia.

Fourth, privatization with the involvement of strategic investors is a lengthy process even in favorable conditions. The property sold must first be valued, and auctions and tenders organized.
The sale itself takes a great deal of time. In other words, with this
approach to privatization, property would spend years at the disposal of old Soviet directors, and await the moment when officials
found the time to finally deal with it. If one takes into account the
spontaneous privatization that took place in many enterprises, it
becomes clear that the assets would be stolen long before official
privatization was carried out. Waiting for a long time would mean
the Russian state losing control of the property.

Fifth, privatization through tenders, which are held together
with the evaluation of property made by officials and experts, inevitably draws criticism from the media and political opponents
of the government. It is alleged that property prices are intentionally undervalued, and tenders held unjustly. Cases that greatly
depend on those organizing the privatization process inevitably
draw accusations of corruption. In Russia in the 1990s, which was
split into warring political camps, charges of corruption became
an important issue in numerous conflicts. Accordingly, any privatization not conducted according to a precise standard scheme established by legal regulations would have been cause for serious
accusations.

Taking all of these issues into account, it is no wonder that
mass privatization in Russia had to be carried out quickly, and
most importantly that it needed to take into account the interests
of enterprise directors and labor collectives. This is indeed what
happened in practice. In the vast majority of cases, labor collec-

tives were able to receive a majority of shares for free. On the advice of the directors, they chose the option, which would lead their enterprise to be privatized. As a rule, outsiders were only able to buy relatively small amounts of shares, acquired through auctions and tenders, and this minimized social tensions within enterprises, at least at the initial post-privatization stage.

Russian mass privatization is often called "voucher" privatization, meaning that it was carried out through state-issued privatization checks, which were distributed to all citizens of the country for free. In fact, this statement is only correct in formal terms, but not in substance. Indeed, Russian citizens had the right to receive privatization checks (often called "vouchers"), as a means of payment for pieces of enterprise property during privatization. This approach was not so much an attempt to ensure equal opportunities for access to state property for Russian citizens as an important element in the policy of appeasement of interest groups. Giving stakes in enterprises to labor collectives only took into account the interests of workers of privatized enterprises and their directors. But what about school teachers, doctors in state hospitals and clinics, professors and lecturers at universities, military and police officers, and everyone else who did not work in privatized enterprises? The voucher mechanism was introduced in order to avoid their alienation from the state property. A teacher or librarian received a privatization check even though schools and libraries remained state institutions.

The experience of mass privatization in Russia demonstrated that while giving controlling stakes to labor collectives fulfilled its task for the most part (there were no cases of serious manifestations of discontent in enterprises), the vouchers had a poor reputation overall. Millions of people did not understand where and how they were to be invested, but expected relatively high revenues in future. Only a few received these revenues, by skillfully investing their privatization checks in competitive enterprises. But the majority of Russians invested them in newly established check investment funds, and received practically nothing from them. This was both because some of the funds were fraudulent, and because these funds themselves were forced to invest the vouchers collected from Russians in uncompetitive enterprises to which strategic investors did not come.[53]

Where for many vouchers were simply lost, the shares of enterprises received by representatives of labor collectives slowly passed into the hands of other owners. At factories and plants that investors were interested in, there appeared purchasers of bonds, who eventually acquired controlling stakes. In many cases, this was done in agreement with enterprise directors, as they were the ones who could provide the purchasers with the most favorable conditions for their actions. These purchasers of bonds were permitted inside the territories of enterprises, where these people could contact workers without hindrance. During the 1990s, lengthy wage arrears were common at many Russian enterprises, and the level of payment was extremely low, so the "shareholders" who used to work at these enterprises were glad to sell the bonds they owned in order to buy food for their family, or simply a bottle of vodka. Clearly, the directors of enterprises received their rewards for working with investors in these cases, which fully corresponded to their mutual interests.[54]

Thus, mass privatization satisfied the investors' interest in shares in potentially attractive enterprises (if indirectly), satisfied the interest of directors in receiving a certain compensation for stopping spontaneous privatization, and even satisfied the interests of workers of labor collectives in receiving at least minimal personal benefit from their factory. Privatization provided the opportunity for strategic investors to gain access to at least some enterprises. Ultimately, it prepared the Russian economy to move from the transformation recession to eventual growth. And this growth did indeed begin in 1999.

---

[53]    For these arguments, see Yegor Gaidar, Anatoly Chubais, *Razvilki noveishei istorii Rossii* (St. Petersburg: Norma, 2011): 66.

[54]    For extended case studies of major Russian enterprises, see Yuko Adachi, *Building Big Business in Russia: The Impact of Informal Corporate Governance Practices* (Abingdon: Routledge, 2010). See also Yakov Pappe, Yana Galukhina, *Rossiiskii krupnyi biznes: pervye 15 let. Ekonomicheskie khroniki 1993-2008* (Moscow: State University – Higher School of Economics, 2009).

A direct push for the post-transition recovery of the Russian economy came from the devaluation of the ruble, which began in August 1998. The currency corridor collapsed because speculators, under the influence of the Asian economic crisis, began to sell Russian bonds, convert their rubles into dollars and invest their funds in the more reliable foreign assets.[55] In 1998, this caused a radical collapse of the system of state-business relations that had formed three years previously, and was a major blow for economic interest groups. While immediately after the "Black Tuesday" of 1994, Chubais had been able to involve business interests in providing loans for the Russian government, it became impossible for him to continue doing so in the atmosphere of panic caused by the crisis. The ruble fell, and the exchange rate for the US dollar quickly quadrupled. The Russian state declared a default on its obligations. Given these conditions, Russian imports dropped drastically. But the devaluation also opened new opportunities for import substitution, and Russian business successfully exploited them. Within seven post-reform years, it was able to recover and experience new levels of post-transition economic growth.

## Intermediate Conclusions

Thus, we can see that the key ideas with which the Soviet Union approached perestroika transformed drastically over the course of fifteen years under the influence of various interest groups. It was impossible to conduct policies on the basis of reformist socialist ideas, as they were based on the illusion that it was possible to build a new socialism "with a human face". When building actually began, it emerged that no one in the Soviet Union was genuinely interested in it. Even the economic interest groups (enterprise directors, cooperators, bankers) who were able to gain major bene-

---

[55]  For detailed accounts, see Andrei Illarionov, 'Kak byl organizovan rossiiskii finansovyi krizis', *Voprosy ekonomiki*, no. 12 (1998), 12–31; 'Krizis finansovoi sistemy Rossii: osnovnye factory i ekonomicheskaya politika', *Voprosy ekonomiki*, no. 11 (1998), 36–64; *Obzor ekonomicheskoi politiki Rossii za 1998 god*, Andrei Poletaev (ed.) (Moscow Bureau of Economic Analysis, ROSSPEN, 1999); Johnson, *A Fistful of Rubles*; Gilman, *No Precedent, No Plan*.

fits from spontaneous privatization strove for private ownership and were not satisfied with half-hearted transformations.

In theory, it was possible to conduct economic policies on the basis of market capitalist ideas, and it was on this basis that the Russian economy moved from recession to growth. The impact of the changes launched by Gaidar's reforms was very strong. But the conduct of reforms was imperfect in many ways. The major interest groups were opposed to the financial stability, which the reformers planned to implement. As a result, Russia became hostage to high inflation, which was essentially a compromise that made it possible to preserve the market economy, satisfying (if only temporarily) the interest groups that strove to lobby for the state's financial support. It was possible to suppress inflation through release of state bonds, built on business interests in favorable investments. But in August 1998, the pyramid of state debt collapsed. Major interest groups not only influenced financial policy, but also had a massive impact on privatization, which was carried out to the benefit of labor collectives and the directorate of former state enterprises. But eventually investors and their capital did come to the potentially profitable enterprises which turned into major drivers of Russia's development in the 2000s.

# Chapter 3.
# The Historical Path and the Slowdown of Changes

From the seventeenth century, Russia was influenced in many ways by ideas coming from the West, and attempted to develop in accordance with challenges from more successful nations. But until the mid-eighteenth century, these challenges could not provide incentives for genuine modernization: the development of a market economy, democratization, or construction of civil society.[56] At that time, Europe itself, taken as a society, had not chosen freedom. When new trends of enlightenment, capitalism, and political change developed in Europe, Western ideas began to enter Russia, gradually transforming the visions and behavior of elites. However, their effects on the historical path being followed by Russia at that time (also known as path dependency) continue to greatly influence the transformation of the elites' mindsets, and hinder further changes in Russia.

## A Patient More Dead than Alive

The first attempts at true modernization of Russian society took place during the reign of Catherine the Great. The German princess who ascended to the Russian throne was very sensitive to trends from the West because of her origin, and an era arrived when the unlimited despotism of the past contrasted greatly with the modernization processes that had begun in other countries. Petrine absolutism, under Peter the Great himself, largely fit into the European picture, but several decades after his death, this absolutism seemed like a total anachronism.

For the further development of Russian society, it was important for Catherine to implement two key changes: The first was to exempt the nobility from mandatory service, so that the intellec-

---

56    For an overview of features of European modernization, see Travin, Marganiya, *Evropeiskaya modernizatsiya*, vol.1, 37–47.

tual potential of the elite could be concentrated in the spheres of economy and culture. The second was to free the peasantry from serfdom, accelerating the development of agriculture and forming a labor market in the cities and towns. No particular problems arose in solving the first task, but the second remained unresolved until 1861, 99 years after Catherine came to the throne. This kind of postponement is very characteristic of Russia, as it shows that on Russia's long historical path, major transformations can only be carried out to the degree to which they are supported by major interest groups.

The decree on the freedom of the nobility had been issued during the short reign of Peter III. The fact that a relatively weak ruler could conduct such an important reform indicates how overdue it was. The nobility benefited from this act, and there were essentially no losers. Even with a free nobility, the state was no longer afraid of being without military officers, as official service in the Russian army was considered prestigious and lucrative, attracting everyone for whom it was a chance to improve their standing in the world. If the societal elite, with alternative sources of income (land and serfs), suddenly preferred to avoid fulfilling its duties, for the Russian army such avoidance was to its advantage. The positions held by noble "ingénues" (who served under the tsar against their will based on their inheritance and status) were now held by people who had a strong material interest in military service.

The lack of a political struggle over the issue of the freedom of the nobility has led to a lack of interest in analyzing it, and it has come to be seen as being only of "secondary nature". Although this reform should have placed Peter III among the key reformers, it is usually taken for granted, and he now has a reputation of being if not a complete fool, then at least a failed leader (having been overthrown by his wife soon after his ascent to the throne). If he had been forced to fight for this reform, the tsar's reputation would have been quite different. But there was no struggle. Or rather, the nobility was able to secure certain concessions under Anna Ioannovna,[57] followed by a new generation, and everyone gradually grew used to the idea of the need for changes. In effect, Peter III only legitimized the inevitable.

Catherine naturally approved of the freedom of the nobility as an objective need, although on the whole she did not hold her late husband in high regard. Of her own achievements, one may note the abolition of the beloved state monopolies of Elizabeth the First: these changes brought every person the full right to establish industrial enterprises.[58] However, Catherine's later changes were less successful: she did not owe her reputation as a great ruler to reforms, but to the territorial expansions made in the south of the country during her reign.

It may be said that at the start of Catherine's reign, the young ruler of German origin found herself immersed in a foreign experience of modernization. "Influenced by Montesquieu, she wrote that the laws are the greatest good that people can give and receive," Vasily Klyuchevsky wrote. In the empress's Instruction to the All-Russian Legislative Commission, which was drawn up in the early years of her reign, 294 of the 655 articles were borrowed from Montesquieu, and many others from other foreign authors. "'My only contribution to this work is the arrangement of the material, and one line and a word here and there,' the empress herself wrote".[59]

However, Catherine increasingly recognized Russia's dependence on its historical path over the years, i.e. she realized that introducing laws, eliminating serfdom and making Russia meet European "standards" of freedom was an extremely difficult task: this bold move would undermine the position of the conservative section of the nobility, a highly influential interest group. Naturally, there were also supporters of major changes among the land-

---

[57]  See Evgeny Anisimov, *Rossiya bez Petra, 1725-1740* (St. Petersburg: Lenizdat, 1994), 292–293.

[58]  See Mikhail Tugan-Baranovskii, *Izbrannoe. Russkaya fabrika v proshlom i nasto-yashchem. Istoricheskoe razvitie russkoi fabriki v XIX veke* (Moscow: Nauka, 1997), 111.

[59]  See Vasily Klyuchevsky, 'Kurs russkoi istorii, Part 5', in Vasily Klyuchevsky, *Izbrannoe*, vol.5 (Moscow: Mysl', 1989), 68–70.

owners, but the majority of the nobility during her reign was completely unprepared to abandon as lucrative a source of income as forced serf labor. Furthermore, as Klyuchevsky wrote, "under the legislation of the eighteenth century, the landowner remained a government agent, an overseer of the farm and a collector of state taxes".[60] In other words, given the absence of a developed bureaucracy, which could be entrusted with managing state finances, the empress was inevitably forced to rely on the country's landowners. The landowner was now less necessary to the monarch as an officer than as a quasi-official ensuring the collection of taxes to be received by the treasury.

One should also note another important fact: whereas the freedom of the nobility during the time of Catherine the Great matched the natural European background, freedom of the peasantry was not yet established in many regions of Central and Eastern Europe. In this respect, Russia was not particularly exceptional. Serfdom was preserved in the Polish lands, in the Prussian lands beyond the Elbe, and in most of the Hapsburg Empire (apart from the western lands inhabited exclusively by Germans). Furthermore, plantation slavery existed across the ocean – in Spanish, Portuguese and British colonies (later on, these areas would become the southern states of the USA).

Overall, freedom had not yet become an absolute value for Europe. One may rather say that there were two different approaches to agricultural labor. One was based on free labor, the other on slavery, and at that time, it was not yet certain which of these approaches yielded better results in economic terms. The choice between these approaches depended on the conditions of historical path of a certain country, and also on the nature of agricultural production. The plantation economy (cotton, sugar, tobacco, and rice in America and grain in Eastern Europe) remained efficient when forced labor was used, while British livestock breeding or French and Italian winegrowing did not involve any serfdom at all.

---

[60]    Klyuchevsky, 'Kurs russkoi istorii, Part 5', 124.

Thus, neither her German origins, nor appreciation of Enlightenment philosophy, nor personal hostility to slavery could render Catherine an uncompromising champion of freedom at that moment, as ideas of the freedom of the peasantry would have faced great opposition. But the situation began to change during the reign of her grandson Alexander I. Austrian emperor Joseph II Hapsburg abolished serfdom in his empire in the 1780s. In Prussia, Baron von Stein did the same in 1807, at the time when Alexander was on the Russian throne. In the same year, Britain outlawed the slave trade. Yet all these changes were very difficult, and involved the conflicts of different interest groups. In the Hapsburg Empire, a number of changes made by Joseph II were annulled after his death, and real land reform took place over half a century after serfdom was abolished. In Prussia, the process took place much more quickly, but did not end until the 1820s, at which point Alexander's reign in Russia was already coming to an end.[61] In the United States, slavery continued in the South until the 1860s, and in Brazil, it lasted even longer.

Alexander I tackled the problem of serfdom with more enthusiasm than his grandmother had. With all the energy of a young man, and one who been educated by the Swiss thinker La Harpe, he attempted to prepare reforms with his friends. The emperor's so-called "circle of young friends" included Prince Adam Chartorysky, Count Pavel Stroganov, Count Victor Kochubei, and also Nikolai Novosiltsev. Later, the emperor entrusted Mikhail Speransky with developing a plan for major political transformation in Russia.[62] But in the early nineteenth century, it remained impossible to implement significant modernization in Russia. The influence of the "free Western world" proved weak: Europe itself was only just discarding the shackles of slavery, and

---

[61] For a more detailed account, see Travin, Marganiya, *Evropeiskaya modernizatsiya*, vol.1.

[62] For more detailed accounts, see Mikhail Safonov, *Problema reform v pravitel'stvennoi politike na rubezhe XVIII i XIX vv.* (Leningrad: Nauka, 1988); Vladimir Tomsinov, *Speransky* (Moscow: Molodaya gvardiya, 2006); Dmitry Travin, Otar Marganiya, *Modernizatsiya – ot Elizavety Tudor do Egora Gaidara* (Moscow: AST, 2011).

Russian society was still insufficiently familiar with the experience of its Western neighbors. At the same time, the influence of conservative interest groups continued to dominate in Russia. Some progressively-minded representatives of Russian nobility, such as Nikolai Turgenev, hoped that the emperor's absolute power would break resistance and free the serfs despite the vested interests of the majority of the nobility,[63] but even the powers of the autocracy proved insufficient for such major changes.

As a result, the "circle of young friends" was unable to launch any serious changes. In the end, Speransky fell out of favor with the monarch, lost his position at the court, and was exiled from the Russian capital. Towards the end of Alexander I's reign, he endorsed experiments aimed at a completely different mechanism of governing the country that was quite opposite to modernization – the military settlements of Alexei Arakcheyev. However, he still continued changes, at least to the extent that progressive ideas borrowed from the West corresponded to the preferences of the dominant interest groups. The official press actively promoted Adam Smith's economic theory.[64] A conquered Poland was granted greater political rights than Russia itself. The Baltic serfs were freed, and reforms in the Baltic region clearly followed the path of reforms carried out in Prussia, the western near-border area of the Romanovs' Empire from which the German landowners took their cue. In Russia itself, serfs could be freed under the 1803 decree on free farmers, i.e. to the extent that the landowners desired. The significance of this decree proved rather small, as on the whole preserving serfdom still corresponded to the interests of the nobility. It is worth mentioning that at this time, the ideas of free trade and serfdom of peasantry combined with little difficulty, as free trade was good for the export of grain and increased the efficiency of landholders' estates.[65] A noble could consider himself progres-

[63]   See Victor Leontovich, *Istoriya liberalizma v Rossii, 1762-1914* (Moscow: Russkii put', 1995), 61–62.

[64]   Tugan-Baranovskii, *Izbrannoe*, 285.

[65]   Tugan-Baranovskii, *Izbrannoe*, 296–297.

sive if he read Adam Smith, but the aspiration to free the serfs was less acceptable, and could be considered dangerous free thinking.

Nicholas I, who succeeded Alexander I, at first glance seemed to pursue a policy that was completely opposed to the freedom-oriented one of his elder brother. But the difference between the paths of the two brothers was determined by objective circumstances rather than by the two monarchs' personalities. At the start of his reign, Alexander I did not see reforms as an extremely difficult task. But when Nicholas came to the throne, he faced the Decembrists' uprising and realized how precarious this throne could be if influential interest groups (especially those supported by the military officers) were to attempt to topple it. Objectively, he was forced to rely on the conservative segments of society from the very first day of his reign, as the progressive nobility (which was close to the Decembrists) associated itself with his brother Konstantin. It proved particularly difficult to conduct any reforms whatsoever in this situation, as he risked losing friends in one camp without gaining them in another. Nicholas I himself understood the need for changes, and continued to prepare them as best he could. This preparation was successfully implemented during the initial period of his rule, in particular by Count Pavel Kiselyov, who had previously succeeded in implementing reforms in the Danube principalities occupied by Russia, where peasants not only ceased to be serfs, but received civil rights. As Yakov Gordin wrote of these reforms: "Free trade enlivened economic thought, and the new system of taxation doubled the state's revenues, burdening the taxable groups less than the previous system".[66]

However, the most important changes during Nicholas' rule did not take place within the state apparatus, but within Russian society. In the 1830s–1840s, it began to change fundamentally. As the historian of Russian liberalism Viktor Leontovich wrote, "This was the era in which one system was subtly replaced by another –

---

[66]   See Yakov Gordin, *Pravo na poedinok* (Leningrad: Sovetskii pisatel', 1989), 59–60.

the serf system became a civil system".[67] A new generation of Russians was much better informed than their fathers and grandfathers about events and developments taking place in various European countries. In addition, Europe itself had changed fundamentally by this time. As a result, the freedom that was gradually becoming consolidated in nineteenth-century Europe had a much stronger influence on Russia than it had had in the past. The emergence of the category of intellectuals known as Westernizers showed that at least one segment of Russian society was consciously and deliberately striving to modernize Russia according to a model taken from abroad. By this time, new ideas had been developed by a certain cohort of people, who had received university education in Germany and regarded German philosophy as the last word in scholarship. Konstantin Kavelin wrote that after 1835, German scholarship "began to be taught by a circle of talented and fresh young professors" at Moscow University, where he had been a student.[68] According to Alexander Herzen, following the defeat of the Polish uprising in 1830, a certain section of the Russian youth, instead of expressing "childish" revolutionary attitudes, began to take an interest in European philosophical thought, ranging from Schelling to St. Simon.[69] As a result, warm relationships were established between progressive professors and thoughtful students. "On the days previously agreed, many students always appeared to hear Granovsky, Kavelin and Redkin," Boris Checherin recalled. "There was lively discussion, not just about scholarly subjects, but about topical issues and works of literature as well".[70]

Some Russian thinkers of the new generation even took on the German philosophy of the special path as a model for a similar philosophy in Russia. But the majority, "without beating about the

---

[67]   See Leontovich, *Istoriya liberalizma v Rossii*, 152.

[68]   See Konstantin Kavelin, *Nash umstvennyi stroi: stat'i po filosofii russkoi istorii i kul'tury* (Moscow: Pravda, 1989) 263.

[69]   See Alexander Herzen, *Byloe i dumy*, vol.1 (Moscow: Khudozhestvennaya literatura, 1973) 192–193.

[70]   Quotation from Leontovich, *Istoriya liberalizma v Rossii*, 168.

bush", were interested in conducting policy reforms in the country that were close in spirit to the German ones, and carry out a technological revolution close in spirit to the English. Yet the most radical Westernizers dreamed of a revolutionary movement in the French manner. This was the exact point when one of Stendhal's characters said that the Russians did the same thing as the French, but with a delay of fifty years.

During this period, the new ideas formed in university auditoriums and narrow intellectual circles began to spread across Russia thanks to literary journals, which, as Alexander Herzen justly noted, "contain[ed] the entire intellectual movement of the country".[71] These journals were complex constructions, optimally suited for the dissemination of ideas. They "lured" readers in with the name of some great writer who published a serialized novel in a number of issues, but at the same time included examples of journalism and op-eds in the same issues, written in the spirit of the times. As a result, modern Western trends, elaborated by small groups of thinkers in Moscow or Petersburg, took on a simplified and stylized form, were adapted for the appreciation of educated readers, and reached the distant provincial cities and towns, isolated rural estates, and conservative clerical families in which nonconformist children were growing up.

It may be said that the influence of Western ideas significantly influenced the situation that emerged in Russia on the basis of its historical path. New generations felt the effect of free thinking more strongly than their fathers and grandfathers, and the pressure of tradition more weakly. As an effect of these changes, well-established interest groups gradually began to transform. Although landowners continued to depend on serf labor and were opposed to plans to free the serfs, an increasing number of aristocrats demonstrated their moral intolerance of slavery. Mikhail Tugan-Baranovsky noted how the views of the free traders had changed by the 1850s. Now, unlike the free traders of the begin-

---

[71] See Alexander Herzen, 'O razvitii revolyutsionnykh idei v Rossii', in Alexander Herzen, *Sochineniya*, vol.3 (Moscow: Gosudarstvennoe izdatel'stvo khudozhestvennoi literatury, 1956), 464.

ning of the nineteenth century, they condemned serfdom and saw the future of the country to be in the development of industry.[72]

From an economic standpoint, serf labor could probably have continued to exist for some time, but from a moral standpoint, it now had an oppressive effect not only for the slaves, but also for the masters, who could no longer feel themselves to be both Europeans and owners of serfs. Influential bureaucrats, refined thinkers and pragmatic landowners were increasingly ready to support the abolition of serfdom. "The serf system had reached a dead end not only because of its low profitability, but because it was impossible to preserve the former level of violence," Russian historian Boris Mironov accurately noted. "(…) The time for abolishing serfdom of peasantry came at the end of the 1850s, when public opinion came to support the idea that serfdom was incompatible with the spirit of the times". [73]

The feeling that slavery was intolerable was intensified by Russia's defeat in the Crimean War of 1853–1856. Although the connection between the weakness of the army, the level of development of industry and the use of non-economic coercion in agriculture was very complex and unclear, the shame felt by the Tsarist regime, together with the opposition from different interest groups, inevitably strengthened the position of supporters of change. This was the intellectual environment that Alexander II found himself in when he came to the throne. As the famous journalist Dmitry Pisarev wrote in 1862, "to attack the idea of abolishing serfdom, a brilliant person is not enough; one must also live in a time when the issue is highly visible, when voices for and against it are heard, when accordingly the importance of this issue even strikes a person who does not yet know whose side logic and justice are on." [74]

---

[72]   See Tugan-Baranovskii, *Izbrannoe*, 488.

[73]   See Boris Mironov, *Sotsial'naya istoriya Rossii perioda imperii*, vol.1 (XVIII – nachalo XX vv.) (St. Petersburg: Dmity Bulanin, 2003), 407–408.

[74]   See Dmitry Pisarev, *Istoricheskie eskizy: izbrannye stat'i* (Moscow: Pravda, 1989), 37–38.

The "post-Crimean" observations of the nephew of Count Kiselyov, Dmitry Milyutin, who later became minister of the military, are characteristic in this sense. "The moribund inertia in which Russia remained until the Crimean War, and then the hopeless disappointment caused by the Sevastopol rout, was now replaced with a youthful enthusiasm, rosy hopes for revival, for the renewal of the entire state system. The former strict ban on the verbal, written and even printed discussion of the truth was removed, and everywhere free, merciless condemnation of the existing orders was heard".[75] In this atmosphere of mass condemnation of the old serfdom system, the monarch was finally able to carry out progressive reforms, as they now had support and did not challenge the interests of the dominant interest groups.

## A Patient More Alive than Dead

Thus, the long-term impact of ideas of freedom borrowed from the West on Russia, and the analysis of foreign experiences of conducting reforms, gradually led to a change in the balance of power between conservative and reformist camps. This shift finally led to the abolition of serfdom in February 1861.[76] But naturally, even given the public hostility towards slavery, this abolition could not seriously undermine the position of the aristocracy as the most influential interest group. The serfs, who had received freedom "at no cost", were forced to purchase plots of land from landowners, thus remaining temporarily indebted (and therefore not fully free), for a long time to come.

One might say that the reform, which arose from the need to take the positions of interest groups into account, determined the new balance of power and the new arrangements of these groups in the post-reform period. Russia's subsequent development up until the Bolshevik revolution was determined by historical path

---

[75]   See Dmitry Milyutin, *Vospominaniya, 1860-1862 gg.* (Moscow: redaktsiya zhurnala "Russkii arkhiv", 1999), 39–40.

[76]   See Mironov, *Sotsial'naya istoriya Rossii*, vol.1, 377–400; Boris Litvak, *Perevorot 1861 goda v Rossii: pochemu ne realizovalas' reformatorskaya al'ternativa* (Moscow: Politizdat, 1991).

dependence, and the great reforms of Alexander II served as an important milestone on this path (along with the abolition of serfdom, they included military and judicial reforms, as well as the introduction of local self-government). The trajectory of Russian modernization from 1861 to 1917 was determined by five main factors:

First, reform created the potential to accelerate economic development, including major industrial growth. Upon the liberation of former serfs, part of the rural population moved to urban areas, and this migration brought a larger workforce to newly emerged industries. At the same time, the process of urbanization contributed to the formation of a large market for consumption, as peasants who left the countryside and became urban workers now needed to buy most consumer goods with their own salaries. In this sense, modernization in Russia corresponded to the path previously taken by other European nations to a great degree, and demonstrated that the combination of capital and labor creates economic growth, despite the preservation of numerous old problems in political, social and ideological arenas. Although the success of Russian industry did not make itself felt immediately after reforms for a number of reasons, nevertheless from the mid-1890s the economic boom became obvious.[77]

Second, for many years reform created conditions for major social tensions, as it was essentially conducted in the interests of landowners. Despite losing its previous influence, the conservative aristocracy was such a powerful interest group that it would have been dangerous for the monarch to ignore it. But among progressive thinkers and radically minded intellectuals, the feeling arose that the changes carried out by Alexander II were halfhearted. Many young people who had hoped for rapid and just reforms believed that "the liberation of the serfs in Russia was a cynical parody of their plans and hopes".[78] Accordingly, the reformer tsar began to be regarded as an obstacle on the path to moderniza-

---

77    See Tugan-Baranovskii, *Izbrannoe*, 338.

78    See Isaiah Berlin, *Istoriya svobody. Rossiya* (Moscow: Novoe literaturnoe obozrenie, 2001), 319.

tion of the country. Terrorists began to hunt him, launched a series of assassination attempts, and finally were able to kill him exactly twenty years after serfdom was abolished.[79] Thus, escalation of social problems was the other side of the reform coin. The success of modernization in the economic arena was inseparable from growing discontent among various societal groups.

Third, while a small group of revolutionary activists became radicalized and resorted to terrorism, the main segments of young people disappointed in politics tended towards pessimism. Their indifference toward the events taking place in the country created a favorable environment for the radicals' actions. They gained a numerical advantage over the moderate reformers, despite being a relatively marginal group. At the same time, the large uneducated segments of the population found themselves in a complex and contradictory situation. Economic growth created new opportunities for them, but the inertia of traditionalism was considerable. As the Russian cultural commentator Igor Yakovenko observed, "The peasant world experiences a split and disintegrates. One group chooses to accept and master new things. Another group feels that the world has collapsed and feels the urgent need to return to the original simplicity of the traditional world". [80] Peasants who moved to the city and attempted to learn to become industrial workers found their lives even more difficult, as they no longer felt the support of the rural community, and were forced to accustom themselves to completely new conditions of life and existence. The "move from the countryside to the town is a complex and extremely painful process, with the migrant feeling constant stress".[81]

Fourth, as growing discontent caused a rise in terrorism, conservative interest groups gained momentum once more. Modernization could not please everyone, especially as it initially resulted

---

[79] See Leonid Lyashenko, *Alexander II: Istoriya trekh odinochestv* (Moscow: Molodaya gvardiya, 2003), 264–321.

[80] See Igor Yakovenko, *Poznanie Rossii: tsivilizatsionnyi analiz* (Moscow: ROSSPEN, 2012), 543.

[81] See Yakovenko, *Poznanie Rossii: tsivilizatsionnyi analiz*, 547.

in the impoverishment of the proletariat, caused by the flood of many rural residents into urban areas, as well as by the active mechanization of labor that left thousands of workers jobless.[82] The country's economic success only became noticeable at the end of the nineteenth century, while "terrorist threats" were observed much earlier. As a result, the Russian authorities developed conservative tendencies as a response to radicalization. The triumph of conservatism, in its turn, caused discontent among radicals, who believed that the reforms launched under Alexander II were to be continued until Russia moved from autocracy to a constitutional monarchy. The newly emerged Marxists looked much further ahead than radical populists and constitutionalist intellectuals, hoping both to destroy autocracy as a political system, and capitalism as a social order.

The terrorism of the "People's Will" and especially revolutionary Marxism did not have their roots in Russia. These destructive phenomena can well be analyzed with the same logic previously mentioned with regard to positive features of modernization. They were generated by the impact of progressive Western ideas on Russia, modified by the country's historical path dependence, which had formed over centuries. Those Russians who desired radical restructuring of society in the shortest timeframe possible looked to the West and appropriated the models that seemed optimal to them. They acted the same way as the reformers who strove to borrow Western institutions and the entrepreneurs who strove to borrow Western technologies and management. But revolutionaries, just like believers in gradual evolution, found that society was far away from their ideals, and that Alexander II's reforms, and their aftermath, were not at all what they wanted.

The history of Russian philosophical thought contains numerous complaints that while the relatively civilized German Marxism had gradually begun to reject its revolutionary nature during the Second International, on Russian soil it became not unlike the concept of Russian rebellion – both meaningless and mer-

---

[82]    See Tugan-Baranovskii, *Izbrannoe*, 422–423.

ciless. As Russian philosopher Nikolay Berdyaev noted, "Orthodox Marxism, which was in fact Marxism transformed in the Russian manner, did not accept the determinist, evolutionary, scientific side of Marxism, but primarily its messianic, myth-making, religious side, allowing the exhalation of revolutionary waves which brought the revolutionary struggle of the proletariat to the fore".[83] In factual terms, this statement is correct. But complaints that Marxism in Russia did not have the outcome its proponents wished for are like complaining that it is, alas, impossible to carry out a painless transplantation of progressive work ethics, or democracy, or a tendency to build institutions of civil society from one national environment to another. Historical path dependence interferes, and causes serious deviations from the original intentions, in every case.

However, neither terrorism nor Marxism could stop Russia's modernization for long. Within the contradictory system in which diverse interests were intertwined, supporters of modernization were able to conduct two more important economic reforms. Firstly, Count Sergei Witte, the finance minister, was able to stabilize the Russian currency and introduce a strong ruble. Later, Pyotr Stolypin, who headed the Russian government after the political changes that took place on the wave of the 1905 revolution, was able to dismantle the Russian rural community (*obshchina*) and allow the peasants to leave it.[84]

Financial stabilization was extremely important for the Russian economy, as the country needed an inflow of foreign capital to develop industry.[85] Though the abolition of serfdom meant there was an abundance of labor force in towns, there were serious problems with capital in Russia. They did not so much lie in

---

[83]  See Nikolay Berdyaev, *Istoki i smysl russkogo kommunizma* (Moscow: Nauka, 1990), 88.

[84]  See Boris Fyodorov, *Pyotr Stolypin: "Ya veryu v Rossiyu:"*, 2 vols. (St. Petersburg: Limbus Press, 2002); Sergei Martynov, *Gosudarstvo i ekonomika: sistema Witte* (St. Petersburg: Nauka, 2002); Igor Arkhipov, *P.A.Stolypin* (St. Petersburg: izdatel'stvo Pushkinskogo fonda, 2017); Travin, Marganiya, *Modernizatsiya – ot Elizavety Tudor do Egora Gaidara.*

[85]  See Tugan-Baranovskii, *Izbrannoe*, 346.

the lack of funds for investing in factories and plants as in poor management. Many landowners, who were forced to adjust to the new economic conditions, were interested in securing revenues by investing in industry, and could have invested their money in business. But in order for these portfolio investments to operate properly, strategic investments were required which would bring not only money but also foreign managerial experience to Russia, as well as technologies that had been developed in various European countries. These investments could have come from most economically successful European countries, but they required a stable ruble. Since the time of Catherine the Great, a weak economy combined with regular costly wars had caused deficits in the Russian state budget, and monetary emission caused further problems. Investing capital in a country where investments could easily lose value because of the speculative policy of the autocracy was a risky undertaking, and so Russia required a strong ruble to accelerate economic growth. Shortly before Witte's reform, a similar task was solved in the Austro-Hungarian Empire by its finance minister Julian Dunajewski.[86] Thus, the Russian monetary changes were based on foreign experience.

The necessity of Stolypin's actions was determined by Russia's historical path dependence, more by its lingering legacy of rural communities than by the effects of Witte's reforms. Development of Russian agriculture was hindered by the division of land within the rural community. Furthermore, according to Boris Mironov's assessment of other forms of Russian communal life, it also slowed the development of agriculture in capitalist terms, through mutual responsibility for tax payments, enforcement of compulsory crop rotation, the work ban on numerous holidays, the public condemnation of excessive diligence, the obligation of the community to help widows, soldiers and orphans, etc.[87] In fact, private ownership as such in terms of rural land ownership did not exist even after Alexander II's great reforms. Solving these problems required new changes: to become the leading grain ex-

---

[86]    See Travin, Marganiya, *Evropeiskaya modernizatsiya*, vol.1, 635–636.

[87]    See Mironov, *Sotsial'naya istoriya Rossii*, vol.1, 459.

porter in Europe, Russia had to improve its agricultural production, attracting significant investments. Giving successful farmers the right to leave the commune and register their land as private property greatly assisted the rapid development of the Russian economy. But while introducing a strong ruble did not particularly concern powerful interest groups, the collapse of the rural community, along with the harsh measures taken by Stolypin to suppress the revolutionary rebellions, increased the split in Russian society. In the end, the reformer was assassinated in 1911.

It may be said that by the beginning of WWI, modernization in Russia had already travelled a long way, and had led to considerable successes. Large cities were developed, urbanization was underway, factories and plants had appeared, and the gross national product rapidly increased. Even the mentality of Russian society began to change gradually. According to Boris Mironov, while the peasant society had previously had difficulty accepting certain features of capitalism, for example, loan operations and interest, after the 1905–1906 revolution the number of credit institutions began to increase swiftly, even in rural areas.[88] In cities and towns, new economic and social ideas spread even more quickly than in villages. People began to act more rationally, striving not to preserve traditions and the old way of life, but to achieve new goals – income, wealth, a career, the ability to ensure a good future for their children, etc.

But in Russia, like other European countries, modernization formed an entire new web of complex contradictions – quite different from the contradictions that had split traditional society. And the tragic events of the twentieth century were not caused by the stagnant nature of the socio-economic system, but rather by the rapid and successful changes in Russia. If for the pre-reform stagnant society, the worst threat was a peasant uprising, unable to overthrow the foundations of the old regime, post-reform society was threatened by revolution, which aimed to destroy the "world of violence" entirely, and to build its own new world on

---

[88] See Mironov, *Sotsial'naya istoriya Rossii*, vol.1, 334.

the ruins, where, as the Communist anthem "The International" put it, "we have been naught, we shall be all".

## Not an Ordinary, but a Permanent Revolution

In 1917, the Russian revolution fundamentally changed the nature of the economic, social and political system. As noted above, in many ways this was caused by the fact that the impact of modernization processes accelerated urbanization and economic development, forming new interest groups, and giving rise to a series of major conflicts between these groups, which were difficult to resolve by peaceful means. In other words, the Russian revolution of 1917 was no accident, although its actual timeframe and parameters could not be strictly predetermined in the early steps of modernization.

Looking at the international experience of modernization, one might say that the revolution in Russia was not some unique event that demonstrated its backwardness. Many European nations had endured a similar ordeal. Revolutions are a harsh but at the same time typical experience for a modernizing society, which comes with a set of major contradictions. But the consequences of such ordeals may be quite different depending on the winners and losers of the revolutionary conflicts emerging upon the collapse of the old regime.[89] The Russian revolution's problems were radical changes in the political system and social organization, which together caused a destructive economic transformation after the Bolsheviks' victory.

Setting aside the discussion on whether the final victory of the Bolsheviks in October was an inevitable consequence of the changes that began with the fall of the monarchy in February 1917, or whether it might not have occurred if circumstances were dif-

---

[89]   For comparative analyses of revolutions, see, for example, Theda Skocpol, *States and Social Revolution: A Comparative Analysis of France, China and Russia* (Cambridge: Cambridge University Press, 1979); Jack Goldstone, *Revolutions: Theoretical, Comparative, and Historical Studies* (New York: Harcourt Brace, 1986).

ferent,[90] the paradoxical connection between the successful pre-revolutionary modernization and the system that arose after the revolution cannot be ignored. Even if one believes that the Bolsheviks' victory was uncertain, one must admit that the revolution, which had not begun as Bolshevik, strongly assisted their final success. It was the success of modernization in Russia that in many ways gave rise to the successes of Bolshevism, and accordingly it contributed to many of Russia's problems in subsequent decades. In other words, Russia's historical path dependence on its pre-revolutionary period complicated its post-revolutionary path, and played a major role in the creation of an economy with a distorted structure, a distorted system of ownership, distorted incentives, and ultimately distorted fates for millions of Russians.

How were the Bolshevik revolution and the Soviet economy connected from a long-term perspective? The nature of Marxist concepts of how a socialist revolution should be conducted is very important for understanding the effect of Bolsheviks' economic policy on Russian modernization. The theory of the dialectic of production forces and production relations set down in Marxism states that at a certain stage, the development of the capitalist economy will enter into irreconcilable conflict with the bourgeois state, and with the very system of capitalist exploitation of one person by another. According to this theory, as class awareness increases over time, workers will strive to change the situation on a fundamental level. For this, the proletariat will launch a revolution that liquidates the practices of private entrepreneurship as its

---

[90] Among the voluminous literature on the Russian revolution, see, for example, Orlando Figes, *A People's Tragedy: Russian Revolution, 1891-1924* (London: Jonathan Cape, 1996); Richard Pipes, *The Russian Revolution* (New York: Vintage Books, 1991); Alexander Rabinowitch, *The Bolsheviks Come to Power: The Revolution of 1917 in Petrograd* (New York: W .W. Norton, 1976); Sean McMeekin, *The Russian Revolution: A New History* (New York: Basic Books, 2016); for Russian-language books, see Vladimir Buldakov, *Krasnaya smuta: priroda i posledstviya revolyutsionnogo nasiliya* (Moscow: ROSSPEN, 2010); Boris Kolonitsky, *Simvoly vlasti i bor'ba za vlast': k izucheniyu politicheskoi kul'tury russkoi revolyutsii 1917 goda* (St. Petersburg: Dmitry Bulanin, 2001).

outcome. Capitalism vanishes, and everything produced by the workers is at the disposal of society as a whole.[91]

According to Marxist theory, the revolution cannot simply take place at any time in any country, but only where the working class is sufficiently strong and aware. This means that the revolution is possible only in truly developed countries with a high degree of industrialization and urbanization, where the size of the peasantry has drastically decreased, the size of the working class has increased, and large cities have emerged. Furthermore, as the existing regime suffers defeats, it may receive military support from neighboring countries (as the experience of several revolutions of the past has shown), and so there is a need for an international unification of proletarian forces. A revolution can only triumph if it takes place in a number of highly developed nations at the same time, such that the bourgeoisie of some countries will be mired in their own concerns, and unable to provide help to the bourgeoisie of others. The thesis on the need for world revolution arose as a practical conclusion from Marxist theory, although in practice, of course, it was assumed that the revolutionary victory of the working class required simultaneous success in only a few key European nations, and not all over the world.

Thus, according to orthodox Marxism, a socialist revolution was completely impossible in Russia, because Russia was primarily peasant-based, with poorly developed cities and towns and a small share of the urban working class, and because an isolated revolution in one country alone was inherently doomed to failure. But Lenin and Trotsky revised Marxist theory to a great degree. They altered it to justify the potential for radical transformation of Russia. According to the revised Marxist theory, a socialist revolution did not necessarily begin when highly-developed productive forces entered into conflict with the existing (capitalist) relations of production, but when a combination of various factors generated a revolutionary situation – when the conflicts already dividing the country began to tear it to pieces, and the lower classes rejected

---

[91]    See Karl Marx, Friedrich Engels, *The Communist Manifesto* (New York: International Publishers, 2014).

their old ways of living, while the upper classes lost their old forms of control. Lenin and Trotsky's changes to Marxism were so radical that they left practically nothing of the previous theory. It must be admitted that it was Lenin and Trotsky, and not the old theorists of Marxism, who properly understood how regimes collapse in practice. That is, they understood the importance for the revolution of the contradictions that have accumulated in society, including those that do not directly relate to the class war between the workers and the bourgeoisie. The Russian revolution confirmed that Lenin and Trotsky were correct. The fall of the old regime took place when dozens of unresolved problems had amassed, and not when the production forces had reached the highest level of development (as, for example, in Britain).

At the same time, Lenin's party was Marxist, and the influence of Marxism on the minds of many Russian intellectuals was very significant. Any changes made to the theory needed to somehow be connected with its foundations. This is why Lenin and Trotsky did not reject the concept of the world revolution, but only formulated the concept of the "weakest link". This stated that the revolution had to initially be launched in the country that was the weakest link in the global chain of capitalist (imperialist) nations, but would then spread in every place where productive forces came into conflict with bourgeois relations of production. In Lenin and Trotsky's understanding, Russia was this weakest link. But for the socialist revolution to triumph, the process that had begun in Russia would have to be developed in other European nations. In practice, this meant that the revolution was to spread from Russia at least to Germany – to a highly-developed, urbanized, industrial country with a large, strong proletariat, and located relatively close to Russia in geographical terms (unlike, say, Britain).

This idea is expressed precisely and laconically in Trotsky's pamphlet "The Permanent Revolution". "Preservation of the proletarian revolution in national boundaries may be only a temporary measure," he wrote, "even if it is a lengthy one, as the experience of the Soviet Union shows. However, with an isolated proletarian dictatorship, the conflicts, external and internal, will inevitably grow alongside the successes. If it continues to remain isolated, the proletarian state will eventually fall victim to these conflicts. The only solution lies in the triumph of the proletariat of advanced countries".[92] The same opinion was also expressed by enemies of the revolution. Immediately after Lenin's death, his harsh critic Alexander Kiesewetter described the concept of the revolution that the Bolshevik leader had stood for, concisely and cynically: "The fool who died in Moscow a few days ago from the very start of his experiment announced in a printed brochure that communism in Russia was impossible, but that Russia was the clump of dry hay which could easily be set alight to start the world social bonfire. Russia will be burned up; but to hell with it, the world will enter the paradise of Communism".[93]

Thus, the specific nature of the Russian revolution lay not in its special destructiveness, brutality or irreconcilability of different parties. Various kinds of revolutionary horrors have been experienced by many countries to a great degree. The distinctive feature of Russian history after the Bolshevik triumph was the spread of the idea that the revolution could not stop, that it needed to be made permanent, and that Russia was only at its first stage and was to prepare for its continuation, which was made inevitable by objective historical laws. These ideas diffused among the new Communist elites both in Russia and beyond. Taken as an ideological position, it was to a great degree a starting point for the Soviet Union's further economic development, which played an important role in how the Russian economy was transformed in the 1990s. Scholarly perceptions of Lenin's NEP, Stalinist industrialization, and the further trajectory of the Soviet economic system from the viewpoint of economic growth and development often ignore the original Bolshevik idea that standard socio-economic categories and indicators were less important than the task of militarization in a country "surrounded by enemies".

---

[92]    See Lev Trotsky, *Permanentnaya revolyutsiya* (St. Petersburg: Azbuka-klassika, 2009), 33.

[93]    Quoted in *Rossiiskii liberalizm: idei i lyudi*, Aleksei Kara-Murza (ed.) (Moscow: Novoe izdatel'stvo, 2004), 489.

On the whole, European experience has shown that an "ordinary revolution" ends sooner or later, and post-revolutionary leaders lose their mystical aura and begin to aspire not towards mythical ideals, but to specific private goods.[94] Many Russians in the early 1920s were aware of this tendency. Accordingly, a certain section of the national intellectual elite did not regard the consequences of the Russian revolution as a tragedy. The authors of the émigré collection *Smena Vekh* ("Change of Milestones"), published in July 1921, believed that the Bolsheviks could sooner or later become ordinary, pragmatic rulers. For them, such a transformation would be a natural, rational reaction of educated people to post-revolutionary events. The historical experience of revolutions demonstrated that though they were undoubtedly terrible, this terror did not last forever. "It cannot be that one Lenin is followed by others," Yury Klyuchnikov wrote optimistically in this collection. "No, from now on, for a long time or forever, revolutionary extremism is over, along with all kinds of Bolshevism in both the 'broad' and 'narrow' sense. There is a lack of fertile soil for it. There is no need for it. A long revolutionary period of Russian history is over. In the future a period of swift and powerful evolutionary progress will begin".[95] In other words, modernization would continue. Klyuchnikov's conclusion was understandable for many of his contemporaries, and quite logical, and other authors in the collection concurred with his comparison of Russian life to the French revolution, which transformed from the horrors of the Jacobin terror to the pragmatism of the Thermidor, Directory and Napoleonic rule. Alexander Bobrishchev-Pushkin believed that "we are already approaching a Directory", and Nikolai Ustryalov even quoted Napoleon, who believed Robespierre would have been prepared to change all his actions if he had been able to hold on to power.[96]

---

[94]   See Arthur Stinchcombe, 'Ending Revolutions and Building New Governments', *Annual Review of Political Science*, vol.2 (1999), 49–73.

[95]   See *Smena vekh* (Prague, 1921), 42–43.

[96]   See *Smena vekh*, 57, 99.

In light of this approach, Lenin seemed to a number of intellectuals to be a kind of reincarnated Robespierre. In particular, they began to believe that the end of the revolution was near because of Lenin's New Economic Policy (NEP), which was passed at a party congress four months before *Smena Vekh* was published. In accordance with the NEP, the Bolsheviks moved away from Communist methods in the economy, replaced expropriation of grain with taxation, and allowed free entrepreneurship on a limited scale. "Obeying the voice of life, the Soviet regime evidently resolved on a radical tactical about-turn to reject the orthodox communist position. In the name of self-preservation, in the name of recreating a 'platform for the world revolution', it undertook a whole series of measures to emancipate the production forces of the country that had been crushed by a chimera". [97]

The question arose that if Russia was returning to the market in the economic system, was it then so important for its future to preserve an authoritarian political system, especially if the mass public was in favor of a change of policy? Sergei Lukyanov, another author in *Smena Vekh*, wrote that the shift was not an accidental, momentary whim of Lenin: "the so-called 'Bolshevik evolution' (…) can be simply explained by the fact that an equivalent evolution is taking place in the masses (…) The proletariat understood that both the intelligentsia and the bourgeois were not only not to be feared by the victorious people, but should and could be used in the interests of the people themselves". [98]

Alas, the intellectuals ignored the fact that for the Communists, the revolution was far from over. The revolution, of course, was not to be an endless horror, but its end was still very far off, and to reach it, first a large number of horrors of various sorts needed to be perpetrated. One of the elements of Bolshevik foreign policy was the attempt to instigate a revolution not only in Germany, but also in other countries – Czechoslovakia, Hungary, Romania, even Italy, not to mention Poland. This was why Mikhail Tukhachevsky's troops moved into Poland in 1920. The or-

---

[97]    See *Smena vekh*, 54.

[98]    See *Smena vekh*, 77.

der given before the start of the Bolshevik intervention left no doubt as to the goals of the operation: "Fighters of the workers' revolution. Turn your gaze to the West. In the West, the fates of the world revolution are being decided. Across the corpse of white Poland lies the path to the world bonfire. On bayonets, we will deliver happiness and peace to working humanity. To the West! To decisive battles, to thunderous battles!"[99] For Tukhachevsky, as he wrote later in a book, the Polish campaign was the "connecting link between the October revolution and the Western European revolution".[100] If he had succeeded, and brought his troops from the Vistula to the Oder, the German workers could have been supported with Red Army bayonets. But the bayonets could not bring Soviet power even as far as the Vistula. The Poles, routing Tukhachevsky and accomplishing the so-called "miracle on the Vistula", prevented the direct merger of Russian and German revolutionary elements.

Nevertheless, the Soviet authorities later attempted to achieve the same goal by different means. On the one hand, they were forced to admit that for some time the Soviet Union would inevitably exist in isolation, surrounded by enemies. Thus, there arose the theory that socialism should first be built in a single country. On the other hand, the problem of survival in a hostile environment was not removed from the political and policy agenda. The fear of imperialist aggression remained. A peaceful interlude was only seen from the standpoint of preparation for a new war, which would inevitably take place.[101] And so the activity of the Communist International was supposed to ensure the intensification of revolutionary forces in various countries of the world. And the Soviet Union, as the only supporter of these forces, was prepared to use its internal resources so that foreign Communists received the opportunity to carry out socialist revolutions.

---

[99] See Yuliya Kantor, *Voina i mir Mikhaila Tukhachevskogo* (Moscow: izdatel'skii dom "Ogonek", 2005), 174.

[100] Quoted in Kantor, *Voina i mir Mikhaila Tukhachevskogo*, 208.

[101] See Oleg Ken, *Mobilizatsionnoe planirovanie i politicheskie resheniya (konets 1920-kh – seredina 1930-kh gg.)* (Moscow: OGI, 2008), 21.

From our present-day pragmatic position, this waste of resources in a poor country, which had barely emerged from the
horrors of the civil war and hyperinflation, seems if not madness,
then an irrational act that violates common sense. But for the Soviet elite, which was deeply absorbed in Marxism, the actions of the
Communist International, aimed at world revolution, seemed very
important, as without them it was impossible to accomplish the
main mission of the Russian revolution. In fact, Orthodox Communists believed at the time that it would be impossible to even
survive in the existing hostile environment without a world revolution. They were obsessed with it, and the renowned Russian historian Vladimir Buladkov gives a series of examples of what he
called "revolutionary psychosis".[102]

If one takes the idea of permanent revolution to its logical
conclusion, then the aspiration of Western imperialists to crush
the young Soviet republic with the use of military force must be
seen as inevitable. In the Orthodox Marxist understanding of the
time, the dominant idea was that the battle between the world of
capital and the world of labor was a matter of life and death. As
the uprising of the working class of developed countries, was according to Marx, inherently to be brought about by the development of production forces, and as Soviet Russia was, according to
Lenin, the foundation that supported this uprising, sooner or later
imperialists would have to launch an intervention against the
young socialist republic simply for the sake of self-preservation.
They were not fools who would sit and wait while the muscular
arms of the proletariat rose up all over the world, and the yoke of
despotism was about to be crushed. It was no accident that Stalin,
in a speech at the Fourteenth Congress of the Bolshevik Party in
December 1925, when discussing the prospects of Soviet industrialization, noted that until the revolution triumphed in Germany or
France, "we absolutely need a minimum of independence for our
national economy, without which it is impossible to protect our

---

[102] See Vladimir Buldakov, *Utopiya, agressiya, vlast': psikhosotsial'naya dinamika
postrevolyutsionnogo vremeni. Rossiya 1920-1930 gg.* (Moscow: ROSSPEN, 2012).
111–114; 345.

country from economic subordination to the system of world capitalism".[103] Stalin and his allies did not consider the possibility of NEP-based agrarian development intended to increase the prosperity of the Soviet citizens. They proceeded from the need for military-industrial development, which would provide the Soviet Union with independence.

In fact, the political leaders of European capitalist countries did not particularly consider the future of humanity in Marxist terms, and held little fear of a permanent revolution. At that time, they had their own share of problems, and were concerned about increasing the efficiency of their economies, which had failed to demonstrate spectacular output after the world war. However, to understand the policy adopted by the Soviet Union, what matters is not what Western leaders actually thought and did, but how the perceptions of their motivations formed in the minds of Soviet leaders. These minds could not accept the concept of the long-term peaceful co-existence of two social systems, of capitalism and socialism. It was only consolidated in the Brezhnev era, when practically all true-believer Marxists had passed away. But until then, while these Orthodox Marxists dominated in the Soviet elite, the central idea was "us or them". War would definitely break out in the foreseeable future, because an absence of war contradicted Marxist-Leninist theory. The Communist elite did not discuss the relevance of this theory, but rather believed in the hostile environment itself, and organized its system of propaganda and agitation accordingly. "Soviet citizens were taught to think of themselves as inhabitants of a besieged fortress, surrounded by enemies from all sides, by imperialists of all countries, who were only waiting to crush them".[104]

---

[103]  Joseph Stalin, 'XIV S''ezd VKP(b): Politicheskii otchet Tsentral'nogo komiteta 18 dekabrya', in Joseph Stalin, *Sochineniya, vol.7* (Moscow, 1947), 299–300.

[104]  See Hosking, *Rulers and Victims*.

## The NEP in Hostile Surroundings

Due to the concept of "permanent revolution", Soviet Russia needed to be transformed into an enormous military camp. This was not a question of choosing a strategy. It was a question of elementary survival in capitalist surroundings. Either you provoke a world revolution, or you are subject to intervention.

In any case, a strong army and powerful military industry was required, one capable of providing the Red Army with weapons. Accordingly, this became one of main objectives of industrialization, or the fundamental transformation of the economy. This transformation was not carried out to fill the market with consumer goods and establish Communism in a single country (such ideas contradicted Marxist-Leninist theory), but in order to provide the army with weapons and arm Communism everywhere within bayonet reach. Soviet industrialization became an element of the irreconcilable battle between the world of labor and the world of capital, a battle to which all existing resources were supposed to be subordinated.

Industrialization in the USSR thus immediately became something fundamentally different from the industrialization that had been carried out previously in capitalist countries. The formation of industry within the market environment inevitably served the task of satisfying consumer demand. Without this, industry could not arise. Even if the state strove to place a strong emphasis on militarization in the process of industrialization (as was the case in Germany or in prerevolutionary Russia), such a maneuver was only possible if enough resources were provided for this market.

In the Soviet Union, militarization of the country essentially became a goal in itself. Naturally, industrialization with a military emphasis could not only involve weapons manufacturing, but required a resource base – production of raw materials and energy supply. During the years of the first five-year plans before 1941, great attention was paid to metallurgy and electricity. But on the whole, all development was aimed at military purposes. As the famous Soviet song put it: "with fire blazing, with the glint of steel flashing, the machines will take to the road, when Comrade Stalin sends us to battle, and the first marshal leads us to fight". Here, a natural question arose: where could the resources for industrialization be found? Theoretically, there could be two answers to this, and their clash was likely at the heart of the major economic debate of the 1920s.

On the one hand, the Bolsheviks were capable of taking a traditional path to military modernization. The declaration of the NEP meant that the existence of a market was permitted, and as the Soviet Union was a peasant country in those years, goods and cash relations should have encompassed the majority of the economy. The peasants grew grain, sold bread, earned money, paid taxes to the state, and these were the funds with which the Soviet regime could have launched industrialization. This model was clear, understandable and tested by practice in many other countries, in other words, absolutely viable. Yet it had one significant drawback, as the speed of industrialization was determined by the volume of resources that the state could collect through fiscal policies. If a serious economic crisis arose, or if the state was unable to collect enough taxes, military modernization would inevitably slow down. The readiness of the country for defense was determined by its readiness for economic development. But what could be done "if tomorrow there is war, if tomorrow we must march"? It emerged that the fateful conflict of the world of labor and the world of capital, and essentially the existence of all humanity, was determined by whether a miserable Russian peasant could sell bread and pay state taxes.

On the other hand, there was the option of ignoring market logic and attempting to confiscate all surplus resources from the countryside to benefit the urban centers. This could be done by the use of coercion, or, as scholars preferred to tactfully put it, by noneconomic means. With this approach, industrialization could be carried out much more quickly. The volume of weaponry that the country needed to receive in a short timeframe could be calculated, the construction of necessary enterprises could be planned, the amount of money needed could be determined accordingly, and finally it could be understood how much grain sold on the market could bring the state the necessary amount of money. Then this amount of money could be confiscated from the peasants by one means or another, irrespective of their own desires.

Movement in this direction corresponded most to the Soviet power's priority tasks, preparing for a confrontation of the world of labor with the world of capital. However, a serious problem also existed here. The Soviet Union had just passed through the years of military Communism, when for the sake of victory in the civil war, the Bolsheviks confiscated resources from the peasants under the food rationing system, without considering any market principles. Military communism led to a significant reduction in agricultural production, and this caused severe problems. The Communist elite could not ignore the danger of this approach. With good reason, it accepted Lenin's policy of the NEP, even though it probably found the idea of allowing a market approach on the path to the world revolution repellent. Thus, the choice between industrialization strategies was not as obvious as it may seem.

The first strategy was advanced by the Communist theorist and relatively competent economist (or at least, a star of Bolshevik economics), Nikolai Bukharin. He spoke of a slow, gradual movement towards socialism through various intermediary forms.[105] Entering into polemics with his opponents, Bukharin positioned himself as a centrist, rejecting both the position of radicals, who strove to confiscate grain from the peasants, and the position of opponents of industrialization, who denied a need to confiscate even part of the surplus product.[106] During the period of the civil war, Bukharin was considered the brightest figure among the so-called left-wing Communists. It is hard to doubt that he remained faithful to Marxist-Leninist theory, and that he aspired towards the world revolution, and therefore agreed with the necessity of militarization. Bukharin attempted to fit the market into

[105]   See Stephen F. Cohen, *Bukharin and the Bolshevik Revolution: A Political Biography 1888–1938* (New York: Alfred A. Knopf, 1973).

[106]   Nikolay Bukharin, 'Zametki ekonomista', in Nikolay Bukharin, *Izbrannye proizvedeniya* (Moscow: Politizdat, 1988) 406, 409–410.

the process of industrialization, demonstrating his ability to achieve temporary compromises on the path to strategic goals. Lenin was a great master of compromise, and it is not surprising that in the 1920s his favorite became the greatest pragmatist. Bukharin attempted to swim the narrow strait between the Scylla of economic collapse and the Charybdis of imperialist intervention.

The second approach was made on the "theoretical front" by the Trotskyist Yevgeny Preobrazhensky. He promoted not only the confiscation of resources from peasants through taxes, but also monopolistically high prices on industrial goods. [107] Initially, Preobrazhensky's position in the debate among Bolsheviks was clearly weaker. First, he did not have the same weight as Bukharin among the Communist leadership. Second, at a time when the Soviet Union needed to determine its strategy of industrialization, the Bolshevik leaders were wrestling for power with his patron Leon Trotsky, and were naturally not very keen to support Trotskyist economic views. Third, after adopting the NEP in 1921, it was difficult to turn the country in the opposite direction without exceedingly serious grounds. So Preobrazhensky was unable to overcome Bukharin on the "theoretical front", although he did not suffer total defeat.

In the first half of the 1920s, events developed practically in accordance with Bukharin's wishes. But soon new problems arose. Although the peasantry had recovered and could adequately feed the urban areas, industrialization had not actually been accomplished. In a country with a standard capitalist economy, with financial markets and guarantees of securing private property, the enriched NEP entrepreneurs and kulaks would inevitably have begun to invest private money in industrial enterprises over time. However, in a country with a market that was only permissible within the limits of the NEP, one could only hope for state investments. It gradually emerged that if business was treated like a milk cow, it would not "grow fat"; sooner or later, it would be turned into meat. In that case, would it not be better to squander the revenues, or hide them?

---

[107]  Cohen, *Bukharin and the Bolshevik Revolution*.

The winners of the NEP faced high taxes from the Soviet government. They were despised by society and ridiculed in the press, threatened with liquidation as a class, and from time to time certain individuals were sent to jail. To preserve their freedom and money, businesspeople were forced to bribe Cheka officers, Soviet functionaries and the party elite. Finally, their children found it much more difficult to receive an education than the children of workers. On the whole, there was a lack of millionaires capable of developing industry in the Soviet Union. This determined the outcome of the entire economic strategy of the Soviet government. "The conclusions were obvious. The policy of moderate growth rates, which would strengthen the position of wealthy groups of the countryside and make it inevitable to balance delicately between these groups and disobedient radicals in the cities, could only be taken as a temporary and forced measure".[108]

By the mid-1920s, it became clear that there was no longer any choice between two paths for building socialism (following Bukharin or Preobrazhensky). The Soviet government would either return to full-scale capitalism, and obtain a chance to accelerate economic growth, or preserve the NEP and bid farewell to plans for industrialization for a long time to come. Alternatively, it could intensify state intervention in the economy and receive funds for strengthening the defense capability of the country at the expense of other goals. The first option, which was the most sensible economically, was completely out of the question for a country that had only just conquered capitalism with enormous sacrifices. The second path's only virtue was that it left a chance for the creeping return of capitalism over time. The Soviet Union could, over multiple generations, slowly establish conditions for effective functioning of the economy. This path looked acceptable to the eyes of the *Smena Vekh* authors, but not to Communist eyes, which saw it as unrealistic given the theory of global revolution. The latter did not wish for the return of capitalism in the near or distant future, and believed that, in hostile imperialist surround-

---

[108]   Alexander Erlich, *Diskussii ob industrializatsii v SSSR, 1924–1928* (Moscow: Delo, 2010), 189.

ings, there would simply be no long-term prospects for the Soviet Union if it lacked a powerful military industry. Throughout the 1920s, this feeling of external threat was gradually internalized by all sides, and as a result Marxist-Leninist perceptions of the world began to be more convincing for the mass public, from the uneducated peasants to the party elite.

First, the Communists constantly discussed various conspiracies of enemies and saboteurs, the need to maintain vigilance, and so forth. The importance of the coercive apparatus of the Soviet state depended directly on the extent to which the Soviet leadership felt its position to be in danger. The more problems the Soviet Union faced in terms of state security, the greater the apparatus's influence became on the general state of affairs, and the greater its staff numbers, salaries and powers. It is not surprising that this "information policy" made nervous even those who had paid little attention to Marxist beliefs about the international bourgeoisie's passionate desire to crush their young Soviet republic.

Second, Soviet citizens, frustrated by post-revolutionary difficulties, began to look for culprits of numerous failures. The working class discovered that capitalist exploitation had vanished, but their lives had not improved. They who were "not naught" actually remained "naught", even though the words of the "International" promised that they would "become all" after the world of violence was destroyed. Blaming the Communist leaders for this situation was dangerous due to the threat of repressions. This is why the Communist leadership found it effective to shift the blame to domestic and foreign enemies as long as it gave rise to constant fear among the mass public. The average person expected aggression from England, France, Poland, Romania, Finland, Estonia, Bulgaria, Japan and other countries where the bourgeoisie could think of nothing but how to harm the Soviet Union.

Third, the search for enemies was to a certain degree based on personal benefits to those who foiled them. The young Communist found an enemy in the old Communist, and claimed their position and salary. Factory workers unmasked an old specialist who held the position of director, and some other expert in finding conspiracies replaced them. With this approach, the idea of unmasking conspiracies gripped the masses, and soon the Soviet leaders, who had a poor understanding of what was actually happening down below, became afraid themselves of the power of spies, saboteurs, and other people with links to treacherous foreigners.

As Vladimir Buldakov noted, "By the end of the 1920s, the Communists saw sedition in almost every sewing group".[109] Could the Bolsheviks calmly allow the NEP to be preserved under these conditions, and postpone industrialization with a defensive emphasis indefinitely? Of course not. The idea of industrialization could only coexist with the NEP at an early stage, but as it developed that under the Soviet conditions of the 1920s, the market in did not guarantee a sufficient volume of investments, the Communists naturally sought to increase state intervention in the economy. They took the resources which were necessary for militarization from the private sector (especially from the countryside). The result was that, objectively speaking, progress followed the path first established by Preobrazhensky. This did not at all conflict with the fact that Trotskyism as a political movement was crushed, and Preobrazhensky himself was repressed in the 1930s. The battle for power, which saw an alliance of different forces from the Bolshevik party, from Stalin to Bukharin, led to the defeat of Trotskyism. Meanwhile, the battle for socialism ended in the victory of Trotskyist views, which consistently reflected his concept of world revolution.

The events that took place in the second half of the 1920s, and led to dramatic consequences for the Soviet Union until its collapse, resulted from a historical path dependency that determined the trajectory of Soviet development. But this trajectory was laid down not because of the revolution as such, but because of the ideological characteristics of the Bolsheviks, who had won the revolutionary conflict. Proceeding from the idea of the world revolution, the Bolsheviks could not prepare for military conflicts with imperialists, and accordingly were forced to carry out indus-

---

[109]   Buldakov, *Utopiya, agressiya, vlast'*, 420.

trialization with a military emphasis over a short time. The claims that continue to be made to this day that the Communists of the 1920s could have chosen the NEP, the market, economic prosperity and the peaceful coexistence of two systems come from the worldview of a completely different era. These claims ignore the post-revolutionary realities and key problems that were the focus of the Communist leadership's attention.

At the Fourteenth Congress of the Bolshevik Party in December 1925, a policy of industrialization was adopted, but in the following year and a half, no fundamental breakthrough took place. The Communists attempted to harness the "restive steed" of state industrialization and the "timid deer" of private ownership to the "socialist cart". But as soon as the issue of choosing an economic policy arose, harsh pressure was placed on the peasantry, with the goal of confiscating all their resources by non-economic means. The year 1927 was a turning point. On the one hand, this was the year of the so-called "military alarm".[110] The UK severed diplomatic relations with the Soviet Union. It is unlikely that "world imperialism" was prepared to attack Soviets at this time, but Moscow, which operated in an atmosphere of fear of hostile encirclement, could not take this potential threat lightly. The feeling arose that the enemy were at the gates, and the Soviet Union was completely unprepared for war. The unstable political balance between the "doves" and the "hawks" in the Soviet leadership had to shift to the latter. At the same time, it was in autumn 1927 that the issue of the state's inability to acquire a sufficient amount of grain from the peasants without expanding the scope of violence came to the fore. In reality, grain supplies were insufficient because the countryside had no desire to surrender the harvest to the state at relatively low purchase prices, and peasants did not have enough earnings to buy consumer goods. They were forced to purchase industrial products at the high prices monopolistically set by the Soviet state, and so were not motivated to sell grain for a pittance. As a result, a large amount of the harvest went to private traders, and the state was left with nothing.

---

[110] Ken, *Mobilizatsionnoe planirovanie*, 42–43.

It was impossible to commence industrialization in this situation. The state needed to feed the workers who were creating "industrial giants", and also to export grain abroad so as to buy modern equipment for the hard currency and hire Western engineers. As a result, pressure on the peasants increased drastically. In order to ensure a sufficient supply of grain, local authorities began to apply methods of compulsion that went far beyond the boundaries of Preobrazhensky's theory. Ordinary peasants were openly harassed, and kulaks fell into the hands of the police. The result, as was to be expected, was contradictory. On the one hand, violence helped patch the holes in the system of state purchases. On the other hand, it was increasingly obvious that, as in the years of military communism, peasants had now begun to hide grain, curtail production activity, and even rebel. "The peasant war developed exponentially," Russian historian Oleg Khlevniuk noted. "In 1926–1927, the authorities recorded 63 mass anti-governmental protests in the countryside. In 1929, over 1,300 protests and 244,000 participants. In January–February 1930 – almost one and a half thousand protests and 324,000 participants".[111] It would seem that the Soviet regime was falling into the same trap again. But this was no longer 1921, when Soviet Russia was drowning beneath the waves of numerous peasant rebellions. The state had grown stronger; it quelled the major centers of rebellion and was prepared to use completely new methods of violence that it had not been strong enough to apply at the end of the civil war.

Thus, the Soviet Union moved forward to collectivization. Depriving the peasantry of the chance to grow and harvest independently, turning peasants into collective farm workers and concentrating control over grain in the hands of the state bureaucracy, the Soviet regime gained resources for carrying out industrialization with a military emphasis. Now it was possible to produce weapons in large quantities, and establish the means of production necessary for the MIC. In addition, there was no need to produce consumer goods. Peasants surrendered their grain and received almost nothing in return. After collectivization, the state

---

[111]   Oleg Khlevniuk, *Stalin: zhizn' odinokogo vozhdya* (Moscow: AST, 2016), 164.

was able to confiscate many more resources from peasants. The export of grain abroad increased drastically in 1930. This was exactly what was needed for industrialization and militarization.

As economic mechanisms for distributing resources between consumption and accumulation no longer functioned, the danger arose that the Soviet bureaucracy would sacrifice reason on the altar of industrialization, i.e. it would confiscate grain to the greatest possible extent. This is probably what led to the tragic famine in Ukraine in 1932–1933, and the terrible privations faced by the peasantry in other parts of the country. In the Don region, Cossacks joked unhappily: "Rye and wheat – all sent abroad. Thorns and corn – left to the Soviet Union". From an economic standpoint, the mass collectivization that began in the autumn of 1929 was a devastating measure that destroyed the already inefficient agricultural system. But the Soviet regime had no other solution with which to oppose world imperialism. Curtailing the NEP was a rational choice for the Communist leaders: facing an increasing external threat, the Soviet Union was transformed into a unified military camp. As Yegor Gaidar justly noted, "as a result of the revolution of the Civil War, Russia's path was closed to dynamic capitalist growth, involving high activity of the private entrepreneurial sector, significant private savings and investments."[112] The country's economy was caught in a trap. The longer it spent dedicated to accomplishing the Bolsheviks' tasks relating to the need to oppose the country's capitalist surroundings, the more inefficient and structurally distorted it became in satisfying society's demands.

The administrative economic system Stalin began to establish in the 1930s was optimally adapted for deepening this trap. Militarization became the goal of existence for the entire economy, while attempts were made to optimize the work of "secondary" sectors only based on the need to channel the maximum resources into the MIC. It is not surprising that over the subsequent sixty

---

[112] See Yegor Gaidar, *Russia: A Long View* (Cambridge, MA: MIT Press, 2012), Chapter 3.

years, this economic system created the grave problems faced by the 1990s reforms, as discussed above.[113]

---

[113]   See Gaidar, *Collapse of an Empire*, Chapters 3–4.

# Chapter 4.
# The Reforms of the 1990s and Modern Institutions

The institutional framework that exists in Russia today is to a great degree affected by the historical path described above. The peculiarities of this path determined the positions of the various interest groups that fought for improvement of their own positions in the wake of the reforms of the 1990s. The outcome of this battle influenced the implementation of the ideas behind these reforms. The ideas themselves transformed during the process of institution building, and in practice manifested very differently from initial theoretical expectations.

## The Law Enforcement System in Present-day Russia

In present-day Russia, there are not many in-depth systematic empirical analyses of how the institutions formed over the post-Soviet decades truly work.[114] In particular, few scholars have analyzed how law enforcement in Russia affected its economic development.[115] Usually, discussions about problems with the Russian economy revolve around analyzing the activities of the ministries of economy and finances, the Central Bank's policy, and anti-monopoly policy.[116] But in fact, today it is not to the agencies formally responsible for economic development that one should pay primary attention. While they have indeed made numerous errors and sometimes even genuine failures, the key problems relate to

---

[114] For some descriptions, see Alena Ledeneva, *How Russia Really Works: The Informal Practices that Shaped Post-Soviet Politics and Business* (Ithaca, NY: Cornell University Press, 2006).

[115] See 'Legality and Violence in Russia', Timothy Frye (ed.), *Post-Soviet Affairs*, no. 2-3 (2014).

[116] For some analyses, see *Oxford Handbook of the* Russian *Economy*, Michael Alexeev, Shlomo Weber (eds.) (Oxford: Oxford University Press, 2013); Juliet Johnson, *Priests of Prosperity: How Central Bankers Transformed the Postcommunist World* (Ithaca, NY: Cornell University Press, 2016); Miller, *Putinomics*.

the state agencies responsible for the rule of law. Thus, the main focus should be shifted to analysis of the influence of the police, prosecutor's office, state investigators and security services on the development of business, in terms of the personal safety of business people and of property rights. Instead of serving as guardians of the rule of law, the servants of these state agencies often break the law themselves. Sometimes these results from bureaucratic over-regulation and the inefficiency of these agencies: it can be easier for law enforcement officers to work and report on their activity to their superiors if they violate some laws. But often these officers can receive additional personal advantages, extra revenues and career advancements by acting illegally and harassing businesspeople. No prudent macroeconomic policy is capable of stimulating the development of Russian business in this environment. Meanwhile, the failures of the law enforcement system have become absolutely destructive for the Russian economy.

One of the best studies of how the law enforcement system in Russia works in reality is the book by Ella Paneyakh, Kirill Titaev and Maria Shklyaruk, "Trajectory of a Criminal Case: An Institutional Analysis". It provides a detailed and step-by-step account of how this system performs, its rules of the game and its major drivers. As the authors themselves put it: "It is important to understand that in Russia, according to statistics, the fact of charging a suspect almost automatically means a guilty verdict by the court, or the termination of the case in court (rarely during the investigation) on non-rehabilitating grounds (i.e. the court finds the defendant guilty, but does not punish him)."[117] In other words, if for any reason a person becomes a suspect, the entire system works so that they are incapable of defending and vindicating themselves. This approach is appalling enough for the individual citizen. But if this citizen does business and owns property, it not only affects their personal fate, but also influences the Russian economy and investment climate.

---

[117]   See Ella Paneyakh, Kirill Titaev, Maria Shklyaruk, *Traektoriya ugolovnogo dela: institutsional'nyi analiz* (St. Petersburg: European University at St. Petersburg Press, 2018), 322.

Police officers in Russia know that there are so-called "good" cases and "bad" cases. "Good" cases are familiar ones, when the police more or less know how to identify the suspect and prove their guilt. These cases fit into routine practice, as police will have already encountered numerous similar incidents.[118] Police officers are roughly aware of who could have committed the crime, and how this person could have acted. It is very likely that the suspect they find does not have influential protectors (such as politicians, state officials, owners of large businesses ("oligarchs"), or law enforcement personnel), whose possible involvement in these cases could cause problems for the police officers themselves. These "good" cases are officially recorded and "disclosed" even if the true culprit is not found. As for "bad" cases, the police simply seek not to register them at all. The victim, who is poorly informed about how the police work, often does not even understand that their case is not being dealt with, and that it is not officially registered in the appropriate official journal. The total annual number of criminal offenses in Russia is approximately 26 million, while just over 2 million are registered every year. For example, it is very difficult to find someone who has stolen one's cellphone, and so the police do not even make the attempt.[119] But police officers have to demonstrate their efficiency in other cases ("good cases") where it is easier for them to achieve the necessary results. And if some innocent person becomes involved in this "good case", it is highly likely that efforts will be made to imprison them, by all possible means. "The cooperation between investigators and police operatives is concentrated on cases that improve detection statistics in certain categories of crimes". [120]

This is the general pattern of how the Russian police operate. To put it simply, Russian police officers are motivated not to catch criminals, not to uphold justice and not to prevent violations of the law, but only to report on crimes resolved (even if only an imitation of resolution actually took place). However, some addition-

---

[118]   See Paneyakh, Titaev, Shklyaruk, *Traektoriya ugolovnogo dela*, 323.

[119]   See Paneyakh, Titaev, Shklyaruk, *Traektoriya ugolovnogo dela*, 328–329, 340.

[120]   See Paneyakh, Titaev, Shklyaruk, *Traektoriya ugolovnogo dela*, 358.

al incentives to portray an innocent person as a criminal are introduced into this system. The police might attempt to present a businessperson as a criminal simply as the result of a bribe from their rival, or from a person who will have the opportunity to seize their company while its owner is in jail. If it is possible to put together a "good" case, which can be brought to a trial and guilty verdict, then both the police and the investigator are interested in doing so. On the one hand, they are able to report that a crime has been resolved, and on the other hand, they receive extra money for this service. In Russia, from time to time police officers are found with enormous cash savings that are completely incommensurable with their official salaries: it is quite possible that this money (or at least a considerable part of it) is the result of cases against businesspeople, "ordered" by those who sought to have them jailed at any cost. If the person in question is in fact innocent, then police may plant evidence themselves. Another method of "proving" guilt is psychological pressure on the suspect. As many intelligent and educated people (including businesspersons) understand how the law enforcement system in Russia is actually organized, and how difficult it will be for them to prove their innocence, they may confess their supposed guilt under this psychological pressure in the hope of mitigating the sentence. Finally and regrettably, in Russia there exists the terrible practice of torture for forcing confessions out of suspects.[121] Formally, police officers who torture people are considered criminals, but as the victims have little ability to prove that torture actually took place, this method is in fact used to force suspects to "confess". Police officers themselves often believe that it is permissible to torture criminals. Furthermore, at the time of torture, the person has not yet been proven to be a criminal. But if the police officers are convinced of this, then most of them do not experience great moral doubts. Even if it emerges that the suspect was not guilty in this particular case, the police still believe they are a criminal guilty of some other crime, and thus deserve their suffering.[122]

---

[121] See Paneyakh, Titaev, Shklyaruk, *Traektoriya ugolovnogo dela*, 376.

[122] See Paneyakh, Titaev, Shklyaruk, *Traektoriya ugolovnogo dela*, 397.

Naturally, the question arises: surely, it is not the police who decide whether a suspect is sentenced? There are investigators, who must directly ascertain whether to charge a person. There is the court, which delivers guilty verdicts. There are lawyers, who should defend the suspect in court. If one considers the matter from a formal viewpoint, there is an entire web of legal and judicial institutions in Russia, which seem similar to their counterparts in democratic countries. But this is not how the system functions in reality. What, then, is the problem?

Investigators are interested in finding a suspect for a crime as quickly as possible, no less so than the police. If the police immediately document that their work is done, then as Paneyakh, Titaev and Shklyaruk note, "the investigator has less risk of working 'blindly': when the guilty person is established and the main information on the circumstances of the crime, potentially registered in the form of proof, has already been gathered, then the chances increase that the case will have a 'procedural future'". In Russia's case, it is much easier for an investigator to work if there is a suspect. Then the judge becomes involved. In many cases, they decide to keep the suspect in custody before the trial. These decisions seem strange if publicly respected people are involved, such as entrepreneurs whom there are no grounds to suspect of committing new crimes or fleeing justice. But the judge most often trusts the work of the police and investigators. They have no other information about the case except what they have gained from these agencies. Willingly or not, the judge proceeds from the assumption that the investigators worked conscientiously, and if they believe a person needs to be held in custody, then this is the appropriate procedure.[123]

Formally speaking, a lawyer can defend the interests of the suspects. But the lawyer's capabilities are severely restricted in present-day Russia. They can, of course, petition for materials to be attached to the case, which prove the innocence of the defendant, or carry out investigative actions, which could clear them – but the final decision remains at the investigator's discretion. Un-

---

[123] See Paneyakh, Titaev, Shklyaruk, *Traektoriya ugolovnogo dela*, 407.

surprisingly, investigators have no desire to add documents for the judge to read that do not confirm their assertions about the case. The investigator's typical argument is 'if you have your own evidence, present it in court'". Judges refuse to acknowledge arguments by the defense, which have not already been presented in the criminal case compiled by investigators. They often operate under the pretext that the defense "concealed" this information from the investigation: if your intentions had been pure, you would have given the investigator the opportunity to check your data beforehand – since you did not, you must be sabotaging the case. As a result, even when the defense works in full force and provides additional proof in the defendant's favor, the court finds a way to ignore them.[124]

The investigative committee in Russia is separate from the prosecutor's office. They are different state agencies. So formally, the state representative at the trial can examine the quality of work by the police and investigators. If they do not find evidence of guilt, then they can reassign the case for further investigation. But in practice, this takes place relatively rarely. Prosecutors are overwhelmed with work and often familiarize themselves with the case directly at the trial. They are unable to study all of its circumstances beforehand. "An unconscientious or overworked prosecutor with a standard, simple case opens the file for the first time in the court. A conscientious one will browse it during the break while he is waiting for the trial to begin".[125]

If one considers the relationship between the court and the prosecutor's office, then the formally existing organizational division does not particularly hinder the practice of cooperation and mutual support, which takes place in reality. Theoretically, the court should display objectivity, hearing both the arguments of the defense and the prosecution. But in Russia, the court is much more closely connected with the prosecution. "In a typical trial at the level of the district court, the judge knows the prosecutor very well – they see each other several times a week at work, if not eve-

---

[124]   See Paneyakh, Titaev, Shklyaruk, *Traektoriya ugolovnogo dela*, 421.

[125]   See Paneyakh, Titaev, Shklyaruk, *Traektoriya ugolovnogo dela*, 437.

ry day. (...) If the state prosecutor has been working for a long time and is on good terms with this judge, they may expect not only that their position will be trusted, but if the judge finds clear discrepancies in the prosecution's case, evidence of violation of the defendant's rights or negligence in registering documents, they will informally hint where errors are present, and in violation of all laws they will allow the prosecutor's office to amend them after the fact."[126]

Employees of the prosecutor's office in Russia themselves say that there are much closer relations between the court and the prosecutor's office than between the court and lawyers. Judges do not trust lawyers, regarding them as greedy and materially interested in winning the trial, while judges and prosecutors are not materially interested in the outcome of a case. Proceeding from this position, the judge often believes that the defense lawyer will break the law in the interests of their client, while the prosecutor will follow the law to a greater extent.[127]

Finally, it is also important that in the superior court's mechanisms for appealing in Russia, innocent verdicts are overturned far more frequently than guilty ones based on prosecutors' appeals. Such annulments may lead a judge's superiors to condemn them for allowing this to happen, as such instances are considered failures by the judge. These practices mean that judges who do not wish their verdicts to be overturned are interested above all in maintaining good relations with the prosecutor's office. If the prosecutor submits an appeal, they will have far greater chance of success (according to statistical data) than a defense lawyer who does the same.[128]

It is also important that in the Russian provinces, where members of elites are less numerous and usually know each other well, judges have very close relations with various influential, powerful and wealthy people. These connections also influence

---

[126] See Paneyakh, Titaev, Shklyaruk, *Traektoriya ugolovnogo dela*, 437–438.

[127] See Paneyakh, Titaev, Shklyaruk, *Traektoriya ugolovnogo dela*, 439.

[128] See Paneyakh, Titaev, Shklyaruk, *Traektoriya ugolovnogo dela*, 443–444.

the outcomes of court hearings.[129] Thus, one might say that in present-day Russia, court hearings are non-competitive. There is a common interest in the case ending as quickly as possible with a guilty verdict and sentence. In particular, if the criminal case was launched on the orders of state authorities to begin with, or was ordered by a rival of the businessperson being charged, then it is extremely unlikely that the law enforcement system will be able to protect the defendant's rights. Business understands this problem very well, and so in many ways these practices contribute to capital flight from a country where business interests are not protected.

## "Expropriation of the Expropriators" in a New Way

There is no need to stress that property rights form the basis of the system of "inclusive economic institutions",[130] which facilitate the inclusion of large groups of the population in economic activity. If the state protects property rights and private ownership, then, all else being equal, business can feel confident. Entrepreneurs strive to attract loans, launch investments, and plan their business activities in the long-term perspective. Their experience becomes tempting for the mass public, and in particular, more young people strive to develop their ideas in business, and build a career through entrepreneurship. However, if the state does not protect property rights, or even attempts to confiscate money from business under the pretext of satisfying state needs, capital either leaves the country or moves into the shadow economy. Entrepreneurship has ceased to be a tempting career for younger generations, who seek other career paths (for example, in law enforcement agencies or the civil service, which may bring high revenues from corruption), leave the country, or invest their efforts in activities with no bearing on Russia's economic development.[131]

---

129   See Paneyakh, Titaev, Shklyaruk, *Traektoriya ugolovnogo dela*, 440.

130   See Daron Acemoglu, James Robinson, *Why Nations Fail: The Origins of Power, Prosperity, and Power* (New York: Crown Business, 2012).

131   Among the voluminous literature, see, in particular, Acemoglu, Robinson, *Why Nations Fail*; Douglas North, John Wallis, Barry Weingast, *Violence and So-*

The problem is that the state's position towards property rights is in many ways determined by societal preferences. If, from the point of view of a country's long historical path, the legitimacy of private property is established, and is considered as the basis of economic prosperity, and the mass public believes that property rights should be protected, the state is generally inclined to support this important institution. Certain powerful interest groups may of course act against private property, seeking to seize property from other owners by pressuring the state, but it is difficult for them to dominate if private property is accepted and endorsed by society at large. On the other hand, if the historical path of a particular country has brought society to the idea that private property is illegitimate, the state may easily expropriate it in the interests of groups that exert sufficient pressure. In this case, society at large may believe that this kind of "expropriation of expropriators", as Karl Marx described the socialist revolution,[132] may be a good solution for the country's problems, and will benefit the mass public. In Russia, in the post-reform years, the mass perceptions of property rights revolved around the belief that private property did not benefit the country's development, but served the maximization of wealth for privileged special interest groups.[133] The spread of these perceptions is not merely a consequence of the privatization of the 1990s, but the result of the entire process of post-Communist transformation. How and why have these transformations affected public perceptions and preferences?

---

cial Orders: A Conceptual Framework for Interpreting Recorded Human History (Cambridge: Cambridge University Press, 2009); for a concise systematic overview on the role of property rights in economic development, see Timothy Besley, Maitreesh Ghatak, 'Property Rights and Economic Development', Handbook of Development Economics, vol.5, Dani Rodrik, Mark Rosenzweig (eds.) (Amesterdam: Elsevier, 2010), 4525–4595.

[132]  See Karl Marx, Capital. Vol.1, Chapter 32.

[133]  For detailed analyses, see Timothy Frye, Property Rights and Property Wrongs: How Power, Institutions, and Norms Shape Economic Conflicts in Russia (Cambridge: Cambridge University Press, 2017); Jordan Gans-Morse, Property Rights in Post-Soviet Russia: Violence, Corruption, and the Demand for Law (Cambridge: Cambridge University Press, 2017).

First, as we noted above, the post-Communist reforms were an intense ordeal for large segments of Russian society, as the structure of the Soviet economy stimulated many people to economic activities which were not in demand by the market. Accordingly, these people faced major economic difficulties, often lost their jobs, and have very mixed memories of the 1990s era of reforms. In other post-Communist countries, where the economic structure was more easily adjusted to market changes than in the Soviet Union, the share of citizens who took a position against private property and privatization was considerably smaller.[134]

Second, the economic transformations in Russia took place over too long a period because the implementation of the economic reforms of perestroika caused macroeconomic imbalance and required a new stage of transformations, which Yegor Gaidar was forced to launch in considerably worse conditions than those that existed when Gorbachev came to power. Such a protracted period of economic reforms (over ten years in total) was difficult to grasp for many Russians, who in general had many difficulties adapting to market changes. In particular, the period of high inflation in Russia lasted too long, and it devalued both the savings and the salaries of the population. Financial instability hindered the transition to economic growth up until 1999. As citizens had a poor understanding of the problems faced by Russian society, many of them came to conclude that the economic reforms were caused by inflation, devaluation of savings, and overall instability, whereas the positive development of the economy began due to causes that appeared much later. Therefore, many Russians may have felt that for some reason the state of the country as a whole was failing to live up to expectations, and that private property and privatization were completely misleading.

Third, the primitive accumulation of major capital and the luxurious lifestyle of the "oligarchs" connected with it preceded

---

[134]   For a comparative analysis of post-Communist countries, see Irina Denisova, Markus Ellter, Timothy Frye, Ekaterina Zhuravskaya, 'Who Wants to Revise Privatization? The Complementary of Market Skills and Institutions', *American Political Science Review*, 103, no. 2 (2009), 284–304.

the period of economic growth. Most Russians could not rationally explain why a small number of people were suddenly enriched
while the economic situation in the country continued to worsen.
Accordingly, they began to believe not only that these large fortunes were illegally acquired (which was true to an extent), but also that private property in general was not legitimate. This was
not a rejection of private property as such (many Russians would
agree that an efficient manager or entrepreneur had the right to
wealth), but specifically of the fortunes of the oligarchs, who
emerged with the spontaneity and ubiquity of mushrooms in
1990s Russia. In many ways, this rejection was not associated with
nostalgia for the Soviet economy, something that could have expressed itself through votes for the Communist Party. Rather, the
Russian voters of the 2000s supported the status quo,[135] wishing to
preserve the existence of a market economy with fully stocked
shops, but at the same time they were prepared for revision of
privatization of major assets.

Fourth, the results of mass privatization could not establish
the legitimacy of private property, despite the participation of
practically the entire population of Russia. The voucher component of privatization was seen by many as a scam due to the inefficiency of investment funds. As for members of labor collectives,
who not only received vouchers, but some shares in their companies, they could not understand why the transition to private
property could not provide them with economic advancement.
Companies which were not especially attractive for investors
would still not earn money effectively in any case; shareholders
did not receive dividends, and were often also deprived of salaries. This state of affairs demonstrated that private property was
not particularly important for the well-being of workers of privatized enterprises vis-à-vis other economic factors, such as quality of

---

[135]   For empirical analyses of voting in Russia in the 2000s, see, for example, Ian
McAllister, Stephen White, 'It's the Economy, Comrade! Parties and Voters in
the 2007 Russian Duma Election', *Europe-Asia Studies*, 60, no.6 (2008), 931–957;
Timothy Colton, Henry E. Hale, 'The Putin Vote: Presidential Electorate in a
Hybrid Regime', *Slavic Review*, 68, no.3 (2009), 473–503.

management, market demand for a company's production, and its support by the state.

Fifth, the perception of privatization was to a considerable degree not even formed by the mass privatization of 1992–1994, but by loans-for-shares deals, conducted prior to the 1996 presidential elections in the hope of generating funds for Yeltsin's reelection bid and obtaining political support from major oligarchs.[136] At the time, the law prohibited the sale of a number of major state companies, but did not prohibit loans from businesspeople. As a result, these companies (including the famous Yukos) moved into private hands, as the state did not pay its creditors (and the government had not intended to do so from the very beginning). This complex scheme was so widely discussed in the media, and so widely criticized in public, that loans-for-shares deals became the symbol of privatization. When Yukos was expropriated by the Russian state from its main owner Mikhail Khodorkovsky in the 2000s, and its assets came under the control of the state-owned company Rosneft, Russian society unsurprisingly regarded this de facto nationalization quite calmly. The legitimacy of Khodorkovsky's property was in itself highly dubious.[137]

Thus, in the 2000s, Russian citizens had no strong grounds to support private property. It had not proven to have any major advantages over state property. The Soviet economy, based on state ownership, had been ineffective as it led to a common shortage of goods, but the Russian economy of the 1990s, based on private

---

[136]   For critical accounts of loan-for-shares deals, see Chrystia Freeland, *Sale of the Century: Russia's Wild Rule from Communism to Capitalism* (New York: Crown Business, 2000); David Hoffman, *Oligarchs: The Wealth and Power in a New Russia* (New York: Public Affairs, 2002); for a more positive assessment, see Daniel Treisman, '"Loans for Shares" Revisited', *Post-Soviet Affairs*, 26, no.3 (2010), 207–227.

[137]   For various assessments of the "Yukos affair", see William Tompson, 'Putting Yukos in Perspective', *Post-Soviet Affairs*, 21, no. 2 (2005), 159–181; Vadim Volkov, 'Standard Oil and Yukos in the Context of Early Capitalism in the United States and Russia', *Demokratizatsiya: The Journal of Post-Soviet Democratization*, 16, no. 3 (2008), 240–264; Thane Gustafson, *Wheel of Fortune: The Battle for Oil and Power in Russia* (Cambridge, MA: Harvard University Press, 2012).

ownership, was seen by many people as ineffective because of the problems mentioned above. Only a small section of educated people understood the importance of private property, but it would have been naïve to expect such understanding from a large section of the Russian population.

By the early 2000s, Russian society had entered a state of uncertainty, waiting for indications to help them understand Russia's further direction of economic development. If the economic growth of the 2000s had been accompanied by consolidation of private property, perhaps property rights would have gradually been reinforced and become legitimate in Russia. But the situation developed in entirely the opposite direction. Economic growth and the increase in real income took place on the basis of major consolidation of the economic role of the state, and the increase in the share of state ownership.

Ordinary citizens, of course, may not have known how ownership problems were related to the Russian economy, but they could see that, according to many indicators, the state was becoming stronger. In a number of cases, this was a feigned strengthening. For example, the perception that the Russian state had entered into a major battle with oligarchic capital did not reflect reality.[138] "Oligarch fortunes" in the 2000s were generally preserved and even increased. But the rhetoric of high-ranking officials and state propaganda in the media produced the notion that the Russian state was re-establishing order in the country after the anarchy of the so-called "roaring 1990s". Perceptions of illegitimacy of private property in Russia led to three negative consequences for Russian economic development.

First, Russian society became indifferent to what might be called "violent entrepreneurship".[139] Criminal groups put pressure on businesses, in many cases seizing control of them, from

---

[138]    For this viewpoint, see Ilya Matveev, 'Big Business in Putin's Russia: Structural and Instrumental Power', *Demokratizatsiya: The Journal of Post-Soviet Democratization*, 27, no.4 (2019), 401–422.

[139]    For an in-depth analysis, see Vadim Volkov, *Violent Entrepreneurship: The Role of Force in the Making of Russian Capitalism* (Ithaca, NY: Cornell University Press, 2002).

the end of the 1980s onwards. The costs of protection rackets reduced the efficiency of business and increased the cost of production, among other similar effects. As Russian sociologist Vadim Volkov noted, these problems are not specific to the Russian economy: they are typical for many countries at certain stages in the process of building their states and economies. Russia's problem was that in the 1990s, after the collapse of the preceding Soviet system, the state was weak and unable to provide any real protection for business. Russian society saw the rise of these issues as "thieves stealing from thieves", and given this indifference, the Russian authorities would not necessarily respond to such problems. Later, when the coercive capacity of the Russian state increased in the 2000s, practices of "violent entrepreneurship" were gradually eradicated by the law enforcement agencies.

Second, criminal entities in Russia became intertwined with certain power structures. If a racket is possible in principle, and there are no mechanisms for suppressing it, a type of violent entrepreneurship arises which is tempting for those with the most power, and who wish to rely on their high status to evade the law. The police and the security apparatus have the greatest power and status, and are also closely linked with certain business actors. When violent entrepreneurship shifted out of private criminal groups into the hands of state officials and law enforcement officers, it soon extended to higher-level authorities. Today, the law enforcement bodies are constantly presenting private business with, as Don Corleone described it in "The Godfather", offers they cannot refuse. The law enforcement agencies may require businesspeople to sell profitable businesses to firms affiliated with them at an unprofitable price. This state of affairs encourages entrepreneurs to sell their businesses and take their money abroad, further contributing to capital flight.

Third, Russian society is not only indifferent to the problem of protection of property rights from numerous attacks, but also to protecting business from numerous instances of bureaucratic harassment in the form of inspections. Formally, these inspections are undertaken by various state agencies in the public interest. Firefighters protect the safety of employees who may be at risk from fire outbreaks caused by managers' carelessness. State education regulators examine whether students receive a sufficiently high quality of education. Tax services protect the interests of the state budget, and therefore all public workers of the country. But in reality, the officials who gain the opportunity to regularly interfere in the activities of business and NGOs with inspections are able to make money from their privileged position, i.e. use it for their personal goals. Under the pretext of protecting public interests, the private interests of the regulated are infringed upon to promote those of the regulators (state bureaucrats, law enforcement agencies). If Russian society were to consider infringement on private property unacceptable, these inspections would be constrained by the supervision of different law enforcement bodies and could not serve as a tool for gaining private profits by state officials. But in present-day Russia, law enforcement officers are more interested in receiving their share of private profits than in ending bureaucratic abuses.

## The Consequences of Inefficient Institutions for Russia

The fact that in contemporary Russia, the law enforcement system does not work for the public interest, and instead of property rights being protected, the blatant confiscation of property promotes special interests closely connected with the "law enforcers" has negative consequences for the Russian economy, and for the country's overall development. Since 2009, Russia has faced economic stagnation, and the pace of economic growth is very slow whereas one regularly observes pure capital flight. This means that Russia is unattractive to investors and the significant sums that could support its development are instead invested in other regions of the world. Of course, it would be an overstatement to say that all these negative consequences are the result of inefficient institutions alone. But there is no doubt that bad institutions are an important cause of the ongoing stagnation.

Russian economist Andrey Zaostrovtsev conducted a comparative analysis of the current state of Russian institutions in relation to those in several other countries. He called the state of its institutions the "Achilles heel" of the Russian economy, noting that "Russia is in 88th place among 138 countries in terms of the overall state of its institutions".[140] Although a certain amount of progress has been made in Russia in recent years in the quality of its institutions, it lags behind not only the Baltic states (which were part of the Soviet Union along with Russia in the past, and are now part of the European Union), but also as authoritarian a country as Kazakhstan. Some countries of the post-Soviet area, which had previously demonstrated extremely poor quality of institutions, are now progressing very rapidly. One such state is Georgia, which has drastically overtaken not only Russia, but even such Baltic countries as Latvia and Lithuania in terms of quality of institutions. As Zaostrovtsev accurately observes: "The success of Kazakhstan and Georgia shows that significant institutional progress is also possible in countries with cultures that are far from the countries that are at the top of the institutional ranking (Finland, Singapore, New Zealand). And even Armenia is clearly ahead of Russia". According to Zaostrovtsev's data, the state of the rule of law is among Russia's most serious institutional problems; it is the reason property rights in Russia are not sufficiently protected. As the state of affairs in this sphere is deteriorating, "Russia has taken the path in the system of property rights from the stage of "expropriation is possible, but takes place rarely" through the intermediary stage of "expropriation is possible" to the stage of "expropriation is just a routine phenomenon".[141]

Expropriation of business has also caused individual attacks on entrepreneurs themselves. According to expert assessments, the number of people imprisoned due to their entrepreneurial activity was over 100,000 in 2007–2009. 80% of the people who were charged had over 10 years of experience in entrepreneurship.[142]

---

[140]   See Dmitry Travin, Vladimir Gel'man, Andrey Zaostrovtsev, *Rossiiskii put': idei, interesy, instituty, illyuzii* (St. Petersburg: European University at St. Petersburg Press, 2017), 233–235.

[141]   See Travin, Gel'man, Zaostrovtsev, *Rossiiskii put'*, 247.

[142]   See Travin, Gel'man, Zaostrovtsev, *Rossiiskii put'*, 266.

The problems with the rule of law are very serious, but Zaostrov-tsev also comments on other important issues besides protecting property rights. In Russia in particular, there is strong state regulation of the economy. The government's interference ultimately aggravates the state of affairs in the economy. Sometimes these effects are connected with the poor quality of state regulations or the low capability of state bureaucracy. However, more often the problem with state regulation is that state officials abuse its capabilities in the name of private profits. According to Zaostrovtsev's assessment, in the post-Soviet area only three countries demonstrate greater abuse of state regulation than those in Russia: Ukraine, Moldova and Kyrgyzstan.[143]

## A Post-Communist Mafia State

It is worth noting that a similar institutional framework in terms of lack of the rule of law and property rights, and the government's encroachment on the economy, was described by the Hungarian sociologist Balint Magyar with regard to Hungary. He used the term "post-Communist mafia state" to describe the state of affairs in that country in the 2010s.[144] Magyar believes that the reasons Hungary evolved in this way under Prime Minister Viktor Orban are a combination of recent political circumstances and the nature of the Hungarian historical path.

"The legacy of Communism was much more cumbersome than expected at the time," Magyar notes. "It soon became clear: there was no direct transition from the half-baked petit embourgeoisement of the Kadar period to real market capitalism. It was more difficult for people socialized in Kadar's world of bargaining and circumvention of rules to adapt to the competition of the world market than it was for other citizens of Central Europe. All at once in the free country it became apparent: Hungarian instincts, desires and hopes, culture and codes of behavior were se-

---

[143]   See Travin, Gel'man, Zaostrovtsev, *Rossiiskii put'*, 238.

[144]   See Balint Magyar, *Post-Communist Mafia State: The Case of Hungary* (Budapest: Central European University Press, 2016), trans. Balint Bethlenfaly, Agnes Simon, Steven Nelson and Kata Paulin.

riously scarred, and had far more in common with East European and Balkan patterns than those of Central Europe".[145]

The so-called "goulash socialism" which existed for approximately twenty years (from the late 1960s to the late 1980s) as a result of Janos Kadar's reforms was able to feed the Hungarians, but did not form a market economy.[146] In this halfway system, state-owned companies had a greater degree of economic independence, but did not fully bear market responsibility for their activity. Success could be achieved not only through effective effort, but also by manipulating rules using informal agreements with officials within the bureaucratic system. By all appearances, Hungarian business brought this experience of hierarchical bargaining through to the post-Communist era.

An equally serious problem was the rejection of democracy by both the right-wing and the left-wing segments of Hungarian society. Of course, this rejection did not openly manifest to the extent that it has in Russia. Hungary became a member state of the European Union, officially accepted European values and obeyed all the norms of behavior imposed by the EU. For a small country which had spent decades in the Soviet Union's sphere of influence the choice to side with Europe was clear and obvious: either align with the European Union, or with Russia, the dangerous heir of the Soviet Union. But the external circumstances that predetermined this choice did not fully correspond to internal developments in Hungary. "The political right- and left-wing of the past were equally undemocratic: after 1989 they were simultaneously engaged in a nostalgic longing for the – undemocratic – past while learning the strings of democratic politics."[147]

The fact was that the right-wing Hungarian politicians, in rejecting Communist ideas, were guided by the influence of pre-Communist times. These had not been times of democracy, but of Miklos Horthy's authoritarian regime. This regime was not particularly effective in economic terms, and most importantly came

---

145   See Magyar, *Post-Communist Mafia State*, 16.

146   See Travin, Marganiya, *Evropeiskaya modernizatsiya*, vol.2., 100–126.

147   See Magyar, *Post-Communist Mafia State*, 19.

to power on a wave of anti-Semitism, and eventually entered into a pact with Nazi Germany. On the one hand, it must be admitted that this regime saved Hungary from the Communist experiment of Béla Kun. On the other hand, left-wing politicians considered themselves heirs not of Béla Kun's destructive regime, but of the pragmatist technocrats who had emerged during the times of the Kadar leadership, and evidently found "goulash socialism" more attractive than Horthy's dubious capitalism. In general, the nature of Hungary's historical path gave rise to a conflict between two authoritarian worldviews in a post-Communist society. Democracy was only seen as an ideal, which Hungarians did not truly identify with, while the real models preserved in the memory of Hungarian politicians were not democratic in essence. This conflict between two autocratic models had its own deep roots. Magyar contrasts Hungary with other Central European countries, which in his opinion adapted better to democratic conditions. However, he does not analyze the historical differences between them, although they do exist.

In the nineteenth century, Hungary was the Eastern part of the dual Hapsburg monarchy. Budapest was the imperial center for the Croatians, Romanians and Ruthenians, as Vienna was for the Czechs, Slovenians and Galician Poles. The Hungarians found it difficult to dismiss this imperial past. After the First World War, they were forced to surrender the lands on which the peoples under their control had lived, and even the lands with an ethnically mixed population. In the blink of an eye, Hungary became a tiny Central European state, and not an imperial center participating in big politics. Peoples who did not belong to dominant ethnic groups and had lacked equal status in the Austro-Hungarian Empire, such as the Poles, Romanians or Czechoslovakians, now appeared more respectable than the former rulers of the empire.

Any empire finds it difficult to bear such humiliation. The Russian Empire dealt with this problem by "restoring itself" in the form of the Soviet Union. Austria gladly submitted to an Anschluss with Germany, which allowed Austrians to consider themselves Germans and thus remain a part of the dominant nation in Europe. For the Hungarians, both of these options for imperial development were impossible, as they were a small nation incapable of restoring the empire by their own efforts. Partnership with Hitler in WWII only aggravated this state of affairs, and led to another defeat. Their strength was exhausted, but ambitions remained.

With great imperial experience but no democratic experience, after the fall of the Eastern bloc Hungary faced the temptation to choose authoritarianism. This choice was not predetermined, but at the same time, there were no significant factors opposing an authoritarian drift. Democratic political institutions appeared in the country, and various political parties gained and lost power accordingly, so formally, the state of affairs was encouraging. However, core authoritarian principles were not rejected by Hungarian society. On the contrary, as the path to Europe proved considerably more difficult than many citizens had previously imagined (unemployment, inflation, major income differentiation), disappointment and the desire to find a scapegoat arose, especially in the wake of the global economic crisis of 2008–2009. Society sought to be proud, but not to improve. As Magyar writes: "the path from unrestrained self-acquittal leads directly to emotional scapegoating: foreign-hearted people, commies, bankers, oligarchs, offshore-riders, liberals, Jews, gays, gypsies, and just about anyone(…) They are all liable for the misfortunes of the Hungarian people".[148]

As in Russia, the process of privatization also affected perceptions of injustice of private property in Hungarian society: "The privatized state property partly landed with the former, largely depoliticized manager elite (…) or foreign investors".[149] Naturally, many Hungarians opposed this transformation. "In the *privatization that followed the regime change* [Magyar's emphasis], it was not merely the growing wealth of the propertied class, but the way they acquired the money that particularly offended the sense of justice of those who lost out in the transformation. This opened the way for political trends whose aim, whether

---

[148]   See Magyar, *Post-Communist Mafia State*, 22.

[149]   See Magyar, *Post-Communist Mafia State*, 175.

openly or in a hidden way, was to reshuffle the ownership situation".[150]

It is important to note that in Hungary, privatization was
conducted in a completely different way than in Russia. The country attempted to sell major assets to strategic investors, primarily
foreign ones, i.e. to those who already possessed large amounts of
capital.[151] Labor collectives received much less opportunity to take
part in the privatization process than they did in Russia. But the
reaction of large sections of the Hungarian population, and even
of elite circles, in the two different countries was approximately
the same. In Hungary, society tolerated the redistribution of property rights, despite the fact that assets were sold effectively, and
not simply handed out. In Russia, the results were nearly the
same. In both cases, the very fact of the emergence of the nouveau
riche was not recognized as legitimate.

In Russia, both specialists and ordinary citizens often criticize
how the privatization process was carried out, noting that because
of the poorly chosen model, "from being the factor of long support
of reformers, privatization rather became an argument of the left
against reform, and seriously complicated internal political life".[152]
Indeed, one may agree that privatization did not help to legitimize
private property and market reforms in general. But in Hungary,
the political outcome was similar even with its different model of
privatization, and this demonstrates that criticism of the specific
models of privatization is often given too much significance. The
problem for both countries is not in the real or imagined mistakes
of the reformers, but in their historical path dependence, which
could not be overcome painlessly in either case.

Returning to Hungary, one should note that the country's
economic problems were especially aggravated by the global economic crisis of 2008–2009. Someone had to be responsible for the
many troubles Hungary faced, and the witch hunting soon began.

---

[150]  See Magyar, *Post-Communist Mafia State*, 174.

[151]  See Travin, Marganiya, *Evropeiskaya modernizatsiya*, vol.2., 147–155.

[152]  See Leonid Grigor'ev, *Ekonomika perekhodnykh* protsessov, vol.1 (Moscow: izdatel'stvo Mezhdunarodnogo universiteta v Moskve, 2010), 498.

In this atmosphere, politicians could manipulate popular perceptions more easily than in an atmosphere of tolerance. "The political right only had to invoke the ideological props of memories from the past (God, motherland, family), to provide points of fixture for people who were also looking for symbolic community and a livable value system."[153] Increased attention to symbols usually reduces attention to rational democratic choice. As a result, the FIDESZ party led by Viktor Orban was able to stay in power from 2010 onwards, and political and economic institutions began to transform without serious popular resistance. Gradually property rights were undermined, and control of major businesses became increasingly concentrated in the hands of powerful officials and the "polygarchs" – politicians ruling the economy – connected to them. The state actors who sought to resist this shift began to be perceived as out of touch with the nation.

Magyar notes that the situation in Hungary differs greatly from the tendencies of typical corrupt regimes. *"The mafia state however is not the qualified case of state capture produced by classical underworld conditions* [Magyar's emphasis], but represents rather a case where the head of a political venture disciplines and domesticates the oligarchs in the capacity, as it were, of the godfather, settling them into his own chain of command. A more fitting description would be *'oligarch capture.'* For in this instance it is not partial economic interests that capture the state, but a political venture that captures the economy through gaining monopoly of power".[154]

This theoretical explanation for the Hungarian case may also be applied to Russia, where the "polygarchs" have also come to dominate in the 2000s and the 2010s. But while their practices are close in nature, their scales prove different. According to Magyar, *"the coercion thresholds* [Magyar's emphasis] of the postcommunist mafia states are different, depending on their geopolitical position. The threshold constraining the use of violence in the case of the EU member Hungary is higher than in Russia, which is not

---

153   See Magyar, *Post-Communist Mafia State,* 27.
154   See Magyar, *Post-Communist Mafia State,* 54.

a member, and even in Russia it is higher than in the case of a post-communist mafia state in Central Asia."[155] Where in Russia it was relatively easy to deprive the richest person in the country, Mikhail Khodorkovsky, of his property, as his control over Yukos was not deemed legitimate by society, in Hungary big business did not suffer to such an extent. The methods, nevertheless, were similar. For example, after the owner of an advertising company refused a government request to sell his property to an oligarch close to the regime, the parliament quickly passed a law prohibiting the placement of advertising on billboards at a distance of five meters from roads, in the interest of safety. This effectively curtailed the company's activity, leaving it all but worthless.[156] One might argue that Hungarian society, by supporting politicians from the FIDESZ party, in fact supports the redistribution of property just like Russian society.

## The Predominance of State Paternalism

Although the illegitimacy of property rights gives rise to inefficiency in the Russian economy, this issue is just one side of the problem. If society does not trust private property and the market economy, it must trust something else instead. In many ways, it is state paternalism that determined the de facto rules of the game in modern Russia. Russian society is little concerned about observation of property rights, but very concerned about opportunities to obtain various goods and services from the Russian state. Unquestionably, paternalism is not a feature specific to Russia. It is typical also for a number of Western European welfare states. But in present-day Russia, large segments of society place their hopes in state support to a greater degree, as (for the reasons described above), they cannot trust in private property or the entrepreneurship connected with it. The average worker does not trust the business owner who provides employment to them. The owner is also not certain of the business's survival over time. But the mass

---

[155]   See Magyar, *Post-Communist Mafia State*, 82.

[156]   See Magyar, *Post-Communist Mafia State*, 181–182.

public did receive certain grounds to trust state paternalism in the 2000s. In the 1990s, these grounds did not yet exist, but a breakthrough took place due to the major increase in global oil prices. Expensive oil stimulated economic growth, and ultimately promoted a rise in real income for the population. The state, supported by its propaganda machine, portrayed these changes as its own achievements. The mechanism of state paternalism has since developed into a complex hierarchy, where various candidates for state support seek state funding at different levels of the pyramid of paternalism.

The upper level is the subsidized regions, which constitute the vast majority of Russia's provinces. The inability to balance the regional budget means that they need to actively lobby their interests before the federal authorities. Depending on how successful this lobbying is, the standards of living in the region may be maintained, as may the potential for regional "barons" to take part in corruption schemes. The middle level is business (including state business), which seeks state orders and various types of support from the state budget. It is in many cases more profitable for business to deal with the state than to offer its production on the market. State orders make it possible to increase profits considerably. The lower level is the broader segments of the population whose life ultimately depends on the budget: police officers, bureaucratic officials, teachers, doctors, professors, pensioners... In present-day Russia, they are not as active in lobbying as the actors on the upper and middle level of pyramid of state paternalism, but their electoral support is fundamentally important for the system's very existence. And finally, the viability of the entire pyramid as a whole is determined by political institutions, which are intentionally created in the interests of ruling groups and designed to strengthen their political and economic dominance. [157]

Thus, the real interests of many Russians are connected with preserving the pyramid of state paternalism. By fitting into the existing state paternalist system, various Russian people, from high-

---

[157] See Vladimir Gel'man, *Authoritarian Russia: Analyzing Post-Soviet Regime Changes* (Pittsburgh: University of Pittsburgh Press, 2015).

ranking officials to low-paid public workers, can pursue their own interests. Paradoxically enough, the existing institutions in Russia enable the economy to stagnate on the one hand, but provide benefits to a large number of people on the other. People have their "own share" in the existing pyramid of state paternalism and do not have sufficient incentive to relinquish it. Nevertheless, it is unlikely that this system will exist forever, since the conditions for its functioning do not remain stable.

Perceptions of benefits are in many ways connected with the difficulties of the post-reform period. Even the low incomes earned today by various groups of Russians may seem acceptable compared with the low incomes and long arrears of wages and pensions of the 1990s. Fearing a return to the difficulties of the era of economic transition, Russian society favors stability at the cost of increased development. But the aspiration to this stability of inefficient institutions is largely a temporary phenomenon. The status quo cannot be preserved in an unchanged form in the face of a change of generations. Those who remember their material hardships in the 1990s, and compare it with the situation nowadays, will sooner or later leave the active stage of their lives. For new generations, the same living standard ceases to look acceptable, as comparisons will be made with the future rather than with the past. In other words, public perceptions correspond to the expectations of economic growth and prosperity. If the development of the economy in the decades to come does not meet these expectations, preference for supporting the stability of institutions may be replaced by a new desire for change. In a certain sense, the current situation in Russia may resemble the status quo of the 1970s, when the generation that compared the Brezhnev stagnation with the wartime hardships of the 1940s was replaced by a generation that had never known these hardships, and strove for higher standards of living in an economic system that was not burdened by a shortage of goods.

If this transformation takes place at a time of more or less stable and not excessive oil prices, with almost zero economic growth, even the objective advantages of state paternalism that exist today for subsidized regions, corrupt officialdom, business fed by state orders, and public sector workers and pensioners existing on state support may disappear. Amidst a constant battle of different interest groups, the economy, in a state of stagnation, is incapable of supporting the living standard of weak groups who have lost the competition for resources. Their "share of the pie" will gradually decrease, as strong interest groups will not be satisfied with a state of stagnation. Even in the absence of growth, strong interest groups will seek enrichment, which will inevitably impact on the weak. A vivid example of redistribution of resources is the Moscow housing renovation program, which began when the Russian edition of this book went to press. The demolition of old residential buildings and the eviction of their residents requires the redistribution of such a large volume of resources for the benefit of the construction business that losses for other interest groups are inevitable. At the moment, it is unclear whether the resettled Muscovites themselves will become victims, or whether there will be an attempt to compensate them in some way.

As the experience of the 1990s demonstrated, when there is a major battle between different groups of interests over a shrinking "pie", it is most likely that besides provincial regions, public sector workers and pensioners will also find themselves on the losing side. Perhaps the list of economic losers will now include also young people, who, unlike the young people of the 1990s, will find it difficult to replace the older generations, as today we do not have the generation gap that existed at the time in terms of knowledge and work skills in the market economy. It is highly likely that young people will cease to understand why the inefficient institutions that their parents passively accepted need to be preserved. If so, then a significant change of perceptions may form the basis for a new stage of changes, both political and economic.

# Chapter 5.
# Public Illusions and Russian Realities

One of the most important arguments set out in this book is that Russian people (as well as people elsewhere around the globe) act rationally and pursue their own interests. As was demonstrated above, among the key ideas that were typical for late Soviet society, in practice the only ones that were realized were those that were aimed at solving urgent economic problems, providing consumers with goods and eliminating the shortages of the Soviet economy. In the process of practical realization, these ideas were transformed under the pressure of dominant interest groups. The ideas that worked well in theory, but did not meet these major interests, remained in the hearts and minds of the Russian reformers. But the ones advantageous for influential actors and the interest groups behind them were formalized in Russian laws and other regulatory acts, as well as in various informal practices, despite the reformers' original intentions. Ultimately, the institutional framework of politico-economic order that has consolidated in Russia is highly advantageous for powerful interest groups. From an economic standpoint, these institutions are inefficient, because they have not facilitated economic growth and societal development, or an increase in real incomes and labor productivity, but for those who established these institutional arrangements, they are very efficient in terms of pursuit of self-interest.[158] In other words, the building of inefficient institutions in present-day Russia is a very rational and logical phenomenon, which arose as an outcome of transformation processes.

However, no society can function solely on a rational basis. This is partly because the interests of the societal groups who are losing in the competitive struggle for money, status, and other re-

---

[158] "Institutions... are created to serve the interests of those with the bargaining power to devise new rules." Douglass C. North, *Institutions, Institutional Changes, and Economic Performance* (Cambridge: Cambridge University Press, 1990), 16.

sources must also be satisfied in one way or another. "The individual is convinced, the mass is indoctrinated," is how the French psychologist Serge Moscovici laconically expressed the essence of this problem.[159] Despite all the economic troubles, poor material conditions, unacceptable social inequality, and other negative phenomena they face, the losers need to feel a certain degree of satisfaction with the current state of affairs, as no regime can function without their support. This is particularly true for electoral authoritarian regimes, which tend to hold general elections on a regular basis. Russia may be considered a prime example of such a regime.[160]

The most powerful interest groups strive to preserve their dominance, despite the fact that they may constitute only a tiny minority of the population. The preservation of their dominance is only possible when the mass public can feel advantaged in certain ways in its current position (even if these advantages are illusory). The status quo may be stable if the dominant interest groups are satisfied with their current position because it actually is advantageous for them. And the rest of the interest groups are satisfied because they experience various non-material advantages (in many cases illusory ones) as compensation for their losses. The list of these illusions may include pride in the country, a feeling of protection from external aggression, hopes for a better future, identification with a strong charismatic leader, myths created by the national culture etc.

## Illusions of the Past

Illusions have always played a major role in Russia's history, as with many other countries. For some time, for example, the quest to build a Communist society in the Soviet Union was one such great illusion. The Bolshevist political system was, of course, not built only on the illusions of large segments of the population. The

---

[159]   See Serge Moscovici, *Vek tolp: Istoricheskii traktat po psikhologii mass* (Moscow: Tsentr psikhologii i psikhoterapii, 1996), 62.

[160]   See Gel'man, *Authoritarian Russia*.

basis for the success achieved by the Bolsheviks in the Civil War was the real interests of many Russians. It was important for the revolutionaries to receive support not only from the working class, but also from the peasantry, as at the moment of the Civil War, Russia was a peasant country. According to Orthodox Marxism, the working class, exploited by the capitalists, was supposed to carry out the socialist revolution; but given the overwhelming numbers of the peasantry, the proletariat was utterly incapable of ensuring power for the Bolsheviks on its own. Lenin therefore took a winning path that contradicted the standard Marxist approach to the Communist revolution: he promised to implement major agrarian reform, transferring control of landowners' lands to the Russian peasants. Thus, the peasants were materially interested in the Bolsheviks' victory, and this is why a large portion of the Russian peasantry supported Lenin and Bolsheviks during the Civil War.

Later on, however, the triumphant coalition of the workers and peasants suffered from a split, as the industrialization of the Soviet Union was implemented in the late 1920s and 1930s at the expense of the peasantry, which was faced with the tragedy of collectivization. Based on a policy of rapid industrialization, Stalin thus split Soviet society and began to rely solely on the urban minority. The standards of living in Soviet cities were much higher than in the countryside, and urban dwellers had grounds to support the Stalinist system based on their material interests. They might experience a considerable shortage of goods, including the most vital, but unlike the peasants, they did not suffer from malnutrition or die of starvation. Thus, by the 1930s, the most important expression of personal success for residents of the rural areas of the Soviet Union was moving to the cities, even if they received the most primitive and low-paying work, poor housing conditions and only basic nutrition. Furthermore, some peasants who moved to the city were able to climb the hierarchical ladder over time. Certain social lifts appeared which enabled yesterday's peasant to become an urban worker, then the manager of a low-tier organization, and subsequently, perhaps, a party functionary, a Red Army officer or an employee of the security apparatus.

Stalin's mass repressions left vacant many positions previously held by people who had risen to the top during the years of the revolution. When the original fighters of the "Leninist guard" were executed or sent to the camps, other Communists occupied their places – those who were loyal to Stalin in the wake of the power struggles. These functionaries left their previous positions vacant in their turn, and these vacancies were filled by their successors. As this pattern of promotion required new personnel, the new recruits were often newcomers from rural areas. A peasant who came to work at a construction site could thus begin by laying bricks and sleeping in barracks, and then become the party secretary of an enterprise, and move on to working at the office of the Bolshevik party, where they were no longer a manual laborer and received a good salary for their work. Finally, during the period of the mass executions of old Bolsheviks (1937–1938), this new member of Stalinist cadres had the chance to join the Communist elite.

Soviet military commanders, directors of factories, and the executioners who carried out the repressions were promoted to their new positions in a similar way. When Stalin decided to exterminate yet another group of leaders, new upward movement took place throughout the entire power hierarchy. Those at the bottom rose to the middle, and those from the middle rose to the very top of the party-state hierarchy. Having made such a successful career for themselves, they became firm supporters of the Stalinist system, and could not conceive of existing without a leader like Comrade Stalin. Nevertheless, these successful new cadres were naturally a minority. The overwhelming majority of the Soviet people continued to live in the countryside. There, they were deprived even of what Lenin had given them in the years of revolution – their own land. Collectivization in practice did not unite the lands of individual peasants into large farms, but deprived rural residents of private property altogether. Working on collective farms, peasants under Stalin received virtually no wages, and were forced to feed themselves primarily from their own subsidiary farms. This resembled the old serf system of statute labor, whereby the peasant worked without pay for several days a week for the landowners, and only on the remaining days provided food for their own family. Naturally, the collective farm peasants, who found themselves practically in the same position as serfs, could not support the Stalinist system based only on their own material interests.

Of course, Soviet urban residents could not always be supportive towards the regime purely based on rational considerations. Although the city lived better than the countryside, many urban residents lived worse than before the revolution. They lost their property to nationalization of factories and residential buildings, their living conditions often deteriorated, and in many cases they were deprived of their high, stable salaries, which they had previously received as a result of quality education and career opportunities. Only a small share of urban dwellers (namely, representatives of the party-state nomenklatura) benefited from Stalin's social lifts and supported Stalinism based on their own rational interests. Rather, rural residents and ordinary city dwellers needed other, irrational incentives to support the regime. "It is primarily ordinary people who suffer from the intolerable pointlessness and aimlessness of life," the Russian writer Alexander Melikhov observes. "They are the ones who are devastated by the lack of any imaginary (and perhaps there is no other kind) involvement in something impressive and long-lasting".[161]

Without a complex of illusions, which portrayed the barbaric Stalinist system as deserving support from the peasantry, it would have been difficult for the Soviet Union to survive. This was especially true during World War II, when the Nazi occupation destroyed the Stalinist state machinery and created the possibility for peasants to serve a different, German regime. Many Soviet people did fight in fact for the Germans, but the majority remained faithful to the Stalinist system. This would not have happened if the complex of Communist illusions had not received broad support and appreciation among the Russian people, including the peasantry.

---

[161] See Alexander Melikhov, *Bronya iz oblaka* (St. Petersburg: Limbus-Press, 2012), 155.

It is easier to survive numerous hardships if you believe that they are temporary, and especially if you believe that you are suffering for the sake of a great mission. The belief in the Communist future of the country formed a motivation for persevering with the work at hand. Soviet peasants lived in extraordinary poverty and frequently suffered from starvation, not to mention lacking any of the forms of leisure available in urban areas (such as visits to theaters, cinemas, concerts, parks with music and dances, or libraries). But the belief in the Communist future of the Soviet Union made it possible to preserve this situation of "spiritual equilibrium" and continue further looting of the Soviet countryside, which was carried out in the interests of Stalin's leadership and its beneficiaries.

A sober view of Soviet realities would have demonstrated to the Soviet people, who believed in Communism, that they had merely been offered a new myth by the ruling ideology. However, in the conditions where the peasantry found themselves, a sober view on the Soviet reality was not necessary. Indeed, it would have been harmful, as in the totalitarian Stalinist system, the Soviet peasants in any case did not have any alternative to their miserable existence. They were forced either to endure their poverty and believe that Communism would improve lives at least for their children and grandchildren, or endure the same poverty and believe in nothing, dooming themselves to hopeless depression. Religious belief was persecuted in those years, and most churches were either closed or demolished, leaving no alternative to the Communist faith. In a way, losers of the Communist regime during the Stalinist period were even more interested in cultivating irrational perceptions of reality in their own milieu than the winners. While the latter could hope to find attractive jobs in the cities, increase their well-being and move up the "career ladder" (if only from low-paid proletarian to qualified worker), the former had no hopes or positive rational expectations, and simply needed to believe in something in order to survive, or at least to preserve their mental health. Soviet people united through their faith in Communist ideology, and experienced enthusiasm that could sometimes reach the level of exaltation.

A similar situation has been observed in many countries where modernization affected the everyday life of traditional society. Interest groups have always included both winners and losers of major societal, economic, and political changes. Even under normal circumstances of economic development, ones not distorted by such cruel experiments as the ones conducted by the Bolsheviks in the Soviet Union, major portions of the population faced an inability to raise their standards of living. This may have been because they lived in depressed regions. It may have been because of the lack of qualification required for high-paid work. It may have been because of extended civil wars and foreign interventions that paralyzed the economy. Although modernization and the market economy improve people's lives in the long term, a given person may not live to see the improvements in the short term. After realizing that they are essentially in a hopeless situation, an average person becomes an active consumer of illusions, which are offered to the mass public as substitutes on the "ideational market". The less opportunity there is to obtain consumer goods, the greater the demand for illusions as a substitute for prosperity.

The well-known philosopher and psychologist Erik Fromm justly noted: "...loneliness, fear and bewilderment remain: people cannot endure them forever. They cannot constantly carry the burden of freedom 'from': if they are incapable of moving from negative freedom to positive freedom, they try to escape from this freedom altogether. The main paths by which the flight from freedom takes place is to submit to the leader, as in fascist countries, or the forced conformism which dominates in our democracy".[162] Carl Jung was even more specific in this respect: "If the individual is overwhelmed by a feeling of his own insignificance and powerlessness, and he feels that his life has lost its meaning (...), this means he is already close to becoming a slave of the State".[163]

---

[162] Erich Fromm, *Begstvo ot svobody* (Moscow: Progress, 1990), 118.

[163] Carl Jung, 'Neraskrytaya samost'', in Carl Jung, *Izbrannoe* (Minsk: Popurri, 1998), 76.

# A New Era, New Illusions

The situation that has formed in present-day Russia resembles, in a certain sense, the conditions of the active consumption of Communist illusions in the several decades after the revolution. Of course, neither the economy nor the political system of the twenty-first century resemble the Stalinist system. Furthermore, Communist ideology itself is now dead. Most Russian citizens will not be able to believe in building the paradise on earth promised a hundred years ago by the Bolsheviks. But the demand for an ideology which helps them to survive at a difficult time still arises in Russian society. And the less a citizen succeeds in real life, the more they need it.

As was mentioned above,[164] a complex of national-patriotic (imperialist) ideas emerged under the surface in Soviet society despite the dominance of official Communist ideology. This complex was little drawn on during the period of perestroika and the reforms of the 1990s, as it could not offer any realistic method for solving acute economic problems. Its ideas were not pragmatic, and they could not be used as practical guidelines for complicated transformations at a difficult time. However, their marginal status did not prevent them from being very attractive for the mass public. While not being a real tool for running the economy, they could be effective as an illusion to help Russian people to adapt to difficult living conditions in the post-reform period.

It is not surprising that national-patriotic ideas became increasingly in demand in Russian society as economic reforms solved the most acute problems faced by the country. Certain elements of Russian society felt themselves to be beneficiaries of the post-Soviet reforms, and had no particular need for illusions. However, another section suddenly found itself blocked by a ceiling, even though their standards of living increased in comparison with the Soviet past and the hardships of the 1990s. Although relative and absolute well-being increased, they did not feel any real prospects for personal growth, for a fundamental change in life-

---

[164]   See Chapter 1.

style, and for opportunities comparable with those enjoyed by the mass public in the West. In other words, they were able to think rationally about the future, but couldn't see any hopes in it for themselves personally. Thus, they felt the need to fill the vacuum of their future with illusions. As a result, national-patriotic ideas became particularly attractive for large segments of the Russian public at a time when rapid economic growth had enriched Russian society.

In present-day Russia, ideology ceased to be seen as a method for solving practical economic problems. New economic and political institutions, inefficient in absolute terms but successful in serving the dominant interest groups, have removed the issue of policy reforms from the practical agenda. Thus, in the aftermath of an ideology that did not support change, only the supply of illusions remains to comfort those who felt dissatisfaction with the changes in Russia over the recent decades. These people are not necessarily the poorest citizens of the country, although those, naturally, have a high demand for various illusions. The poor hope for a strong, paternalistically oriented state, which takes care of them, provides them with highly paid work or social support, restrains the oligarchs, redistributes property and acts effectively. These illusions appeal to the normative ideal of "a good Soviet Union" – a combination of the stability ensured by Soviet power with shops filled with goods, and other advantages of the market economy.[165] Those who became the losers of reforms wish for new changes. They see the state as a social reformer, but do not understand that it will not act in their interests by punishing the rich.

Strangely enough, many of the Russians who have found a place for themselves in the new world, found work and can satisfy their family's needs also require a strong ideology that provides an illusion, and to the same great extent. These people can provide for themselves, but do not see significant prospects for their life. They often have a dull, monotonous job (such as a driver behind

---

[165] See *Obshchestvennoe mnenie – 2016* (Moscow: Levada-Center, 2017), 22, 76, 77, 79. On the "good Soviet Union" as a normative ideal, see Gel'man, Marganiya, Travin, *Reexamining Economic and Political Reforms in Russia*.

the wheel of a car, or behind a cash register). They have a strong need for something to give new meaning to their exhausting existence. On the one hand, this existence involves earning enough money to survive, but on the other hand, when this survival is ensured, a person wants to receive some stronger and better impressions from their life. They wish to be involved in some great undertaking; to feel that their life has involved not merely earning money, but fighting for a great cause.

For a long time in the Soviet Union, this kind of illusion was provided by the Communist ideology, but today, that ideology is completely irrelevant. The average Russian citizen is forced to seek another source, which can furnish them with illusions. While some people devote their lives to their families in the hope of providing for a happy future for their children and grandchildren, others attempt to identify themselves with the Russian state, and feel emotional about the country's successes and failures. These emotions cannot be connected with something as boring as economic reforms, which are not understood by the mass public. The average Russian citizen, however, is capable of becoming emotional about the Russian state when it begins to resemble a football team – when it battles with rivals, conquers territory, raises its international prestige, and takes certain steps against others, which demonstrate its strength and its ability to dominate the international arena.

Thus, the demand for national-patriotic ideas is very high among large segments of the Russian population, as a strong and successful state is an ideal object of identification for those people who are dissatisfied with their everyday lives. We emphasize that these ideas are not addressed at solving practical problems. There are not all that many people in Russia who are prepared to join the army voluntarily in order to conquer the territory of other countries, or are prepared to sacrifice their money and property to strengthen the state's defensive capacity. National-patriotic ideas serve as an optimal supplier of illusions. Those who strive to identify themselves with a strong Russian state are not prepared to act to make it stronger. They wish to receive a strong state in ready-made form, and if this is impossible, they are prepared to believe the propaganda provided by the mass media that the Russian state is moving from victory to victory, from success to success. As a result, they may believe in this propaganda until their need for illusions comes into sharp contrast with the growing economic problems. Such a contrast is often expressed in present-day Russia with the formula of "the war of the television and the fridge"; this war may end with the victory of the latter.

Last but not least, one should note that the need for illusions even exists among citizens who are clearly successful. Many of them do not compare themselves with losers in their own country, who are hopelessly behind in their career and wealth, but rather with those people who have equivalent positions in the West. Then it emerges that that these comparisons are not in the Russians' favor. Successful Russian citizens often travel abroad, for both business and leisure. They are able to compare the way of life of their counterparts in the West with their own. Even if in Russia it is currently possible to achieve personal material success, it is rather difficult to ensure an acceptable lifestyle as a whole. Problems of transportation, personal safety, environmental issues, self-expression and self-realization in present-day Russia are much more acute than in the majority of Western European nations.

Many Russian citizens would like to live in the West, but do not have an opportunity to do so, as they face problems which cannot be solved by money or education. Russian citizens lack the ability to compete for prestigious jobs in the countries where they would like to live. Some who reside in economically developed countries, but do not truly fit into Western society, begin to worship patriotic and imperial values while living abroad. Young people who have not assimilated, lack good jobs and have a poor knowledge of foreign languages are no longer prepared to "acquire" illusions produced in Russia and consume them without leaving the United States or Germany. For them, these problems may serve as an incentive for self-improvement that enables them to apply their efforts and become more competitive. But those whose personalities have already fully formed cannot start anew and achieve the superior positions in the United States or Germany that they once achieved in Russia. These people feel their inferiority, but often do not blame themselves for their problems, rather blaming those in the West who refuse to accept them.

It is well known that many people in Russia resent the fact that NATO accepted a number of countries from Central and Eastern Europe which were previously members of the Warsaw Pact or part of the Soviet Union, but its leaders did not invite Russia to join with a status which would match the country's importance as the legal successor of the Soviet Union. A similar situation exists in many other fields. Successful Russian citizens would like to become accepted in the West as equals, but when this is not possible, they display anti-Western sentiments and come to subscribe to ideas of revenge. At the same time, these patriotically minded people do not desire a further deterioration of relations with the West that might extend as far as a new Cold War. This is the fundamental difference between the present-day situation in Russia and the one observed in many other modernizing countries. Present-day Russian "patriots" do not wish to fight for a socialist homeland, or for a national-socialist one. Russian patriots want to travel to the West, spend some time there, relax at resorts and stock up in shops. Their rhetoric is anti-Western, but their lifestyle, paradoxically enough, is completely Western. In a certain sense, the supporters of national-patriotic imperialist illusions resemble football fans who wish to identify themselves with their favorite team, but are incapable of playing for it at the required level, and cannot even attain the necessary level of fitness to play sports seriously. With a bottle of beer, in front of the television, one can root for a football club contending for a title, or for one's native country as it conquers distant lands. The sociologist Michael Mann even uses the expression "spectator-sport militarism" to describe a situation when a certain society is prepared to sympathize with the state in its battle, but is not truly prepared to sacrifice its interests.[166]

Thus, for a sizeable part of Russian society, the complex of national-patriotic illusions is a form of psychological compensa-

---

[166]   See Michael Mann, *Vlast' v XXI stoletii* (Moscow: Higher School of Economics Publishing House, 2014), 45.

tion for problems that it has experienced in the process of modernization. The rational and irrational motives constantly intertwine
in the minds of Russians. In the wake of major transformations,
they often acted quite rationally, defending their economic interests and challenging interest groups that opposed them. Some
Russians won in this battle, and others lost. Some political and
economic actors were able to adjust the reforms to their own benefit and gain large revenues and high status, but others gained little
or practically nothing. As new institutions were established and
new rules of the game were consolidated, many people began to
feel dissatisfied with the current situation. Dissatisfaction gave
rise to a need to find scapegoats responsible for all problems. For
some Russians, these enemies are wealthy and successful people
such as oligarchs. For others, the main source of problems is foreign countries, which lead better lives and shut themselves off
from Russia with all kinds of barriers. In the end, the "oligarchs",
NATO member states, "foreign agents" and the pro-Western liberals merged into one "fifth column", which came to personify the
enemy who hindered people from realizing the ideals that they
had formed in their minds. These ideals, of course, are unattainable, but the irrational features that are typical for a considerable
section of Russian society do not allow them to reconcile themselves with this unattainability. Hence the need to find a specific
enemy who must be conquered. However, Russian society is prepared not to sacrifice its specific rational interests in order to battle
this irrational enemy, but to support the illusions, which help to
make the imperfect world psychologically comfortable.

## The Crimean Problem

The annexation of Crimea by Russia in 2014 took place in a situation when the need for a mass illusion was increasingly felt by
Russian citizens. Hopes for a further rise in the living standards
had become empty fantasies by the beginning of 2014. The economy was growing much more slowly after the crisis of 2008–2009
than in the pre-crisis period. In 2013, the growth rate was only just
over 1%, and even this rate of economic growth was achieved

mainly because global oil prices remained at the level of over $100 per barrel. Inefficient institutions slowed Russia's economic development even with relatively favorable conditions on the global energy resource market. It became clear that with a lack of further growth of oil prices, the Russian economy could expect stagnation, and with a new fall, a serious recession with a fall in standards of living. This did in fact happen later on, in 2014–2016.

The lack of rational hopes for economic development was augmented by the lack of rational hopes for political development. The mass protests of 2011–2012 were short-lived, and enthusiasm for protests died quickly. Furthermore, the subsequent repressions demonstrated that in certain cases, the law enforcement agencies could inflict harsh coercion on protesters. After that, there were no grounds to hope for successful political development of the country. By early 2014, Russian society was on the verge of falling into apathy. However, those Russians who did not wish to fall into apathy, which would be fraught with social degradation and worsening public health, were intuitively inclined to look for illusions, which could help them endure difficult times. The Russian leadership's decision to annex Crimea greatly contributed to these illusions.[167] It drastically changed the mental atmosphere in a severely frustrated society, which no longer had rational grounds to hope for successful economic development. The television-driven media machine devoted enormous amounts of coverage to the Crimean annexation, presenting it to the viewer in the most attractive light.[168] As a result, large segments of the Russian population gained the illusory feeling of a great mission being pursued by the Russian state, and a feeling of pride in its realization.

It is indicative that in the public discussion that arose after the annexation of Crimea, opponents of the act often asked its supporters what they actually gained along with this peninsula. Material benefit? Or an opportunity for a better holiday? This

---

[167] See Dmitry Travin, *Prosuchestvuet li putinskaya sistema do 2042 goda?* (St. Petersburg: Norma, 2016), 235–271.

[168] See *Politicheskoe razvitie Rossii, 2014-2016: Instituty i praktiki avtoritarnoi konsolidatsii*, Kirill Rogov (ed.) (Moscow: Liberal'naya missiya, 2016), 39–43.

question presupposed that the respondent would approach the problem rationally, and weigh the annexation's costs and benefits. But the responses usually came from a completely different realm: this was the realm of completely unfounded fantasies of saving the residents of the Crimea from the terrible neo-Nazi disease that was allegedly spreading through the Ukraine. Additionally, there were suggestions that NATO was planning to station a military base in the Crimea capable of threatening Russia. No rational counter-arguments with data about the tiny influence of the right-wing nationalists on the political life of Ukraine, or that NATO already had the opportunity to station military bases directly next to Russia's borders in the Baltic countries (and so it did not need Crimea), were accepted by the opponents. Such a denial was not connected with a lack of logic and knowledge. Supporters of the Russian annexation of Crimea did not need this specific territory as such, but an illusion allowing them to identify themselves with Vladimir Putin, the political leader of the country who had fulfilled a great mission. In any given person's eyes, such a mission would validate a personal life without development, without progress. A lack of practical opportunities to change life in reality resulted in the need for the illusory possibility of experiencing the greatness of Russia and possessing a satisfactory place in this overall greatness. In this illusory vision, Russia had saved Crimea from Ukrainian neo-Nazis, fought for brotherly Ukraine against America, and strengthened Russia's own security, depriving the aggressive NATO bloc of the opportunity to threaten Russia from the shores of the Black Sea.

Russian public polemics over the Crimea seemed to be take place in different languages. One side spoke in the language of reality, and the other in the language of illusions; without a "translation", they could not even understand each other. Supporters of reality – in many cases successful, accomplished people, with a clear understanding of the meaning of their own lives, or even their own missions – could not understand the rational sense of immersing oneself into a world of illusions. They attempted to wrest their opponents from the world of illusions, as if these people could listen to their opponents in the world of reality. It was not surprising that supporters of the annexation of Crimea did not even wish to learn the language of their ideological opponents. Quite the opposite, they did not want to "go to a country where that language is spoken", as they would be unhappy there. In their turn, they could not understand the opponents of the Crimean affair, as they could not even imagine their rational logic. They could not understand why a successful person should not have an internal need to identify themselves with a strong state and a strong leader.

In a certain sense, the ideational movement that became informally known as "Krymnash" ("Crimea is Ours!") attempted to reproduce the set of uplifting illusions from the times when there was true belief in the possibility of building Communism. Of course, the tasks of that era were incomparable in scale with the tasks of the twenty-first century. "Krymnash" is merely a low-quality substitute for the "great idea" of the past. Yet this kind of substitute was used many times by other peoples and in other countries in difficult periods of modernization, when societies needed mass illusions. After defeat in World War I, Germany dreamed of annexing the Sudetenland and Danzig (Gdansk). The drive to fulfill the general mission of reviving the country and annexing land manifested itself most strongly in the years of the Great Depression, when hopes for prosperity and personal success were rapidly dashed across Europe. France attempted to hold on to Algeria at any price, Great Britain to Ireland, Poland to Vilnius, etc. The recent Crimean annexation, with its "little green men", is very reminiscent of these illusions.

## The Empire's "Divorce" with the Nation

Until very recently, national-patriotic and imperialist ideas were treated as a single unit in Russia. This was the way things were in the late Soviet Union, where the empire was not separated from the nation in which the so-called "new historical communality: the Soviet people" featured. However, more recently, the concepts of "empire" and "nation" have slowly begun to diverge in Russia. Furthermore, since the collapse of the Soviet Union, it would be more appropriate to speak of ideas of Russia as a superpower, rather than ideas of imperialism, as this set of ideas more accurately reflects the current mood of many Russians.

A considerable portion of Russian citizens strive to identify themselves with the country as a whole, i.e. Russia with its current borders. Furthermore, some people feel nostalgia for the old Soviet Union, which was considerably larger in territory, included closely ethnically related people — the Ukrainians and the Belarusians — and most importantly, had such great military strength that it could be considered a superpower alongside the United States. The current patriotic convictions of this segment of Russian citizens are that the country must be as powerful as possible, and if necessary may include neighboring territories in its sphere of influence. However, the majority of Russians are not prepared to sacrifice their prosperity for such a bold move. They are personally unwilling to join the military to defend Russia's borders, even though they fully support strengthening of the state's power. The vast majority of Russian society was in favor of the annexation of Crimea, and also supported the recognition of independence of South Ossetia and Abkhazia, which for a long time were in conflict with Georgia.[169]

Previously, Russian society had also supported President Vladimir Putin in his firm resolve to maintain Chechnya as an integral part of the Russian state. For supporters of the idea of preserving Russia as a superpower, it is not important that the Chechens are not ethnically related to Russians. Uniting in a struggle in the name of the state, many Russians experience a feeling of community and involvement with a great undertaking, as they understand it. The ordinary Russian citizen may not be particularly successful in their life, may have a low income, a low status and a job that brings no moral satisfaction, but if they feel themselves to be part of the great Russian people, then they believe that they are making a contribution to preserving the superpower and expanding its borders, or if not a contribution, they are at least providing moral support to the state in its efforts. These kinds of

---

[169] See *Obshchestvennoe mnenie – 2016*, 199, 208–210.

superpower illusions are not a feature unique to Russia. They were typical for some countries in the recent past when they had to pass through difficult periods of modernization. A feeling of involvement in a great undertaking supports people in difficult situations even if the ability to achieve these goals is an unattainable illusion.

Superpower illusions were formed in the era of modernization, and may gradually vanish (as demonstrated by the experience of many foreign countries with imperial pasts), when the tasks of modernization are essentially fulfilled. In a society with high standards of living, low income differentiation, decent social services and welfare protection, good opportunities for leisure and sound environmental standards, there will be significantly less grounds for a spreading of superpower illusions among the mass public. Additionally, superpower illusions weaken as international integration processes develop (as demonstrated by the experience of the European Union): these tendencies draw the residents of a modernizing country onto the international scene. If Russian citizens have more opportunities to live, study and work in Europe, to own property there and gradually become integrated into European societies, the aspiration to superpower status will gradually vanish, making the way for the aspiration to satisfy rational social and economic interests.

For the modern world, the problem is not so much a matter of empire as of dangerous and violent ethnic nationalism,[170] which in modern political science is usually distinguished from "good" civic nationalism (although it is cannot be separated completely).[171] Russian ethnic nationalism is much less widespread in Russia today than superpower illusions, although from time to time it manifests itself in conflicts between Russians and various migrants, and also with representatives of certain other ethnic groups that live in the country. Around half of the respondents

---

[170]  See Urs Altermatt, *Ethnonatsionalizm v Evrope* (Moscow: Russian State University for Humanities, 2000).

[171]  See Alexei Miller, *Natsiya, ili mogushchestvo mifa* (St. Petersburg: European University at St. Petersburg Press, 2016), 96, 137.

surveyed by the Levada Center (the leading public opinion survey agency in Russia) believe that the principle of "Russia for ethnic Russians" should be implemented in the country, at least within reasonable limits. Some respondents (considerably less than half) believe that people of various nationalities should be barred from living in Russia.[172]

Ethnic nationalism is based on the same irrational ideas about the presence of enemies, and the belief that someone is benefitting from the citizens' difficult material position. These views are the illusory compensation for the misfortunes (real or imagined) one suffered in the wake of modernization. Blaming other ethnic groups for these problems, some people shift responsibility for their failures from themselves to others, and may thus gain relative psychological comfort in a difficult situation. Ethnic nationalism, unlike superpower illusions, does not currently receive the official support of the Russian authorities. Leaders of nationalist movements and their most extremist figures are in jail. However, ethnic nationalism and superpower illusions grow in the same soil. In the political sense, they aim in different directions, but they are very similar as methods for providing psychological comfort in a complex situation of incomplete modernization.

The inefficient Russian economic and political institutions mutually complement the illusions, which are dangerous for Russia's development. Institutions that give rise to corruption, the violent confiscation of property, and damage to business activity may only exist to the extent that society, inspired by illusions, is indifferent to its severe socio-economic problems. In turn, illusions may persist for a long time if the economy, which guided by these institutions, is in a state of long-term stagnation. A stagnant country, which presents no interest for investors, may be cut off from the world economy. If considerable income differentiation persists, then marginalized social groups will be deprived of prospects in the long term. The only comfort for them will be to preserve illusions of being surrounded by numerous enemies who are harming the superpower. Thus, the country's primary direc-

---

[172]   See *Obshchestvennoe mnenie – 2016*, 190.

tion of development is associated not with constructive economic cooperation, not with investments or property rights, but with an escalation in military expenditures, intensification of defensive capacity, and restriction of the rights and freedoms of suspicious persons. This direction is perilous for Russia, as history knows no examples of successful development for such a society.

Illusions must disappear sooner or later, and for those people who crave psychological comfort, this will be a serious ordeal. A well-known example for Russians is the disappearance of Communist illusions, which united the people for a long time and helped them to endure a miserable life surrounded by a capitalist world hostile to the Soviet Union. When the illusions vanished, the Soviet people found the transformation extremely difficult – both in the material sense (as they discovered that they severely lagged behind Western countries) and in the moral sense (as it was very difficult for people in a society with a distorted economic structure, where reforms had destroyed many jobs, to maintain high self-esteem). If illusions once again prevail the attainment of rational interests, problems in society will only be exacerbated. Illusions resemble a drug. For a while, they create a feeling of psychological comfort and even euphoria, but they undermine the individual's strength, and make a person weaker over time. They deprive individuals of the ability to act in their own rational interest. Russia should not only reject the inefficient institutions that hinder development, but also reject the illusions that support these institutions.

# Chapter 6.
# Bad Governance in Russia: A Vicious Circle?

More than a quarter-century of post-Communist socio-economic and political transformations in Russia has brought unpromising results. Examining these transformations from the perspective of a "triple transition",[173] i.e. modernization on the three fronts of democratization, market economy and nation- and state-building, their outcomes are contradictory at best. The post-Soviet political regime in Russia turned into a form of electoral authoritarianism.[174] Market reforms in Russia and other post-Soviet countries form the basis of "crony capitalism", built around ruling groups' control over key economic assets and market agents.[175] The very low quality of state governance in Russia, which has been commented on ubiquitously,[176] is severely criticized by all observers, regardless of their views on any other issues. These outcomes of post-Soviet development in Russia may be described as "bad governance", which is characterized by such phenomena as lack and/or perversion of the rule of law, a very high level of corruption, poor quality of state regulation and government ineffectiveness.

Although optimistically minded experts hope for positive changes in Russia as the economy grows and new generations of political leaders emerge in the decades to come,[177] the issue of the

---

[173] See Claus Offe, 'Capitalism by Democratic Design? Democratic Theory Facing the Triple Transition in East Central Europe', *Social Research*, 58, no.4 (1991), 865–892.

[174] See Gel'man, *Authoritarian Russia*.

[175] See Gulnaz Sharafutdinova, *Political Consequences of Crony Capitalism inside Russia* (Notre Dame, in University of Notre Dame Press, 2011); Åslund, *Russia's Crony Capitalism*.

[176] See *Worldwide Governance Indicators, 1996–2014* (Washington, DC: The World Bank, 2016). http://data.worldbank.org/data-catalog/worldwide-governance-indicators.

[177] See Henry E. Hale, *Patronal Politics: Eurasian Regime Dynamics in Comparative Perspective* (Cambridge: Cambridge University Press, 2014); Daniel Treisman,

causes and mechanisms of this trajectory of development of Russia remain very relevant. Why is the quality of governance in Russia much worse than one might expect based on the degree of its socio-economic development? According to numerous international assessments – both integral and addressing specific issues (such as corruption, rule of law, and property rights)[178] – Russia is on the same level as poor and undeveloped countries of the Third World, and far below a number of other Eastern European countries. The search for an answer to this question requires a closer look at the political and economic constraints on post-Soviet modernization in Russia in a theoretical and comparative context. This chapter and the next will investigate the institutional foundations for economic and political development, which set limits and constraints on modernization processes in Russia, and sometimes led to unintended and undesired outcomes.

## Introduction: Russia's Greatest Rent Machine

At the beginning of 2015, the residents of over twenty Russian regions received an unexpected and unpleasant New Year's present. They were informed about a large-scale reduction in the number of suburban commuter trains, which connected cities and regional centers with neighboring areas (and in some regions, their total removal). Although the frequency of commuter trains had dropped dramatically in previous years, and fares had permanently increased, the complete cancellation of routes caused a major wave of public discontent: in a number of areas, suburban trains had been the only type of public transportation available for local residents. The public authorities and the top management of the Russian Railways holding company were even accused of "geno-

---

'Income, Democracy, and Leader Turnover', *American Journal of Political Science*, 59, no. 4 (2015), 927–942.

178  See Andrey Zaostrovtsev, 'Authoritarianism and Institutional Decay in Russia: Disruption of Property Rights and the Rule of Law', in *Authoritarian Modernization in Russia: Ideas, Institutions, and Policies*, Vladimir Gel'man (ed.) (Abingdon: Routledge, 2017), 73–94.

cide" of Russians,[179] and collective protests took place in a number of regions, including threats to block railroads by local residents. Social tensions were made public, and in February 2015, President Vladimir Putin demanded on television that government officials and the Russian Railways management restore suburban train transportation to its previous level of frequency. Officials immediately reported that they had carried out this demand by the head of state, thus restoring the previous status quo.

The cancellation of suburban trains was a logical consequence of the changes, which had taken place in Russian railway transport in the previous decade.[180] In 2003, on Putin's initiative, the state company "Russian Railways" (RR) was created (and later reformed as an open shareholders' society) by the Ministry of Transportation, and given the key assets of the entire industry. Following this, structural reforms designed to liberalize the transportation market were conducted in Russian railway transport. According to the plan of the initiators of these reforms, who were guided by foreign models,[181] a division was to be made between profitable cargo and unprofitable passenger transportation, and the market itself should become a field of competition for private companies. But in fact, RR not only preserved but reinforced its monopoly, practically dictating fares for transportation, which were increased by several times, and forcing the regional budgets to cover the ever-increasing losses of suburban train companies (firms affiliated with RR). These companies rented infrastructure and trains from RR and paid the monopolist for repair and operation of trains according to rates it set, while the costs of transportation were covered by these companies from the budget subsidies. From 2011 onwards, the federal government made regional budg-

---

[179]   See Alexey Navalny, 'Khroniki genotsida russkikh: Ob odnom deistvitel'no uzhasnom i simvolichnom sobytii' *navalny.com*, 24 December 2014. https://navalny.com/p/4036/ (access 3 January 2020).

[180]   For an overview, see Russell Pittman, 'Blame the Switchman? Russian Railways Restructuring After Ten Years', in Oxford *Handbook of Russian Economy*, Michael Alexeev, Shlomo Weber (eds.) (Oxford: Oxford University Press, 2013), 490–513.

[181]   See Pittman, 'Blame the Switchman?'

ets responsible for subsidizing passenger transportation, although these budgets did not have enough funds (to some extent, because they were forced to bear many other expenses arbitrarily forced on them by the federal government), and did not have enough resources to oppose RR pressure. The last blow to passenger transportation in the regions was the Russian government's decree of 8 January 2015, which increased fees for regional budgets' use of RR infrastructure by twenty-five times.[182] Putin's intervention and the subsequent restoration of suburban commuter trains did not change the economic model of passenger transportation in any way, but simply moved the expenses and subsidies from the regional budgets to the federal budget (according to some estimates, its expenses grew by at least 22 billion rubles).

The problem of subsidizing unprofitable but socially significant passenger transportation and subsidizing commuter trains was characteristic for reforms of railways in a number of countries, and Russia was far from being an exception. But the RR case clearly stood out from the rest, not only in terms of the scale of the problems arising in the wake of reforms, but also as a method for solving them. Essentially, the result of the reforms was the transformation of a former state agency, which had served as part of the centralized planned economy into a gigantic market monopoly, which was formally controlled by the Russian government, but in fact went beyond its control, and operated almost exclusively in its own interests. The CEO of RR from 2005 onward was Vladimir Yakunin, a member of the "inner circle" of Putin's long-term allies. He was also known for his predilection for the prestigious consumption of material goods (his secondary suburban estate outside Moscow was dubbed the "fur coat depository" because of the outstandingly large luxury collection of furs owned by Yakunin's family), and the no-less-prestigious consumption of symbolic goods on the international level. Yakunin, a doctor of political science, serves as a patron of the Russian Society of Political Scien-

---

[182] See Alexey Navalny, 'Problema elektrichek, likbez ot FBK (a takzhe fil'm "Dozhdya" besplatno), *navalny.com*, 5 February 2015. https://navalny.com /p/4107/ (access 3 January 2020).

tists and president of the international forum "Dialog of Civilizations", as well as a consultant at the Economic Council of the United Nations. Among other things, this forum sponsored the publication of an English-language book where Yakunin himself was included in the list of "World's Foremost Thinkers" alongside Nobel Prize winners.[183] Despite the vocal criticism of Yakunin in the media, and attempts to prevent him from extending his contract as the CEO of RR, his closeness to Putin has made him almost untouchable, and given him virtual carte blanche in all respects. As a result, RR has essentially been transformed into a "fiefdom" of one of the Russian president's allies, and operates through numerous offshore firms connected with Yakunin. Although in August 2015 Yakunin was finally dismissed from the post of head of RR (he is presently working in Berlin as the president of "Dialog of Civilizations"), subsequent changes in company management did not greatly change the principles of governance, though the most odious features that characterized the RR leadership under Yakunin are now a matter of the past.

Thus, one of the outcomes of Russia's reforms was an enormous monopoly, the largest employer in Russia, formally managed by the state, being given to a private individual who transformed RR into a tool for maximizing rent and placing the expenses (which he arbitrarily determined himself) on taxpayers' shoulders. To paraphrase the 1970s pop song "Rasputin" by Boney M, this practice of governance could be called "Russia's Greatest Rent Machine". Its social expenses were much higher than under the Ministry of Transportation's model of governance, formed (with the ministry itself) in the 1930s, when the sector was headed by Stalin's close ally Lazar Kaganovich. The Ministry of Transportation was one of the pillars of the Soviet economy, and because of its strategic importance, it had priority access to resources, including a labor force (at first, Gulag, and later, railway military divisions) and state investments, as well as access to dis-

---

[183] See 22 Ideas to Fix the World: Conversations with the World's Foremost Thinkers, Piotr Dutkiewicz, Richard Sakwa (eds.) (New York: New York University Press, 2013).

tribution of material goods (including medical services for employees). Later, the status of the ministry fell as technological changes took place and the Soviet economy declined, and by the time the Soviet Union collapsed, its contribution to rent extraction was relatively modest. Although the crisis of the ministry in the 1990s and the need for structural reforms in the sector were perceived by all observers,[184] the consequences of the reforms of the 2000s–2010s should be characterized as a turn from bad to worse.

The case of RR is not unique; it is far from the only example of the failure of one of the sectoral reforms, which served as part of the ambitious socio-economic modernization plans adopted in the early 2000s.[185] But why did the good intentions of liberal reforms ultimately pave the road to the hell of crony capitalism in post-Soviet Russia? We assert that the reason for these metamorphoses of post-Soviet modernization is that after the collapse of the Soviet Union, deliberately constructed mechanisms of bad governance began to dominate in Russia. These mechanisms were not so much inherited from the Soviet and pre-Soviet past as intentionally created in the interests of ruling groups and designed to consolidate their political and economic dominance. Bad governance removes the possibility of implementing projects of socio-economic modernization, meaning that individual reforms have at best a partial effect, and at worst become a "vicious circle" of socially ineffective changes, serving privileged special interests. We also assert that this vicious circle cannot be broken by attempts to borrow and/or cultivate socially effective institutions within the existing political constraints. Furthermore, as bad governance becomes established, there is an increasing risk that its mechanisms may be reproduced regardless of the possible consequences of political regime changes. Is there any possibility of rejecting the insti-

---

[184]    See Pittman, 'Blame the Switchman?'; Farid Khusainov, *Zheleznye dorogi i rynok* (Moscow: Nauka, 2015).

[185]    See Vladimir Gel'man, Andrey Starodubtsev, 'Opportunities and Constraints of Authoritarian Modernisation: Russian Policy Reforms of the 2000s', *Europe-Asia Studies*, 68, no.1 (2016), 97–117.

tutions of bad governance, and replacing them with "inclusive" political and economic institutions?[186]

## Bad Governance in the Making

Although the causes and mechanisms of bad governance have been a key issue for political science since the times of Machiavelli (if not Aristotle), modern discussions of this phenomenon are relatively new. This has been brought about less by the growth in specialists' interest in the problem of state governance than by the emergence of new analytical tools and international databases. Many researchers regard bad governance from the standpoint of its compliance (or rather, non-compliance) with the ideals of good governance, and examine deviations from these ideals in terms of normative rather than positive analysis. As an example, although the detailed Oxford Handbook of Governance[187] includes a chapter that provides a survey of good governance[188], the problems of bad governance are barely discussed. Similarly, the Quality of Government Institute (QOG) at the University of Gothenburg gives primary attention to studying the "best practices" of state governance. A change in the approach to understanding bad governance requires a shift from normative judgements to positive analysis: it should be recognized that bad governance is not merely an antonym of good governance, but a manifestation of a fundamentally different political-economic order. This political-economic order, in its turn, may be seen as an instance of "limited access order",[189] and the dominance of "extractive" political and economic institutions[190] demonstrates a number of certain features that distinguish it from other political-economic orders. We believe that bad governance in post-Soviet Russia in many ways

---

[186]  See Acemoglu, Robinson, *Why Nations Fail.*

[187]  See *The Oxford Handbook of Governance*, David Levi-Faur (ed.) (Oxford: Oxford: Oxford University Press, 2012).

[188]  See Bo Rothstein, 'Good Governance', in *The Oxford Handbook of Governance*, David Levi-Faur (ed.) (Oxford: Oxford University Press, 2012), 143–154.

[189]  See North, Wallis, Weingast, *Violence and Social Orders.*

[190]  See Acemoglu, Robinson, *Why Nations Fail.*

emerged as a result of intentional actions by the political and economic actors who strove to maximize their profits in the process of
redistributing power and resources after the collapse of the Soviet
Union. In the case of RR discussed above, Yakunin's governance
of the largest state company was not shaped by the Soviet "legacy" in this sector or in the Russian economy as a whole: neither
Kaganovich nor his successors had dreamed of the degree of freedom enjoyed by Yakunin in running this sector of the economy.
On the contrary, RR's transformation into a fiefdom of the company's CEO was the result of a distribution of access to sources of
rent among members of the informal "winning coalition"[191] headed by Vladimir Putin and his allies. In a similar way, the maximization of power in politics and the maximization of rents in the
economy should be perceived as the rational goal of ruling
groups, which were able to achieve it in a number of post-Soviet
countries in the process of political regime changes and market
transitions.

A number of analyses of the dynamics of changes in the
"rules of the game" in the political and economic arena since the
collapse of the Soviet Union[192] have demonstrated that the processes of complex transformations made it easier to achieve these
goals, which would have been very difficult in a different situation. Bad governance serves as a means for achieving the goals of
ruling groups, and they build institutions in order to achieve these
goals, to consolidate the current configurations of political and
economic actors and to ensure that the existing political-economic
order continues to function for as long as possible. However,
while some political leaders were able to maximize power and
rent, others were not. In our opinion, the development of bad
governance may be compared to the effects of a deliberate "poi-

---

[191]  See Bruce Bueno de Mesquita, Alastair Smith, *The Dictator's Handbook: Why
Bad Behavior is Almost Always Good Politics* (New York: Public Affairs, 2011).

[192]  See Konstantin Sonin, 'Why the Rich May Favor Poor Protection of Property
Rights', *Journal of Comparative Economics*, 31, no.4 (2003), 715–731; Anders
Åslund, *Russia's Capitalist Revolution: Why Market Reforms Succeeded and Democracy Failed* (Washington, DC: Peterson Institute for International Economics. 2007); Hale, *Patronal Politics*; Gel'man, *Authoritarian Russia*.

soning" of a social organism by actors belonging to ruling groups. But it is not so easy to answer the question of whether this disease can be treated.

The major principles of post-Soviet bad governance as a political-economic order, which determines the nature of political regimes and the mechanisms of state governance, may be defined as follows:

- rent-seeking is the primary goal and the primary substance of state governance at all levels;
- mechanisms of power and governance tend to form a hierarchy ("power vertical") with a sole center of decision-making that claims a monopoly (what may be called a "single power pyramid");[193]
- the autonomy of domestic economic and political actors within the country vis-à-vis this center is defined arbitrarily and may be changed and/or restricted at any time;
- the formal institutions that set the boundaries for exercising power and governance are side effects of the distribution of resources within the "power vertical"; they may influence real "rules of the game" only to the extent to which they support (or at least do not hinder) rent extraction;
- the government apparatus within the hierarchy of the "power vertical" is divided into organized segments and informal cliques competing for access to rents.

These principles constitute the informal institutional "core" of the politico-economic order of bad governance, around which ruling groups have created a "shell" of formal "rules of the game". This shell is more than a smokescreen designed to conceal the unsightly appearance of bad governance; it also partially moderates the risk of regime changes and maintains the balance of forces between actors involved in the informal "winning coalition".[194]

---

[193]  See Hale, *Patronal Politics*.

[194]  See Milan Svolik, *The Politics of Authoritarian Rule* (Cambridge: Cambridge University Press, 2012).

There are risks involved because monopolization of decision-making may be undermined, and suppression of actors' autonomy may reach its limits. But if these risks can be minimized, then bad governance proves almost invincible under the current political regime, at least if one does not take into account the risk of exogenous shocks.

The long-lasting and stable nature of bad governance in Russia requires a rethinking of this phenomenon, and a more in-depth, detailed and nuanced analysis. Despite considerable attention by specialists to the problem of bad governance in Russia, many studies are more descriptive than explanatory. One might say that there is a "dismal consensus" among the authors, even though they often differ in their views and scholarly approaches:[195] durable bad governance has become a commonplace of practically all works, which present a picture of post-Soviet reality. The picture is that of "state capture"[196] by rent-seekers within the state apparatus and influential businesspeople connected with them. In striving for privatization of gains and socialization of losses in the process of state governance, rent-seeking actors, who serve as the core of ruling groups in Russia and certain other post-Soviet states (in various arrangements), deliberately and purposefully create and support socially ineffective "rules of the game".[197] But as their planning horizon is limited to the short-term because the legitimacy of their dominance is performance-based,[198] and because the prospects for dynastic power succession are dubious at best[199] these actors behave like "roving" rather than "station-

---

[195]   See Åslund, Russia's *Capitalist Revolution*; Karen Dawisha, *Putin's Kleptocracy: Who Owns Russia?* (New York: Simon and Schuster 2014); Gerald Easter, *Capital, Coercion, and Postcommunist States*, (Ithaca, NY: Cornell University Press, 2012); Alena Ledeneva, *Can Russia Modernise? Sistema, Power Networks, and Informal Governance* (Cambridge: Cambridge University Press, 2013); Taylor, *The Code of Putinism.*

[196]   See Hellman, 'Winners Take All'.

[197]   See North, *Institutions*, 16.

[198]   See Samuel Huntington, *The Third Wave: Democratization in the Late Twentieth Century* (Norman, OK: University of Oklahoma Press, 1991), 55.

[199]   See Jason Brownlee, 'Hereditary Succession in Modern Autocracies', *World Politics*, 59, no.4 (2007), 595–628.

ary" bandits, to use Mansur Olson's term.[200] They embezzle state resources at all levels of governance, and the term "kleptocracy"[201] comes to look not only like a journalistic cliché, but also like a fairly adequate description of the dominance of "crooks and thieves". Thus, the result is a vicious circle: mechanisms of bad governance are reproduced under different rulers, and attempts to overcome it (if any) meet with strong resistance, and usually provide limited effects from the standpoint of the quality of state governance.

However, beyond the limits of this dismal consensus, the question of the causes and mechanisms of bad governance remains open. Opinions range from invectives against political leaders and their circles and/or the contrasts between "good guys" and "bad guys" in the process of post-Communist transformations[202] to ideas about the inescapably warped nature of Russia itself, which makes any attempts to overcome bad governance impossible.[203] This is why we need a critical reassessment of existing explanations for the phenomenon of bad governance as a whole and in Russia in particular.

## "Bad Governance": Why?

Although in the present day, bad governance is perceived as an anomaly, in reality, human history primarily consists of the history of ineffective corrupt governments, while the rule of law and high quality of governance are relatively recent phenomena, which only emerged in modern times in the wake of development of modern nation-states.[204] Good governance did not appear by itself through the good will of wise leaders, but was a forced response by ruling groups to two interconnected challenges. Firstly,

---

[200] See Mancur Olson, 'Dictatorship, Democracy, and Development', *American Political Science Review*, 87, no.3 (1993), 567–576.

[201] See Dawisha, *Putin's Kleptocracy*.

[202] See Åslund, *Russia's Capitalist Revolution*.

[203] For a critical overview of these arguments, see Dmitry Travin, *"Osobyi put'" Rossii ot Dostoevskogo do Konchalovskogo* (St. Petersburg: European University at St. Petersburg Press, 2018).

[204] See North, Wallis, Weingast, *Violence and Social Orders*.

international competition was accompanied by numerous bloody wars: states that demonstrated insufficient military and economic effectiveness risked severe losses or even conquest by their more successful opponents. Secondly, ineffective and corrupt governments also caused escalation of internal political conflicts and numerous instances of political violence. These instances often challenged major political and economic actors as well as various societal groups, and caused reshuffling of informal "winning coalitions", and revolutionary regime changes.[205] In fact, the textbook example of the establishment of the rule of law and the beginning of a transition to good governance as a result of the "glorious revolution" in England in the late seventeenth century[206] serves as a clear illustration of the effects of these challenges. The fiscal crisis provoked by the monarchy led to a chain of violent political crises (revolution – dictatorship – restoration), which continued for decades until the warring actors reached a decision to establish a parliamentary monarchy and limit state borrowing. It was only later that a long and stable trajectory of economic growth, which was also a consequence of good governance, helped Britain to strengthen its position in the international arena, securing itself from domestic and foreign policy challenges.

However, in the contemporary era, the nature of international and domestic political challenges of bad governance changes significantly. When wars become a matter of the past, corrupt and ineffective governments' risks of losing power in military defeats are not so high. As for international economic competition, although losing may be unpleasant for those who exercise bad governance, these challenges are not overly painful. A low economic growth rate, capital flight, shortage of investments, and the inefficient use of human resources have negative consequences, but in and of themselves they do not contain risks of losing power and wealth for ruling groups – on the contrary, these consequences of bad governance often make it possible to maintain the internal po-

---

[205]   See Bueno de Mesquita, Smith, *The Dictator's Handbook*.

[206]   See North, Wallis, Weingast, *Violence and Social Orders*.

litical status quo.[207] The "winning coalitions" are capable of both incorporating individual rent-seekers and using various means of suppressing dissidents. These statements apply to Russia in full. International challenges of bad governance are not seen as immediate challenges to its ruling groups, while instances of political pressure from various social groups manifest only sporadically, and can for the most part be brought under control. In this sense, post-Soviet bad governance in Russia and beyond may be regarded as a natural course of events in a situation where ruling groups feel a lack of immediate challenges that directly threaten their ability to remain in power, and are typically left unchallenged, not encountering strong resistance from within the country or in the international arena. This leads them to rationally and purposefully organize a politico-economic order, which could be unavailable to ruling groups under other conditions.

What are the causes of bad governance in Russia? If one discards ad hominem arguments, which ascribe bad governance to abuse by specific individuals, these causes are usually linked to the configurations of political and economic elites in the wake of the construction of autocracies after the Soviet collapse. There is no need to prove that the formation and consolidation of authoritarian regimes as a whole and in Russia in particular creates a political and institutional environment which promotes bad governance. The rare cases of high-quality state governance in authoritarian regimes may be summed up concisely by the statement by Dani Rodrik: "For every President Lee Kwan Yew of Singapore, there are many like President Mobutu Sese Seko of Zaire (now called the Democratic Republic of Congo)."[208] Furthermore, electoral authoritarian regimes (such as Russia's) often demonstrate the worst combination of features in terms of bad governance. They combine dependence on political business cycles (which is also a feature of democracies) with vulnerability to the risk of re-

---

[207]  See Bueno de Mesquita, Smith, *The Dictator's Handbook*.

[208]  See Dani Rodrik, 'The Myth of Authoritarian Growth', *Project Syndicate*, 9 August 2010. http://www.project-syndicate.org/commentary/the-myth-of-auth oritarian-growth. (access 3 January 2020).

gime collapse due to mass protests (as could be seen after the post-electoral protests of 2011–2012). These factors narrow the planning horizon of authoritarian leaders, enabling the politicization of management in administrative and economic fields – from mobilization of voters at companies[209] to, ultimately, the transformation of the entire state apparatus into a "political machine" to ensure the provision of votes for the ruling groups.[210] The consequence of this state of affairs is the inability to develop adequate incentives to improve the quality of governance – in particular, regular rotation of personnel and the dependence of upward career mobility of officials on the performance results they attain.[211] On the contrary, within the framework of the "power vertical", incentives for officials are connected to demonstration of political loyalty at the expense of efficiency[212] – these tendencies are a weak point for many authoritarian regimes.[213]

## The Long Arm of the Past?

Along with this approach, deterministic and path-dependent explanations of bad governance in Russia are also popular. The proponents of these theories believe that it finds its source in the repressive and inefficient autocratic state machine that is rooted in the depth of centuries of Russian history, a "matrix"[214] that fun-

---

[209] See Timothy Frye, Ora John Reuter, David Szakonyi, 'Political Machines at Work: Voter Mobilization and Electoral Subversion in the Workplace', *World Politics*, 66, no.2 (2014), 195–228.

[210] See Grigorii V. Golosov, 'Machine Politics: The Concept and Its Implications for Post-Soviet Studies', *Demokratizatsiya: The Journal of Post-Soviet Democratization*, 21, no.4 (2013), 459–480.

[211] See Michael Rochlitz, Vera Kulpina, Thomas Remington, Andrey Yakovlev, 'Performance Incentives and Economic Growth: Regional Officials in Russia and China', *Eurasian Geography and Economics*, 56, no.4 (2015), 421–445.

[212] See Ora John Reuter, Graeme Robertson, 'Subnational Appointments in Authoritarian Regimes: Evidence from Russian Gubernatorial Appointments', *Journal of Politics*, 74, no.4 (2012), 1023–1037.

[213] See Georgy Egorov, Konstantin Sonin, 'Dictators and their Viziers: Endogenizing the Loyalty-Competence Trade-off', *Journal of European Economic Association*, 9, no.5 (2011), 903–930.

[214] See Hedlund, *Russian Path Dependence.*

damentally cannot be changed. Others focus on deterministic explanations for state-society relations, based on the scheme of the "Soviet personality" – an ideal type, a concentration of numerous negative feature, reproduced through generations,[215] and serving not only as a product of the inescapable "matrix", but also as a tool for maintaining it. This viewpoint is vulnerable to criticism, as it is insufficient heuristically and is in many ways constructed on the principle of "tailoring" a theory to a previously constructed answer.[216]

In any case, the argument of the "legacy of the past" is very structural; it assumes that bad governance is the equivalent of a chronic hereditary illness of a social organism, one which cannot be treated in the foreseeable future, at the very least. Yet, there is also no reason not to acknowledge that "history matters"[217] for an analysis of bad governance. The question is rather different: how does this legacy become part of the present and future in the practice of state governance?

The "legacy of the past", considered as the historically established set of obstacles on the path of good governance, is often seen as a list of unfavorable starting conditions which existed at the moment of the Soviet collapse and have been performing their role as obstacles ever since. However, this view of the legacy does not explain why it has a different impact on different countries in the region and different spheres of governance, or the nature of the mechanisms through which the legacy of the institutions and practices formed after the Soviet collapse made its impact. In seeking to avoid determinism, Steven Kotkin and Mark Beissinger redefine "legacy" as "a durable causal relationship between past institutions and policies on subsequent practices or beliefs, long beyond the life of the regimes, institutions, and policies that gave

---

215   See Yuri Levada, *Ishchem cheloveka: sotsiologicheskie ocherki* (Moscow: Novoe izdatel'stvo, 2005).

216   For critiques, see Travin, *Osobyi put' Rossii.*

217   See North, *Institutions*, 3.

birth to them".[218] They focus on a number of mechanisms by which this causal chain works, transferring institutions and practices of the past into the present and future – including "cultural schemata" connected with perceptions of certain practices as normal or unacceptable as inherited from past experience, in the field of state governance and elsewhere. Cultural schemata – ways of thinking and perception that are rooted in the past, but have outlived the previous order – create concepts of an imaginary "good Soviet Union"[219] as a kind of normative ideal, and serve as a basis for "mental models"[220] for post-Soviet actors, and for societies as a whole.

Although analysis of the legacies is not limited in application by chronological boundaries, it seems reasonable to concentrate on the Soviet period, and not to retreat to the depths of history. The legacy of the past has a limited effect on the present and future by itself. "History matters" to the extent that various actors use it to achieve their goals, including in the field of state governance, and their reflections are limited to a relatively recent horizon of the past, related to the living experience of one or two generations. The "legacy of the past" is a social construction to a significant degree, both in Russia and beyond. With regard to state governance in Russia, cultural schemata are important tools for maintaining bad governance in at least two ways. First, they make the Soviet (and more rarely pre-Soviet) past the main or even solitary reference point in public discussion. History ceases to be the domain of historians, and penetrates all aspects of life in present-day Russia. The experience of the past and the imaginary elements, which play the role of normative "markers" (whether of the Brezhnev period, the Stalinist era or other times) are perceived as

---

218   See Stephen Kotkin, Mark R. Beissinger, 'The Historical Legacies of Communism: An Empirical Agenda', in *Historical Legacies of Communism in Russia and Eastern Europe*, Mark R. Beissinger, Stephen Kotkin (eds.) (Cambridge: Cambridge University Press, 2014), 7.

219   See Gel'man, Marganiya, Travin, *Reexamining Economic and Political Reforms in Russia*.

220   See Athur Denzau, Douglass North, 'Sharing Mental Models: Ideologies and Institutions', *Kyklos*, 47, no.1 (1994), 3–31.

the alpha and the omega in planning for the future, including mechanisms of state governance. This is why past institutions and practices become building blocks of sorts in institution building and policy-making. Second, since references to one's own past experience serve as virtually the only tool for legitimizing political decisions, other mechanisms of control, institutions and policy-making are often not perceived as legitimate by society (regardless of whether or not they correspond to the best practices of governance).

The "good Soviet Union", i.e. the politico-economic order, which resembles the late Soviet system in some way, but is devoid of the defects inherent to it, in fact has little in common with the real experience of the late Soviet Union. Elements of this experience become a "legacy" which is selectively used to ensure the maximization of power for Russian ruling groups. They include the hierarchy of the "power vertical", "stability of cadres" at all levels of governance (i.e. preservation of elites in their high-level jobs), narrow pools of elite recruitment and formally and informally guaranteed privileged status of ruling groups, state control over important media channels, a repressive approach to combating dissent,[221] and several others. At the same time, elements of the politico-economic order of the late Soviet times, such as a relatively low level of inequality and certain state social guarantees, have been discarded without any serious resistance from society. The "good Soviet Union" also includes very important features for ruling groups, which the real Soviet Union did not have at all. These features include not only the creation of a market economy without shortages of goods, but also a lack of the institutional constraints that existed in the late Soviet period to limit ruling groups' acquisition of rents, and opportunities for legalizing their status and incomes in the West. It would be no exaggeration to say that the "good Soviet Union" was deliberately constructed as a normative ideal by ruling groups in post-Soviet countries, allowing them and their servants to receive, through privatization of gains and

---

[221] See Vladimir Gel'man, 'The Politics of Fear: How Russia's Rulers Counter their Rivals', *Russian Politics*, 1, no.1 (2016), 27–45.

socialization of losses, everything that their predecessors in the late Soviet decades wished for but could not achieve.

An appeal to such a legacy as the basis for post-Soviet institution-building and practices of state governance enables the consolidation of the existing status quo, including by moving certain elements of this ideological construct onto the level of specific decisions in the field of politics and governance. This has also applied to a number of policy reforms,[222] in particular the organization of bureaucracy and incentives for its performance.[223] The "good Soviet Union" as a normative ideal did not create incentives for rejecting "bad governance", even as the authorities declared raising the quality of state governance to be a policy goal. On the contrary, the "good Soviet Union" as the foundation of the post-Soviet "mental model" serves as an effective tool for legitimizing, at least in the mid-term perspective, the politico-economic order of bad governance in Russia, the boundaries of which are set by the lifecycle of the current generations of post-Soviet ruling groups.

To summarize, we may argue that the legacy of the past that hinders good governance in Russia and beyond is not so much material as ideological in nature. The "long arm of the past", which supposedly dooms various countries to overwhelming corruption and inefficiency, is largely a social construct, created and supported by ruling groups with the aim of maximizing their own power. Countries, which have at least partially rejected the ideological "legacy", such as a number of Eastern European states, may improve their chances of rejecting the principles of bad governance, although success on this path is far from guaranteed. But those who see the sources of modern state governance in the imagined (glorious or inglorious) past of their own countries may turn bad governance into an endless vicious circle.

---

[222]   See Gel'man, Starodubtsev, 'Opportunities and Constraints'.

[223]   See Eugene Huskey, 'Legacies and Departures in the Russian State Executive', in *Historical Legacies of Communism in Russia and Eastern Europe*, Mark R. Beissinger, Stephen Kotkin (eds.) (Cambridge: Cambridge University Press, 2014), 111–127; Paneyakh, Titaev, Shklyaruk, *Traektoriya ugolovnogo dela*.

## The Power Vertical as a Mechanism of Bad Governance

The term "power vertical" is usually used to describe the hierarchical model of sub-national governance in Russia.[224] It involves the formal and informal subordination of lower tiers of governance to their superiors, and numerous systems of informal exchange of resources between them (for electoral authoritarian regimes, votes at elections are one of the most important resources, although not the only one). However, the mechanisms for the territorial dimension of state governance are complex, as are those for other segments of the state apparatus, as well as for governance in the public sector. Sectoral "verticals" are typical for law enforcement agencies, academia, and a number of NGOs. The private sector of the economy is also included in the system of exchanges within the "power vertical", although it may have somewhat broader autonomy (in particular, workplace mobilization of voters during the Russian federal elections of 2011–2012 was less common among private companies, and applied to a lesser degree, than among state-owned companies).[225] Exchanges concern both distribution of rents and observance (or non-observance) of legal norms and rules within formal institutions, and also opportunities for changing them. The "power vertical" as a mechanism of governance is legitimized by the fact that it is seen in public opinion as the only possible means of control over the activity of low-level tiers of governance. The post-Soviet experience of the 1990s encouraged this perception, as there was a protracted economic recession while state capacity weakened, and a number of basic functions of state governance performed extremely poorly.[226] This is a strong argument in favor of the "power vertical" as a tool of governance. Adam Przeworski justly noted: "since any order is

---

[224] See Vladimir Gel'man, Sergey Ryzhenkov, 'Local Regimes, Sub-National Governance, and the "Power Vertical" in Contemporary Russia', *Europe-Asia Studies*, 63, no.3 (2011), 449–465.

[225] See Frye, Reuter, Szakonyi, 'Political Machines at Work'.

[226] See Volkov, *Violent Entrepreneurs*.

better than any disorder, any order is established".[227] Insofar as the lower levels of the "power vertical" distribute the minimum necessary resources entrusted to them by the people, and are able to secure patronage, this mechanism of control (not only of territories, but of companies, institutions and organizations) is perceived as legitimate.

The reliance on the "power vertical" as the basis of the politico-economic order of bad governance involves a drastic increase in agency costs against the background of intensifying principal-agent problems within the hierarchy of governance.[228] While in China these problems in the system of territorial governance are to some extent solved by competition between agents (the heads of provincial committees of the Communist party who achieve the greatest success in development of territories receive positions in the central leadership), different approaches are typical for post-Soviet countries. They may be described as the politics of redundancy[229] at all layers of governance. In other words, within the system of governance, there are parallel structures, which manage political control over subordinated actors: the presidential administration is in charge of control over the government, presidential representatives at the sub-national level (in Russia since 2000, federal districts) are in charge of control over governors and mayors, etc. Another tool of control is creating numerous regulatory and supervisory agencies in various fields with their own territorial branches (i.e. their own "verticals"). One might think that administration, when it runs contrary to the interests of those who occupy the middle and lower levels of the "power vertical", should require superior agents to punish their subordinates for any deviations from their orders. However, in practice, the large apparatus of control, which has broad powers, does not often resort to re-

---

[227] See Adam Przeworski, *Democracy and the Market: Political and Economic Reforms in Eastern Europe and Latin America* (Cambridge: Cambridge University Press, 1991), 86.

[228] See Sharafutdinova, *Political Consequences of Crony Capitalism*; Gel'man, Ryzhenkov, 'Local Regimes'.

[229] See Eugene Huskey, *Presidential Power in Russia* (Armonk, NY: M.E.Sharpe, 1999).

pressions (outside the context of individual campaigns initiated by the high-level political leadership): there is no way to keep every last person in line as a military hierarchy would.

The popular perception of the "power vertical" as only a tool of control and the subordination of the lower-ranking levels to their superiors is only partially true. It does not take into account the numerous "zigzags", "turns" and "twists" connected with supporting the politico-economic order of bad governance. We may say that the "power vertical" is a successful tool of control not so much because of the threat of top-down sanctions as because it creates individual incentives for the actors who belong to this hierarchy. To put it more simply, maintaining the "power vertical" is beneficial for its insiders because of the possibility of access to sources of rents, which are unavailable to those outside it, or those who are at the lowest levels of the hierarchies. If these agents are to pursue their own interests, they need to also help the political leadership achieve its strategic goals (or at least not hinder it). These goals may be defined as maintaining a stable economic and social order (under the slogan of "stability"), in which the relative economic well-being of the population and patronage over the masses deprived of material goods is determined by the ruling groups. In turn, they aim to preserve power (promoting support of the political status quo) and continue economic growth (or at least a lack of major economic failures). Thus, through the use of economic resources, the principals at the top of the "power pyramid" become able to reward politicians and bureaucrats at lower levels, and representatives of various sectors of the economy and persons connected with them, with the opportunity to gain access to rents in an amount sufficient for motivation of their activity as agents. In other words, corruption is not merely a negative side effect of low quality of governance, but an integral part of the mechanism of state governance within the "power vertical".

At the same time, along with positive incentives within the "power vertical", there is widespread use, or threat of use, of mechanisms for selective punishment of disloyal and/or ineffective agents. The tools of control here are not limited to personal decisions regarding appointments, and reshuffling or dismissals of agents, but also exclusion of individual participants from the electoral process, and criminal cases opened against various politicians, officials and businesspersons. The fact that practically all actors included in the "power vertical" pursue interests connected with rent seeking in the process of political and economic governance not only ensures their loyalty, but also gives the principal an additional leverage of control. Compromising material (kompromat) may be used at any given moment against a certain actor, and this threat may be an even more effective mechanism of control than its actual use. As a result, in order not to lose, and perhaps even to increase access to rents, actors are genuinely interested in implementing policies that secure both the interests of the principals and their own. One should note that the top-down punishment of actors is usually applied when lower-ranking actors begin to steal beyond certain limits and act against the interests of the principal, rather than being accused of ineffective governance which would undermine the legitimacy and stability of the regime; cases of that kind may be considered exceptional.

As a consequence, the "power vertical" has relatively low costs of control, and is successful as a solution to principal-agent problems, by means of the mechanism of "feeding" of agents with the informal agreement of the principal. It makes it possible to support and develop the capability of the Russian state to control socio-political and economic processes at all levels. The state acts in the collective interests of all groups included in the "power vertical", from the president to the director of a rural school who embezzles part of funds allocated by the local administration in exchange for the "proper" voting result from the school's polling station, as required by the authorities. For those Russian citizens who are not normally included in this system of exchanges, the actual opportunity for access to sources of rent is a strong incentive not only for political loyalty, but also for social advancement. Thus, the goal of higher education for a number of graduates of Russian schools is the ability to receive a job in the state apparatus and/or at major state-led companies such as Gazprom.

This scheme of political and economic governance, typical for "crony" capitalism in a number of countries, has distinctive features in the post-Soviet environment. These include: (1) a certain degree of room for agents to maneuver, while actions that contradict the interests of the principal are punished; (2) unquestioned freedom of action for the principal, and the arbitrary nature of his assessments and decisions connected with these assessments; (3) specific division of the control process into levels and branches of the state machinery. Governance is further complicated in the "power vertical" by the division of elite groups: the politico-economic order of bad governance is characterized by competition between various controlling agencies, and groups within them, for distribution of rents, and for positions in the informal hierarchy of centers for decision-making at different levels and/or in different policy areas. Among the Russian law enforcement agencies, the harsh conflict between the Prosecutor's Office and the Investigative Committee is a good example, and at the level of Russian big business, there is the conflict between Rosneft and Gazprom.[230] These conflicts are structural by their nature: they stem from the fact that separate sectoral "verticals" function in state government agencies and in state-led companies (including Russian Railways, outlined above), connecting lower-ranking agents with individual "patrons" or groups at higher levels of the hierarchy, or even personally with the head of state. This mechanism plays a significant role in informal decision-making, as it is impossible to bypass it in receiving an appointment even at a low level of the "power vertical", or to defend one's position in the hierarchy if a threat arises from competing bureaucratic rivals, let alone make an anticipatory counter-attack against them if the need arises.

In the Russian journalistic discourse, on the national level, this phenomenon is often described in terms of "the new Politburo" or "the battle of the Kremlin towers", but these descriptions are only partially correct. Popular parallels between the "power vertical" in post-Soviet Russia and the Soviet system of governance clearly do not take into account the fundamental difference both in the objectives and incentives, and the lack of an institu-

---

[230]  See Gustafson, *Wheel of Fortune.*

tionalized mechanism of centralized control. In the Soviet Union, the Communist Party controlled the state apparatus at all levels, and if necessary could unilaterally apply sanctions to violators of formal and informal "rules of the game". By contrast, in post-Soviet Russia, the personalist nature of the political regime sets different conditions: personnel decisions on appointments, dismissals and reshuffling are made at the very highest level of authority in all important cases, based on the need to maintain the balance of power between different "verticals" and cliques, including preemptive actions on the principle of "divide and conquer". As such, it is inevitable that alliances of actors competing for sources of rents often emerge on various grounds. This is a side effect of the informal distribution of resources between agents, which drastically increases the agency costs the principal must endure: he is forced to restrict competition between agents, and at the same time reduce his own risk of becoming completely buried under mountains of kompromat from every quarter. Competition between agents does not increase the quality of politico-economic governance – rather, it does the opposite. Although economic growth and the flow of resources make it possible to satisfy the interests of the most influential rent-seekers and smooth over these contradictions, the top political leadership remains incapable of eliminating them.

If the "power vertical" did not receive signals from the leadership over an extended period, was not engaged with various reforms, and was simply reproducing the status quo, it could easily remain self-enforcing even without any flow of resources and at low (or zero) economic growth, given the lack of meaningful alternatives. However, the imperative of modernization and ongoing reforms forces the political leadership to implement a number of changes, which must involve agents of the "power vertical" at various levels. This is not limited to, and indeed not focused on, structural reorganization – such as creating new agencies or administrative units, and aiming to change target indicators and/or criteria for assessing the activity of various agents. Instead, officials and managers are required to demonstrate "effectiveness", which is understood as reaching certain formal standards, from holding tenders in the system of state purchases to publishing articles by university employees in international scholarly journals. Ruling groups are interested in growth and development not only as a means of increasing the amount of rents and satisfying the appetites of numerous rent-seekers, but also as a tool for legitimization of the political status quo[231] and the foreign policy conducted by ruling groups. Furthermore, the results of successful reforms in terms of publicly recognized achievements – such as holding global events in the country (from the Olympics to meetings of the G8/G20), or universities appearing on the top-100 list of world rankings – perform an important function of prestigious consumption for ruling groups and other actors, and serve as a source of status rents. Reforms, however, have had a considerable destabilizing effect on the "power vertical"; their consequences in terms of improving the quality of governance are far from clear, and in a number of cases they have even worsened the state of affairs in comparison with the former status quo. Thus, the result of a number of post-Soviet policy reforms has been often no more than a replacement of Kaganovichs with Yakunins, with the lamentable consequences described above.

Paradoxically, bad governance in post-Soviet Russia and beyond is indirectly based on the imperative of a ("narrow") program of socio-economic modernization. In other words, Russian ruling groups set the goal of achieving high indicators of socio-economic development (both in relative and absolute terms), and implement a number of socio-economic changes directed towards achieving these goals. At the same time, the "broad" program of political modernization, including democratization and expansion of civil and political rights and freedoms, while not publicly rejected, is at best limited to cosmetic and ad hoc measures.[232] The "narrow" program of modernization, the goals of which are shared by the Russian ruling groups and a significant portion of

---

[231]   See Kirill Rogov, 'Forty Years in the Desert: The Political Cycles of Post-Soviet Transition', in *Russia 2025: Scenarios for the Russian Future*, Maria Lipman, Nikolay Petrov (eds.) (London: Palgrave Macmillan, 2013), 18–45.

[232]   See Gel'man, *Authoritarian Russia*.

the Russian population, in many ways was a reaction to the unsatisfactory resolution of the "dilemma of simultaneity" in the context of the 1990s–2000s.[233] After the collapse of the Soviet Union, Russia was unable to successfully solve the simultaneous tasks of democratization, market reforms and nation- and state-building. This is why "narrow" modernization as a means of achieving economic growth and development was designed to maintain the politico-economic order of bad governance at least in the medium term.

However, the "narrow" program of modernization in post-Soviet Russia encounters a whole range of contradictions. First, it proposes major policy reforms that rely on the state bureaucracy,[234] against the background of a low-quality state apparatus.[235] Second, policy reforms that infringe the interests of influential rent-seekers often bring very minor effects, especially if no influential coalition of potential reform supporters has been established. Third, policy reforms, especially those that propose comprehensive managerial solutions, often have unexpected and unpredictable consequences. These contradictions and consequences are only partially caused by the content of specific policy measures in various policy areas. They are connected, to a much greater extent, with mechanisms of governance within the "power vertical" and possible policy changes caused by their constraints. The question is how these contradictions can be resolved in post-Soviet Russia, and why many policy reforms enable the consolidation of bad governance. The next chapter is aimed at addressing these issues.

---

[233]    See Offe, 'Capitalism by Democratic Design?'

[234]    See Gel'man, Starodubtsev, 'Opportunities and Constraints'.

[235]    See *Worldwide Governance Indicators.*

# Chapter 7.
# Policy versus Politics:
# Technocratic Traps of Post-Soviet Reform

How can politics and policy be connected: how has the struggle to obtain, exercise and preserve power affected policies in various fields? Often, the power struggle between the two prevents policies from being successfully implemented, and the plans of those who propose various policy reforms are at best only conducted partially and/or with severe distortions; at worst, they result in the opposite of what was intended. There are many reasons for this, from political "business cycles" which hinder reforms during election periods to ideological confrontation between various political actors, whose priorities differ greatly, the destructive role of veto players in blocking policy decisions, and the like. There are countless examples of these policy failures in different countries and different eras. So it is not surprising that many politicians in power, and many policy experts, may easily subscribe to the statement made by the former minister of economic development of Russia:

"The main question of any evolution is limitation of power: how to make decision-making competent, depending on knowledge and experience and not on voting results; how to achieve a "non-intervention regime" of the political sphere to other spheres of public life". [236]

In fact, even if a "non-intervention regime" is established in the political and institutional contexts where decision-making does not depend on the voting results, this rarely brings positive effects in terms of the quality of decisions, let alone their implementation. Above all, this criticism applies to authoritarian regimes, where voting results do not influence the exercise and

---

[236] See Alexey Ulyukaev, 'Liberalizm i politika perekhodnogo perioda v sovremennoi Rossii', *Mir Rossii*, 4, no.2 (1995), 8.

preservation of power (at least not directly).[237] Leaders of a number of authoritarian regimes often have a vested interest in the ineffectiveness of the policies they pursue, taking advantage of it as a means of maintaining their own power,[238] although they usually strive for the effective implementation of policies directed towards economic growth and the successful development of their nations (though criteria for "success" may vary). In democracies, when politicians try to achieve "insulation"[239]of policy-making from political conflict, the results of policy implementation often fail to meet the expectations of advocates of the "non-intervention regime".

The inevitable and unavoidable contradiction between politics and policy often stimulates a search for mechanisms of state governance directed towards improving the quality of policy-making, which ideally should not depend on the nature and direction of politics. These mechanisms of governance are regarded as "technocratic" (juxtaposed with "political" mechanisms, when politics and policy-making are conducted by the same actors). The technocratic approach and aspirations towards creating and supporting a "non-intervention regime" predominated among liberal reformers in Russia throughout the entire post-Soviet period. In the 1990s, one could observe fierce conflicts between politics and policy-making, which clearly did not support the success of market reforms.[240] In the 2000s, certain policy successes were achieved against the background of a major decline of competitive politics.[241] However, the insulation of policy reforms from political struggles was far from always conducive to their success,[242] and

---

[237]  See Svolik, *The Politics of Authoritarian Rule*.

[238]  See Bueno de Mesquita, Smith, *The Dictator's Handbook*.

[239]  See Barbara Geddes, *Politician's Dilemma: Building State Capacity in Latin America* (Berkeley, CA: University of California Press, 1994).

[240]  See Shleifer, Treisman, *Without a Map*.

[241]  See Åslund, *Russia's Capitalist Revolution*; Gel'man, *Authoritarian Russia*.

[242]  See Gel'man, Starodubtsev, 'Opportunities and Constraints'.

the achieved policy outcomes often paved the way to reinforcing a number of authoritarian tendencies.[243]

Why do technocratic solutions work successfully in some cases, but not in others? Our argument is that when ruling groups are focused on rent-seeking, attempts to conduct large-scale policy reforms and improve the quality of state governance through technocratic mechanisms encounter strong resistance from influential veto players, such as special interest groups and various segments of the bureaucracy, and sometimes their informal coalitions. At the same time, the "non-intervention regime" leaves few opportunities to create broad and stable coalitions in support of policy reforms. Thus the main, if not the only source of policy reforms is the personal priorities of the top political leadership: even under the most favorable circumstances, this is not always sufficient for achieving policy goals, and indeed often becomes a major obstacle on the path of reforms. The Russian experience of the 1990s–2010s demonstrates that technocratic policy reforms can face major problems if conducted in an unfavorable political and institutional context.

## The Technocratic Trap: Dictators, "Viziers" and "Eunuchs"

There is nothing new about technocratic policy reforms: historically, the majority of policy changes, both successful and unsuccessful, were carried out in various countries according to a technocratic model. Under the influence of foreign and/or domestic policy challenges, leaders who held firm control over politics (monarchs and dictators of all types) made decisions on major policy reforms aimed at reducing losses and strengthening their own positions and those of their countries. As conduct of such reforms requires professional qualifications and expertise, and their results are unpredictable by nature, it is not surprising that the role of

---

[243] See Ivan Grigoriev, Anna Dekalchuk, 'Collective Learning and Regime Dynamics under Uncertainty: Labour Reform and the Way to Autocracy in Russia', *Democratization*, 24, no.3 (2017), 481–497.

policy reformers is given to officials and/or professionals, who (1) are qualified to perform the task and (2) can have blame shifted to them in the event of policy failures. In other words, the reformers who are responsible for policy-making in various areas are in the position of hired workers whose functions are limited to the tasks that the hiring politicians assign to them. At the same time, however, they have sufficient autonomy in their policy fields, and are only accountable to their employers. The employers, in turn, have a monopoly on decision-making and policy evaluation, and are capable of "insulating" the content of policy reforms from the impact of both public opinion and at least part of the special interest groups. One might regard the experience of such diverse figures as Colbert and Turgot, Witte and Stolypin, the "Chicago boys" under Pinochet, and the technocrats from Opus Dei in the last decades of Franco's rule in this light.[244]

At first glance, with this division of labor, technocratic policy reforms are autonomous from the logic of politics (both in authoritarian regimes and in democratic ones, despite obvious differences in the nature of their politics). However, here principal-agent problems come to the fore, and their acuteness depends on the scope of the reforms. Politicians are unable to assess the extent to which the plans of technocrats are adequate solutions to the problems of the country, or to what extent implementing these plans will achieve the goals they have set. At best, informational signals on policy outcomes reach them with a delay (or prematurely, if reforms assume a long-term perspective); at worst, they are accompanied by major distortions, especially in authoritarian regimes.[245] Relations between politicians and technocrats often resemble the conflicts between stakeholders and managers of companies: their interests and incentives are very different by definition. The opposite of the technocratic model of policy-making is the political model, where ruling politicians and/or parties make policy decisions themselves (though these decisions are usually prepared for with the assistance of experts), and bear responsibility for policy

---

[244] See Travin, Marganiya, *Modernizatsiya: ot Elizavety Tudor do Yegora Gaidara.*

[245] See Svolik, *The Politics of Authoritarian Rule.*

outcomes: it is difficult for them to blame the experts for policy failures. But in terms of relations between politicians and technocrat reformers, principal-agent problems are aggravated by the fact that policy-makers can use the power delegated to them for political goals. Unlike managers in a company, who cannot overthrow the stakeholders who hired them, high-ranking technocrats are not only able to join coalitions of their employers' political rivals, but also (in the most extreme scenario) to come to power themselves, casting out the former leaders and changing their own roles from technocrats to politicians. The risk of this increases if the situation in the country deteriorates (not necessarily due to the actions of the policy reformers), and tensions between politicians and technocrats become more acute. Successful technocratic reformers may bring politicians even more harm than unsuccessful ones – especially in authoritarian regimes, where political leaders usually lose power because of intra-elite conflicts.[246] This is why politicians face the temptation of favoring loyal but not always efficient technocrats. As dictators' positions weaken, the chances of replacing efficient technocrats ("viziers") with more loyal counterparts increase, which often causes a decline in the quality of policy-making.[247]

Although there are many examples of efficient but not particularly loyal technocrats challenging their (former) politician employers (one might recall the former Ukrainian prime minister Viktor Yushchenko and the former Georgian minister of justice Mikheil Saakashvili), these instances may still be regarded as extreme. However, politicians have to make an effort to ensure that efficient technocrats remain loyal and successfully perform their functions, using both standard and non-standard solutions to principal-agent problems in state governance. Besides controlling and monitoring the performance of technocrats so as to minimize information costs, politicians also have to stimulate internal competition between agencies and informal cliques within the state apparatus, and limit the technocrats' discretion. The technocrats

---

[246] See Bueno de Mesquita, Smith, *The Dictator's Handbook*.

[247] See Egorov, Sonin, 'Dictators and their Viziers'.

that find some of their intentions are blocked by a formal or informal veto from politicians. Owing to these constraints, technocrats' ability to conduct reforms is narrowed in terms of the policy areas in which politicians grant them discretion, and in terms of the scope of their influence on implementation of their own plans. The weakest link here is not developing plans and programs for various policy reforms, but implementing them through the efforts of the state apparatus, which is under the technocrats' control only to a small extent, if at all, and is usually not interested in policy reforms, regardless of their content. Where the quality of the state apparatus is low, the technocrats' chances – even when their hands are "untied" for reforms – of implementing their plans adequately are low.

The most significant challenge to technocratic reforms is not the conflict between politicians and reformers, but the latent or explicit resistance to them from the bureaucracy, and influence on policy-making from various interest groups acting both within and outside the state apparatus. For many rent-seekers, new opportunities arise to advance their self-interest, while technocrats' ability to successfully build informal (let alone formal) coalitions in support of the policy reforms they have launched is considerably limited. For the most part, technocrats fight against the opponents of reforms – rent-seekers[248] – over influence on politicians and their preferences and choices, but the subordinated status of technocrats in the decision-making process makes them very vulnerable politically. Within the political model, a mandate received from politicians gives them a window of opportunity to conduct reforms. However, within the technocratic model, this window may be closed at almost any time if the efforts of rent-seekers are successful, and especially if losers of policy reforms establish a successful informal coalition on the basis of a negative consensus.[249] Although the "insulation" of policy reforms and reformers from the influence of these interest groups reduces the risk of policy changes being curtailed, it also makes pro-reform coalitions

---

[248]   See Shleifer, *Treisman, Without a Map*; Åslund, *Russia's Capitalist Revolution*.

[249]   See Przeworski, *Democracy and the Market*, especially Chapter 4.

unstable and vulnerable. Policy changes may be interrupted half-way, as early winners of the first stages of reforms may be uninterested in their further implementation.[250] Reformers may expect successful implementation of their plans only if their preferences coincide with the priorities of political leaders (or at least do not conflict with them). In fact, their main resource becomes the ability to "sell" their policy solutions to leaders under various attractive covers for a relatively long period of time. The success of this undertaking by reformers is uncertain at best, and it is not surprising that policy reforms are at risk of being unstable and subject to distortion, crippling, or partial or full revision – frequently even due to the influence of factors not connected directly with the content of the policies. Failure of reforms does not completely put an end to plans for policy changes, but makes their implementation by the technocrats themselves problematic (in this political model, these reforms are likely to be postponed indefinitely).

The unfavorable combination of features of the technocratic model, namely:

- aggravation of principal-agent problems;
- risks of disloyalty and attempts to mitigate them;
- limited resources and power of technocrats against the background of
- resistance from interest groups and
- limited opportunities for building pro-reform coalitions, makes technocratic policy reforms an unreliable and unsustainable undertaking.

Technocratic reformers may fall into a trap where their role in decision-making is significantly reduced, and there are limited opportunities for policy reforms. The scope of reforms is narrowed to a very small number of "pockets of efficiency"[251] with low potential to spread changes to other policy areas, and the discretion of technocrats is narrowed to participating in development of policy programs as advisors and consultants, without the power to

---

[250]   See Hellman, 'Winners Take All'.

[251]   See Geddes, *Politician's Dilemma*.

take key decisions and implement them. To put it crudely, one might say that as the loyal "viziers" are removed from control over policy leverages, they risk turning into "eunuchs". The formally high status of these figures is often a reward for loyalty, but is designed to conceal their inability to significantly influence policy, let alone politics, in their countries.

The limitations of this kind of technocratic approach to policy reforms are more or less universal, regardless of countries and eras. But in Russia, these limitations are also aggravated by the principles of state governance aimed at rent seeking. "State capture" by rent seekers[252] does not happen only from outside government (by representatives of business), but also, and mainly, from inside (by politicians and officials who are part of informal "winning coalitions").[253] This situation cannot be remedied, and forces politicians and policy reformers to concentrate their efforts on a narrow set of priority policy areas at best or change their policy priorities in favor of a coalition of bureaucrats and rent-seekers at worst. Furthermore, dependence on "regime cycles"[254] prioritizes reforms, which may demonstrate relatively quick success – often to the detriment of long-term plans, many of which remain only on paper. So even when technocrats are able to obtain a mandate from politicians to pursue reforms and overcome resistance from rent-seekers, they are severely constrained in terms of time and space.

In discussing policy reforms (in Russia and beyond), two important caveats should be made. The first concerns ideas about the logic of these reforms as a process driven by "wrong" ideas (as critics describe them). Left-wing commentators tend to see post-Communist policy changes as a manifestation of a global conspiracy of neo-liberals, who aim to eliminate social guarantees throughout the world. Their opponents, in their turn, unmask the "tyranny of experts", who propose ill-conceived solutions which are not always suitable for the countries and regions in ques-

---

[252]   See Hellman, 'Winners Take All'.

[253]   See Bueno de Mesquita, Smith, *The Dictator's Handbook*.

[254]   See Hale, *Patronal Politics*.

tion.[255] Whatever the angle of criticism, it assumes that a number of policy reforms developed on the basis of "hollow paradigms" ultimately fail when confronted with reality.[256] In fact, however, ideas in the realms of both politics and policy in Russia in many ways depend on the interests and resources of important actors,[257] and this is equally true for neoliberalism (as a basis for policy changes) in post-Communist countries. [258] In essence, governments' inability to defy the interests of influential business actors and/or rent-seekers resulted in a reduction of public social expenditures. At the same time, this rarely met with protests from trade unions and/or interest groups that sought support from the state, and the ideological preferences of the heads of state agencies were a secondary factor at most. The second caveat is that, in Russia and beyond, any policy reform is often seen by actors from the very beginning only as a method of privatization of gains and socialization of losses for ruling groups, and technocrat reformists are only seen as implementers of the selfish plans of oligarchs and/or bureaucrats. Although the history of post-Soviet privatization, and especially the case of the Russian loans-for-shares deals,[259] gives reasonable grounds for these arguments, it would be incorrect to see the embezzlement of resources as the only goal of post-Soviet policy reforms. At least on the level of policy programs, reformers declare goals of economic growth and social development. The problem is that it is often very difficult to recognize the original intentions when looking at the results of these reforms. However, the task of researchers is not to blame the technocrats, but to explain the causes of their successes and failures.

---

[255] See William Easterly, *The Tyranny of Experts: Economists, Dictators, and Forgotten Rights of the Poor* (New York: Basic Books, 2014).

[256] See Marina Khmelnitskaya, *The Policy-Making Process and Social Learning in Russia: The Case of Housing Policy* (London: Palgrave Macmillan, 2015).

[257] See Stephen E. Hanson, *Post-Imperial Democracies: Ideology and Party Formation in Third Republic France, Weimar Germany, and Post-Soviet Russia* (Cambridge: Cambridge University Press, 2010).

[258] See Hilary Appel, Mitchell Orenstein, *From Triumph to Crisis: Neoliberal Economic Reform in Postcommunist Countries* (Cambridge: Cambridge University Press, 2018).

[259] See Freeland, *Sale of the Century*; Hoffman, *Oligarchs*.

How do the technocratic models of policy reforms function in Russia and beyond? And why do technocratic approaches to reforms succeed in some cases, but fail in others? How sustainable are technocratic models of policy reforms, and how acceptable and realistic are the alternatives?

## The Origins of Post-Soviet Technocracy

In the spring of 1992, two post-Communist reformers met in a Prague pub – Vaclav Klaus (who then held the position of Prime Minister of Czechia) and Yegor Gaidar (then the first deputy prime minister of the Russian government). According to Gaidar, their discussion about the problems of economic *policy* soon turned to one on the political strategy of reformers in terms of *politics*.[260] Klaus, in particular, advised in his expressive manner that Gaidar and other Eastern European reformers should not limit themselves to developing and implementing policy measures, but should act as independent political actors who would fight for power by building political parties and running for election. Otherwise, in Klaus's opinion, reforms in Russia and other post-Communist countries could be terminated and even reversed. Gaidar took Klaus' advice with a large dose of skepticism and did not particularly follow his suggestions. The election coalition "Vybor Rossii" led by Gaidar in 1993, as well as its successors, the "Democratic Choice of Russia" party (1995) and the "Union of Right Forces" (1999), only claimed the role of junior partners of the ruling group in an informal "winning coalition", not aspiring to political autonomy. When the Kremlin no longer had any need for allies, they were quickly removed from the political arena, losing their impact on politics.[261] Overall, throughout the entire period of the 1990s, Gaidar and his allies consistently played the role of "viziers", acting under the protection of the political leadership under Yeltsin, and not striving to play an independent role in the

---

[260]   See Yegor Gaidar, *Days of Defeat and Victory* (Seattle: University of Washington Press, 1999), 259.

[261]   See Vladimir Gel'man, 'Political Opposition in Russia: A Dying Species?', *Post-Soviet Affairs*, 21, no.3 (2005), 226-246.

political arena. [262] Similar tendencies were also observed during the early 2000s, when the same technocratic reformers also played an important role in policy-making in Russia, accepting formal and informal "rules of the game" and political constraints as indisputable conditions.[263] In the 2010s, reformers still acted as "viziers", although political room for maneuver narrowed even more. But in many analyses of policy reforms in Russia, including those conducted by the technocrats themselves, politics is still not considered the major factor of success and failure of policy-making.[264]

Of course, it would be misleading to ascribe the far greater success of the economic reforms of the 1990s in the Czech Republic than in Russia exclusively to differences in relations between politics and policy-making. Gaidar recognized the differences in the initial conditions of policy reforms and structural problems facing both countries.[265] Furthermore, on a political level, in the 1990s, Russia faced high political polarization and severe intra-elite conflicts in the context of a weak state. These processes left little room for conducting consistent policy reforms, many socio-economic changes were compromised,[266] and the decision-making process in a number of cases was more than chaotic.[267] This is why even if Russian technocratic reformers had ceased to limit themselves to the role of "viziers", and had striven to determine the political agenda themselves, the policy outcomes would probably not have been much more successful. At best, Russia could have taken the path of "polarized democracy", like Bulgaria in the 1990s, when policy-making was very inconsistent and ineffective,

---

[262]  See Åslund, *Russia's Capitalist Revolution*.

[263]  See Gel'man, Starodubtsev, 'Opportunities and Constraints'.

[264]  See *Analiz faktorov realizatsii dokumentov strategicheskogo planirovaniya verkhnego urovnya: Analiticheskii doklad*, Mikhail Dmitriev (ed.) (Moscow: Center for Strategic Research, 2016). http://csr.ru/news/analiz-faktorov-realizatsii-dokumentov-strategicheskogo-planirovaniya-verhnego-urovnya/ (access 3 January 2020).

[265]  See Gaidar, *Days of Defeat and Victory*, 259.

[266]  See Shleifer, Treisman, *Without a Map*.

[267]  See Gilman, *No Precedent, No Plan*.

against a background of fierce political struggles and instability of governments.[268] At worst, the reformers' defeat in the political arena might have further aggravated the negative effects of policies implemented by the authorities before the Soviet collapse, and led the country to chaos, if not to collapse. The strategic choice in favor of the role of "viziers" by the Russian policy reformers brought certain short-term benefits for realizing reforms in a number of policy areas in the 1990s and 2000s.[269] But in the long term, this choice brought them and the country as a whole, considerable costs in terms of both politics and policy-making.

In practice, implementation of the technocratic model of policy reforms in Russia faced numerous problems. Perhaps the most significant was the ineffectiveness of the state apparatus, against the background of the construction of new post-Soviet states and the influence on policy of various interest groups. Although the technocratic model assumed that politics, with all its formal actors capable of interfering with policy – voters, parties and deputies – would be removed, it stealthily crept in together with influential informal actors – oligarchs, lobbyists, and cronies of political leaders, who in fact interfered with policy to a much greater extent.

At the same time, complete "insulation" of policy from politics was impossible in a number of cases, i.e. the technocratic model had little chance of implementation in "pure" form. At least for as long as political leaders depended on the support of public opinion to maintain their power, policy-making suffered more pressure from politics than within the framework of the political model. Although mass support for political leaders relied on mass evaluations of economic performance[270] and could have stimulat-

---

[268]   See Timothy Frye, *Building States and Markets after Communism: The Perils of Polarized Democracy* (Cambridge: Cambridge University Press, 2010), Chapter 8.

[269]   See Shleifer, Treisman, *Without a Map*; Gel'man, Starodubtsev, 'Opportunities and Constraints'.

[270]   See Richard Rose, William Mishler, Neil Munro, *Popular Support for an Undemocratic Regime: The Changing Views of Russians* (Cambridge: Cambridge University Press, 2011); Daniel Treisman, 'Presidential Popularity in a Hybrid Regime: Russia under Yeltsin and Putin', *American Journal of Political Science*, 55, no.3 (2011), 590–609.

ed reforms in a number of policy areas, the short-term expenses of unpopular measures created risks relating to public discontent for political leaders. Even failures that were not particularly great – such as the ill-conceived "monetization of social benefits" in Russia in 2005, which caused a wave of public protests[271] – led to postponement of changes in a number of policy areas, and the very notion of "reform" became taboo in official discourse. Furthermore, the dependence of political leaders' survival in electoral authoritarian regimes on mass support[272] stimulated them to use the state apparatus primarily for political goals, from ensuring the desired election results to giving important positions in governance to political allies in "winning coalitions". These factors created almost insurmountable barriers for policy reforms, even when there was the political will to conduct them; at best, these changes reached a certain "saturation point", after which further advancement of reforms became impossible.[273]

As a result, the post-Soviet technocratic reformers found themselves between the rock of expectations of policy successes from the political leadership and public opinion, and the hard place of resistance to their policies from interest groups and bureaucrats from the state apparatus. The well-known description of "privatization of gains and socialization of losses" in the wake of reforms can be applied to the reformers as well. It was not only that the socialization of losses affected society at large, while gains from reforms went to oligarchs[274] and/or rent-seekers connected with political leaders;[275] the reformers themselves, even if they managed to implement their plans, usually did not draw benefits from these undertakings, but were criticized from all sides and

---

271   See Suzanne Wengle, Michael Rasell, 'The Monetisation of L'goty: Changing Patterns of Welfare Politics and Provision in Russia', *Europe-Asia Studies*, 60, no.5 (2008), 739–756.

272   See Hale, *Patronal Politics*; Gel'man, *Authoritarian Russia*.

273   See Ketevan Bolkvadze, 'Hitting the Saturation Point: Unpacking the Politics of Bureaucratic Reforms in Hybrid Regimes', *Democratization*, 24, no.4 (2017), 751–769.

274   See Hellman, 'Winners Take All'; Hoffman, *Oligarchs*.

275   See Åslund, *Russia's Capitalist Revolution*.

had their reputations undermined. Their achievements were cast into doubt and could be reconsidered under changing political circumstances. Nevertheless, for as long as there was a need for economic and social changes in post-Soviet states, there remained a demand for the presence of technocratic reformers in governments, who provided the necessary supply of reforms. But the scope of this demand declined over time. According to some evaluations, of the technocratic reformers' proposals for the government program "Strategy-2010" (the "Gref Program"), adopted in Russia in 2000, less than 40% were fully or partially implemented. The similar "Strategy-2020" program, developed partially by the same reformers in the early 2010s and continuing the policy of its predecessor, was gravely curtailed, and less than 30% of its proposals were implemented.[276] In this light, the fate of new reform programs and strategies seems highly dubious.

This does not mean that the technocratic model of policy reforms in Russia is now exhausted. On the contrary, there seems to be almost no alternative to it. Professional expertise (often of high quality) remains an important resource for the post-Soviet technocracy, especially in important areas as tax policy[277] and the banking sector,[278] where the political leadership cannot implement effective policies without professionals. Essentially, political leaders have prioritized avoiding crises in governing their countries, and require "foolproof protection", especially in running the economy and finance. In turn, the involvement of technocrats in the ruling "winning coalition" has in many ways increased its stability, allowing political leaders to act on the principle of "divide and conquer" in relations with their junior partners,[279] and from time to time to reward the technocrats for their successful combination of loyalty and efficiency. Furthermore, the perceptions by

---

[276]  See *Analiz faktorov.*

[277]  See Hilary Appel, *Tax Politics in Eastern Europe: Globalization, Regional Integration, and the Democratic Compromise* (Ann Arbor, MI: University of Michigan Press, 2011).

[278]  See Johnson, *Priests of Prosperity.*

[279]  See Daron Acemoglu, Georgy Egorov, Konstantin Sonin, 'Coalition Formation in Non-Democracies', *Review of Economic Studies*, 75, no.4 (2008), 987–1009.

economic agents (including international business) of technocrats' involvement in decision-making as a barrier, albeit a weak one, against possible expropriation of their assets by rent-seekers connected with officialdom (the "piranha effect")[280] and arbitrary changes to the "rules of the game" are not groundless.

By conducting reforms or simply supporting the status quo, technocrats legitimize the politico-economic order, and thus bring benefit both to the political leadership and to themselves. Furthermore, political leaders interested in the success of their policies may easily blame technocrats for the failures of various changes, while positive effects of reforms can broaden opportunities for rent-seekers, increasing benefits for participants of "winning coalitions". Even the potential replacement of efficient "viziers" with loyal ones, if it takes place, does not mean a review of the technocratic model as such, but (in the worst case scenario) only a decline in the quality of policy-making. This is how the technocratic model works, and why its effects on both politics and policy-making are so contradictory in Russia and beyond.

## Technocracy at Work: Reforms in the Crossfire

It would seem that there is nothing worse for reformers than implementing policy changes within the framework of the political model of policy-making. They face hostility to reforms from public opinion, opposition parties in parliament, social movements in street protests, and interest groups behind the scenes of the political process. If one imagines a certain reform – such as the introduction of the Unified State Exam (*Edinyi Gosudarstvennyi Ekzamen*, EGE)[281] in Russia – being conducted by the government, politically accountable before a parliament chosen under free and fair elections, then the reform would probably come up against

---

[280]   See Stanislav Markus, *Property, Predation, and Protection: Piranha Capitalism in Russia and Ukraine* (Cambridge: Cambridge University Press, 2015).

[281]   See Andrey Starodubtsev, 'How Does the Government Implement Unpopular Reforms? Evidence from Education Policy in Russia', in *Authoritarian Modernization in Russia: Ideas, Institutions, and Policies,* Vladimir Gel'man (ed.) (Abingdon: Routledge, 2017), 148–165.

almost insurmountable obstacles. The coalition of angry parents, unhappy representatives of school bureaucracy, teachers and university rectors would not allow the education ministry to submit the project to be approved by parliament, and deputies from opposition parties would block this decision in voting, and subject it to review up until the next elections. At best, a reform could be postponed for a long time and implemented in a completely different way than the reformers planned, and at worst case it would be buried completely.

Under the technocratic model of policy-making, the EGE was introduced in Russia according to a different scenario. Facing resistance from opponents of the reform, the education ministry, on the one hand, coopted their representatives into creating a bombastic national doctrine of education, which had no practical significance at all. On the other hand, it secretly implemented the EGE under the guise of an "experiment" which encompassed increasingly broad circles of school graduates. When the "experiment" became so extensive that practically all graduates sat the EGE, legislative approval of the decision at the State Duma became inevitable. The provision of the reform which initially proposed to link the results of the EGE to the amount of state funding to pay a school graduate to study at university was sacrificed by the reformers. Its rejection was an element of the deal between officials and deputies in exchange for their support of the EGE, but was partially caused by the difficulties of introducing the complex model, and the reformers' own lack of interest in this innovation.[282]

At first glance, this outcome of policy change could be considered a "success story" for technocratic reformers – they were able to overcome resistance from society and interest groups using a series of bureaucratic tricks, and bring their plans to implementation, even if not to their full extent. Although the introduction of the EGE was accompanied by a number of instances of fraud caused by incentives from the subnational bureaucracy (the results of the EGE were part of the criteria for performance evalua-

---

[282]   See Gel'man, Starodubtsev, 'Opportunities and Constraints'.

tion of the regional chief executives' work), in the end it became irreversible. However, the side effects of introducing the EGE were problems of a different nature. The content of the EGE became emasculated over time: under pressure from interest groups, blind testing of school graduates was increasingly replaced by a mechanism of assessment that contained a considerable subjective component.[283] After the change of education minister in 2016, it was announced that Russian universities would receive the right to hold enrollment exams in addition to the results of the EGE, which in many ways made the original purpose of the exam irrelevant. As the legitimacy of the EGE itself came under question (a considerable section of the population assessed it negatively), the revision of the previous reform and the rejection of some of its elements did not meet with significant resistance. The question of what was worse – (1) a long preparation of the reform, including public discussions and cooperation with the main stakeholders, its gradual introduction and subsequent adoption or (2) a relatively quick introduction of the reform as a special operation, bypassing the key actors, and its subsequent revision and emasculation – clearly requires a different study in the comparative perspective. The Russian experience, however, provides great evidence for this type of analysis. In the context of post-Soviet Russia, a number of policy changes combined the worst features of options (1) and (2), including the pacification and cooptation of stakeholders on the one hand,[284] and the privatization of gains and socialization of losses on the other. The consequence of this approach may be turning the tactic of selective pacification of stakeholders into a strategy where the loyalty of veto players becomes the goal of policy reforms. The cost of achieving this goal will not only be increased influence by stakeholders, but the legitimacy of reforms themselves coming under question.

---

[283] See Alexander Chernykh, 'Sdachnyi roman: vo chto prevratilsya Edinyi gosu-darstvennyi ekzamen', *Kommersant-Vlast'*, 15 February 2016. http://www.kommersant.ru/doc/2911647 (access 3 January 2020).

[284] See Shleifer, Treisman, *Without a Map.*

The privatization of state enterprises in Russia in the 1990s is illustrative here. It involved coopting "red directors" in exchange for their loyalty to reforms, and taking the most attractive assets outside the general rules of privatization through loans-for-shares deals, which led to transfer of assets into the hands of oligarchs close to the government.[285] Although the reform was successful as a whole, and many privatized enterprises demonstrated better performance,[286] the legitimacy of privatization in Russia was seen as low compared to a number of other post-Communist countries, and many felt that its results should be reconsidered.[287] It is not surprising that the counter-reform implemented in the 2000s by the Russian state – creeping nationalization of privatized assets, and of a number of other private assets ("business capture")[288] – was seen as much more legitimate than privatization, undoing some of the results of the previous reform in the 1990s. According to assessments by the Federal Antimonopoly Service of Russia, over 70% of all assets were held by the Russian state by the end of 2016.[289]

While reform projects and plans are developed from time to time by independent experts, they usually continue to not be in demand by the top political leadership, which in practice remains the only group that can order reforms. These are proposed by both technocrats, sometimes motivated by ideational considerations, and by policy entrepreneurs from the mid-range bureaucracy, motivated by opportunities for career advancement. Implementation of these reform plans is conducted at different layers of the "pow-

---

[285]   See Freeland, *Sale of the Century*; Hoffman, *Oligarchs*.

[286]   See Sergey Guriev, Andrey Rachinsky, 'The Role of Oligarchs in Russian Capitalism', *Journal of Economic Perspectives*, 19, no.1 (2005); Adachi, *Building Big Business in Russia*; Treisman, 'Loans-for-Shares Revisited'.

[287]   See Denisova, Eller, Frye, Zhuravskaya, 'Who Wants to Revise Privatization?'

[288]   See Andrey Yakovlev, 'The Evolution of Business-State Interactions in Russia: From State Capture to Business Capture?' *Europe-Asia Studies*, 58, no.7 (2006), 1033–1056.

[289]   See Maria Leiva, 'FAS zayavila o kontrole gosudarstva nad 70% rossiiskoi ekonomiki', *rbc.ru*, 29 September 2016. http://www.rbc.ru/economics/29/09/2016/57ecd5429a794730e1479fac (access 3 January 2020).

er vertical", and the monopoly on policy evaluation belongs to the top political leadership. This does not mean that policy evaluation is inherently arbitrary – it usually takes into account the interests of the most important participants in the "winning coalition", as well as public opinion. But overall, in authoritarian regimes, the top political leadership has greater room to maneuver in pursuing policy changes than presidents and prime ministers in many democracies.

These conditions also appear to create opportunities to "protect" technocratic reformers from negative influence by interest groups and public opinion,[290] but they place virtually insurmountable obstacles before many policies. The most important obstacles are connected with the fact that under conditions of bad governance, policy reforms are faced with an irreplaceable informal institutional "core" by definition, and mostly affect only the "shell" of formal institutions. It is not surprising that many reform plans are of a partial, incomplete, and compromised nature even at the preparation and decision-making stage, to say nothing of implementation. In other words, the reforms are not only undermined after the fact, but they are also deliberately "spoiled" in advance by rent-seekers interested in the privatization of gains and the socialization of losses. Reformers often factor in such expectations, meaning they can affect initial plans for policy reforms and mechanisms for their implementation.

To some extent, "spoiling" reforms is a side effect of the design of executive power within the presidential-parliamentary model of government in Russia.[291] While the role of the parliament and political parties in decision-making is secondary in nature,[292] the popularly elected president personally appoints and dismisses the government as a whole and individual members of the cabinet (including the prime minister). Meanwhile, the government only

---

[290] See Geddes, *Politician's Dilemma*.

[291] See Matthew Shugart, John Carey, *Presidents and Assemblies: Constitutional Design and Electoral Dynamics* (Cambridge: Cambridge University Press, 1992).

[292] See Jennifer Gandhi, *Political Institutions under Dictatorship* (Cambridge: Cambridge University Press, 2008).

has minimal autonomy and performs technical (rather than political) functions, implementing political decisions taken by the president. This mechanism fully correlates with the practice of bad governance: the government only manages affairs of secondary importance. This organization of executive authority contributes to the fragmentation of government: it does not act as a collective decision-maker, but as a functional set of top officials hired by the president on an individual basis, and responsible for specific tasks in various fields of governance. The function of coordinating the government's work should theoretically be performed by the prime minister, who in turn relies on his numerous deputies in charge of various agencies, while the president is often directly in control of a number of agencies (primarily in law enforcement), bypassing the prime minister. As a result, decision-making at the top level of the "power vertical" is a complex and often ineffective process of negotiations between different agencies, and key officials have to spend considerable effort on internal bureaucratic battles, which greatly complicates conducting reforms[293] (and this is to say nothing of the problems of coordinating policy-making between levels of the "power vertical"). As the bureaucracy in general is interested in preserving the status quo, and not interested in change, many reform initiatives are ultimately drowned in the routine of negotiations.

It is not surprising that under these conditions, the most effective strategy of reformers may be to appeal directly to the president, who for various reasons may be personally interested in successful policy reforms in a certain area, and consider them a personal priority project. In a number of cases, support from the top political leadership can allow reformers to overcome various segments of the state machinery, and implement their plans using "manual control". A successful example of this kind is the Russian experience of tax reform in the early 2000s, which was implemented by the ministers of finance and economy and their team of ex-

---

[293] See Gilman, *No Precedent, No Plan.*

perts with the active support of the president.[294] But the other side of the coin is the very fact that the number of priorities for the president is inevitably limited, and so implementing one set of reforms may close the path to implementing others. Furthermore, the head of state's decisions regarding reform policy priorities and/or approaches to conducting them may prove incorrect. This threatens to remove modernization from the agenda altogether, or at least drastically reduce the incentives for reforms. Finally, in an authoritarian regime, leaders' political prospects depend on the outcome of reforms even more than in democracies. For electoral authoritarian regimes, the "window of opportunity" for policy reforms closes with the approach of the next elections, which may deal a heavy blow to the survival of the regime as a whole.[295] In "hegemonic" authoritarian regimes,[296] incentives for reforms drastically decrease as given political leaders continue to remain in power: over time, they become less inclined to implement major policy changes.

But the main problem for conducting policy reforms under conditions of post-Soviet bad governance lies in the fact that the informal institutional "core" not only blocks various changes to the formal "shell", but has a fundamental distorting effect on the nature and direction of policy changes. In practice, reforms always have significant redistributive consequences. In political terms, the process of their implementation involves building coalitions between their direct and potential beneficiaries, and the complex process of coordinating their interests with the positions of those who bear the expenses in the wake of reforms. This process often leads to a decline in quality of policy-making. Distributional coalitions of interest groups may render any positive changes impossi-

---

[294]   See Appel, *Tax Politics in Eastern Europe*; Gel'man, Starodubtsev, 'Opportunities and Constraints'.

[295]   See Hale, *Patronal Politics*.

[296]   See Marc Morje Howard, Philipp Roessler, 'Liberalizing Electoral Outcomes in Competitive Authoritarian Regimes', *American Journal of Political Science*, 50, no.2 (2006), 365–381.

ble.[297] In democracies, these phenomena can often contribute to populist policies (some Latin American countries in the 1980s, such as Peru, Mexico, or Brazil, can serve as prime examples); similar concerns were typical among Russian reformers in the 1990s.[298] However, under conditions of bad governance, distributional coalitions do not disappear: on the contrary, their influence only increases over time.[299] Although populist rhetoric of political leaders is also a feature of the post-Soviet politico-economic order, in reality, the major beneficiaries of its policies are "narrow" groups of rent-seekers. Essentially, the "power vertical" with all of its "zigzags" becomes a mechanism for coordinating the division of rents between participants of "winning coalitions", who transfer the expenses of reforms to other actors and/or society as a whole. Rent-seekers not only do not face political and institutional constraints in achieving their goals, but in fact the institutional "core" of the politico-economic order is designed to achieve these kinds of distributional effects. Therefore, the consequences of post-Soviet reforms are the privatization of gains and the socialization of losses. In a situation of economic growth, these trends are partially mitigated by the increasing flow of resources, but if the country faces protracted crises, conflicts of this kind come to the surface. These distributional effects may become aggravated and increase until a significant decline in the amount of rents causes open conflicts between rent-seekers.

The reforms of Russian Railways described above serve as a vivid illustration of this trend. The CEO of the company, as one of the key participants of the "winning coalition", successfully maximized benefits for RR: the company became a monopolist holding managed by Yakunin as his own fiefdom on behalf of the Russian state, with no possibility for external control of its activity. The

---

297   See Mancur Olson, *The Rise and Decline of Nations: Economic Growth, Stagflation, and Social Rigidities* (New Haven: Yale University Press, 1982).

298   See Vladimir Mau, *Ekonomicheskaya reforma skvoz' prizmu konstitutsii i politiki* (Moscow: Ad Marginem, 1999).

299   See Anton Shirickov, *Anatomiya bezdeistviya: politicheskie instituty i byudzhetnye konflikty v regionakh Rossii* (St. Petersburg: European University at St. Petersburg Press, 2010).

benefits of the reforms for RR top managers were clear: freed from the need to subsidize loss-making commuter transportation, the company set the tariffs for its services unilaterally, accepted payment from the regional authorities for leasing trains and infrastructure to its own affiliated companies, and blocked any opportunities for market competition. Costs were not so much placed on passengers (individual customers of monopolist services) as on budgets (i.e. taxpayers). While the regional budgets were capable of satisfying RR's appetite, this situation was seen as unacceptable only by opposition activists,[300] but did not draw broad public attention. Shifting the costs of commuter transportations to the federal budget resolved the issue for a while, but did not influence the causes that gave rise to it. Notably, as an alternative solution to the problem of commuter transportations, the management of RR offered regional administrations the chance to purchase the depot and wagons of commuter trains from the company – of course, at prices set by the RR top management.

Yet another important problem for policy reforms under the politico-economic order of bad governance is that the bureaucratic "power vertical", with all its defects, is the main, if not the only, tool for their implementation. Reformers and their patrons in the top political leadership believe by default that without systematic top-down supervision and control, the lower levels of the "power vertical" do not have incentives for carrying out even their routine duties. In the extreme case, this would mean that without threats of punishment and promises of rewards, no one will do anything at all: janitors will not clear snow, university lecturers will not teach students, and police will not pursue criminals. Given a lack of other mechanisms of accountability (elected local authorities, self-regulation, public opinion) these expectations are not groundless. In particular, it is difficult to imagine that the mid-level officials and/or directors of state enterprises and organizations will implement policy reforms in order to increase their own efficiency. Good intentions of providing effective management of policy

---

[300] See Navalny, 'Khroniki genotsida russkikh'; Navalny, 'Problema elektrichek'.

implementation often face a lack of incentives in various political and institutional contexts, and post-Soviet countries are no exception.[301] But the politico-economic order of bad governance proves most harmful of all for implementing policy reforms.

As only a small number of rent-seekers benefit from top-down policy reforms, reformers have problems with of compelling other actors, those who do not stand to benefit in any apparent way in the wake of policy changes, to participate in reforms. However, the very programs of reforms are based on the principles of "high modernism",[302] which evaluate the success of policy implementation at the lower levels of the "power vertical" using a great number of formal indicators. The use of formal, easily quantifiable indicators is partially a means to decrease high agency costs within the "power vertical". But the result of this approach is that regulation is tightened – essentially, almost every step on the path of reforms involves an increase in the density and scope of regulation in almost all aspects of performance at the lower levels of the "power vertical". In practice, this leads to a snowball effect in the growth of paperwork and related costs – police officers, teachers, doctors and other ordinary workers of various organizations are occupied with paperwork, instead of fulfilling their immediate professional duties. As a result, the policy goals are replaced by required indicators, achieving which at any cost becomes the most important, and essentially the only criterion for assessing their work.

In the Russian law enforcement system, the system of appraisal of police work on the basis of percentage of resolved crimes and other incident reports has provoked the aggravation of numerous pathologies, replacing the task of combating crime.[303] For supervisory agencies, a similar mechanism has stimulated the discovering those violations of the law which would be easy to

---

[301]   See Jeffrey Pressman, Aaron Wildavsky, *Implementation* (Berkeley, CA: University of California Press, 1973).

[302]   See James C. Scott, *Seeing Like a State: How Certain Schemes to Improve the Human Condition Have Failed* (New Haven: Yale University Press, 1998).

[303]   See Paneyakh, Titaev, Shklyaruk, *Traektoriya ugolovnogo dela.*

identify and prove. A more vivid example may be the practice of passing the above-mentioned unified state exam by graduates of secondary schools in various regions of Russia.[304] Soon after the EGE was introduced, the presidential administration began to calculate the percentage of school graduates failing the EGE as one of the criteria for assessing the performance of regional chief executives.[305] As a consequence, regional and local levels of the "power vertical", from heads of education departments to school teachers, were taught to minimize the number of pupils failing the EGE every year, and the exams were accompanied by numerous scandals. Finally, in 2014, the indicators for evaluation of performance of the regional chief executives were changed, and they were no longer threatened with punishment for their school graduates' poor EGE results. But since in this case the percentage of those who did not pass the exam might surge with no clear explanation, clearly showing that performance had worsened compared to the previous years, the requirements for graduates were drastically reduced by the organizers of the exam themselves: passing it at the minimum acceptable level now required much less knowledge.[306] It hardly bears saying that with this approach, reforms in many policy fields achieve partial and incomplete results at best, and at worst, end up as pointless busywork and construction of "Potemkin villages", and ultimately reduce them to nothing.

## "Borrowing" and "Cultivating" Institutions: Any Possibility of Success?

When observing the public statements of many experts who participated in developing policy reforms in Russia, it is difficult not to receive an ambiguous impression. On the one hand, the majori-

---

[304] See Starodubtsev, 'How Does the Government'.

[305] See Reuter, Robertson, 'Subnational Appointments in Authoritarian Regimes'.

[306] See Lev Lyubimov, 'Ne nuzhno vsem vydavat' attestaty: pochemu v Rossii pora menyat' podkhod k obucheniyu v shkolakh', *lenta.ru*, 19 February 2015 http://lenta.ru/articles/2015/02/19/school/ (access 3 January 2020).

ty of experts, even if they disagree about specific policy measures, agree about the harmful effect of the informal institutional "core" on policy outcomes. On the other hand, by serving as experts for the government, they are forced to refrain from criticizing the main obstacle to implementing their own proposals. This is why they attempt to conceal their unshakable skepticism behind euphemisms such as "unfavorable institutional environment", "low quality of institutions", or refer to the "legacy of the past", "cultural matrixes", or numerous "institutional traps". Being not only unable to solve the problem of the informal institutional "core", but even to publicly raise the issue of the need to change it (which would involve the replacement not only of ruling groups, but of the entire political regime as a whole), experts attempt to avoid this obstacle. The main approach they use is not dismantling existing informal institutions, but creating new formal institutions "from scratch" in parallel with them, built on completely different principles than the "core" of bad governance. It is thought that these new formal institutions may, through their effectiveness, gradually become rooted in society. If so, even if they are unable to replace the existing "core", they can at least overcome its pernicious effects, thus expanding room for subsequent consolidation of "inclusive" economic institutions,[307] and in the long term, a possible transition to "inclusive" political institutions.

This viewpoint, which corresponds to the logic of "narrow" modernization, in practice involves two complementary strategies for creating new formal institutions – "borrowing" and "cultivating".[308] "Borrowing" involves transferring to post-Soviet countries the norms, rules and mechanisms of state governance which have successfully proved themselves in the political and institutional contexts of other countries, and which may be adapted to solving tasks of economic growth and development (in parallel with the

---

[307] See Acemoglu, Robinson, *Why Nations Fail.*

[308] See Yaroslav Kuzminov, Vadim Radaev, Andrey Yakovlev, Evgeny Yasin, 'Instituty – ot zaimstvovaniya k vyrashchivaniyu: opyt rossiiskikh reform i vozmozhnosti kul'tivirovaniya institutsional'nykh izmenenii', *Voprosy ekonomiki*. no.5 (2005), 5–27.

existing informal "core"). "Cultivation" is based on the building of new norms, rules and mechanisms of governance in certain areas of governance under special experimental conditions, and later their spreading as general practices. Although in theory both of these strategies look reasonable, in practice, in the context of post-Soviet bad governance, they demonstrated critical defects, which cast doubt on their relevance.

"Borrowing" institutions, which involves the transfer of best practices of governance, faced a process that Andrey Zaostrovtsev called "bastardization".[309] Initially, he used this term to describe the deteriorating quality of products and services made in Russia by local subsidiaries of foreign firms. The causes of this phenomenon are the intentional non-observance of technological standards, and low quality of governance by domestic managers (who do not have incentives to maintain a high level of quality of products and services). The same can be said of the "bastardization" of borrowed institutions, as encouraged by those actors who transfer and subsequently adapt them on post-Soviet soil. To some extent this process is caused by the fact that transfer of borrowed institutions is an expensive undertaking which is often unaffordable for mid-developed countries such as Russia. For example, when the EGE was introduced in Russia, the same tests were used for assessing the knowledge of graduates as for holding competitions for enrolment in universities, while the United States, among other countries, uses two different types of tests for these purposes.[310] The choice in favor of the cheaper option gave rise to many problems with the utilization of this mechanism. However, the much more widespread causes of "bastardization" are driven by the interests of those who adopt and implement the borrowed institutions.[311] In the process of their adaptation to post-Soviet conditions, purposeful and deliberate "spoiling" is conducted by local

[309] See Andrey Zaostrovtsev, 'Zakon vseobshchei shitizatsii', *fontanka.ru*, 11 August 2009 http://www.fontanka.ru/2009/08/11/116/ (access 3 January 2020)
[310] See Starodubtsev, 'How Does the Government'.
[311] See North, *Institutions*, 16.

actors interested in maintaining and consolidating bad governance.

A typical example of "bastardization" of borrowed institutions in Russia is the experience of introducing an "open government" during the presidency of Dmitry Medvedev. The idea of
creating a new model of openness and transparency of state government, involving the active participation of citizens in preparing
policy decisions using modern information technologies, was actively promoted by Medvedev as part of his political rhetoric of
"virtual liberalization".[312] Some resources were allocated to "open
government", and a special minister in charge of these issues was
appointed to the government. This mechanism itself was borrowed from the practice of e-government, which has become
widespread in some Western countries, involving the use of the
Internet for providing state services and developing feedback
mechanisms between governments and society (in particular, civic
legislative initiatives etc.). In the initial context, e-government was
complementary to existing institutions of democratic governance –
free elections, parties, independent media, rule of law etc. In Russia, the "open government" was supposed to act as their substitute,[313] i.e. it was aimed at replacing political mechanisms which
were destroyed and/or undermined in the 2000s. From the viewpoint of governance, e-government served as an additional tool
helping a state apparatus built on modern "post-Weberian" principles. In Russia, introducing an "open government" was a substitute for the administrative reform that had all but failed in the
2000s[314] due to the efforts of Medvedev himself, who was in
charge of this policy area during his work in the presidential administration.[315] One should not be surprised that the project of

---

312   See Gel'man, *Authoritarian Russia*.

313   See Nikolay Petrov, Maria Lipman, Henry E. Hale, 'Three Dilemmas of Hybrid Regime Governance: Russia from Putin to Putin', *Post-Soviet Affairs*, 30,
no.1 (2014), 1–26.

314   See Mikhail Dmitriev, 'Administrativanaya reforma', in *Istoriya novoi Rossii:
ocherki, interv'yu*, Petr Filippov (ed.), vol.1 (St. Petersburg: Norma, 2011), 198–
216.

315   See Gel'man, Starodubtsev, 'Opportunities and Constraints'.

"open government" did not meet the expectations that had been placed on it, and in reality involved nothing more than the development of websites by state agencies, and giving citizens the opportunity to send complaints and suggestions to them using modern technology. But the citizens themselves were nothing more than petitioners in relation to officials, who could respond (or not respond) to their appeals at their own discretion. The final chord in the process of "bastardization" of "open government" was an incident, which took place in February 2015: a legislative initiative was submitted for inspection by the Foundation for Combatting Corruption, led by the opposition leader Alexey Navalny, which called for ratification of the UN anti-corruption convention which stipulated the responsibility of state officials for illegal self-enrichment. Approval of this initiative, supported through the Internet by the signatures of over 100,000 Russian citizens, was a necessary condition for subsequently submitting this draft for discussion in the parliament. But as this proposal did not suit the ruling groups, the "open government" removed the draft from further examination under a formalist pretext.[316] In this case, any openness, transparency of governance, and active participation by citizens were utterly out of the question.

Another approach to building new formal institutions, designed to restrict the sphere of influence of the informal "core", involves the purposeful "cultivation" of new norms, rules and mechanisms of governance and their subsequent export to most policy fields. This involves cultivating spontaneously emerging norms, rules and mechanisms, and intentionally designed experiments under the patronage of reformers and with the support of the top political leadership. As large-scale institutional changes are often rejected both by the "power vertical" and by public opinion, "cultivation" of new institutions makes it possible to prepare the soil for their subsequent full-scale introduction, and also to develop various details of given innovations in advance in order

---

[316] See Alexey Navalny, 'Dlya bor'by s korruptsiei v pravitel'stve net kvoruma', *navalny.com*, 9 February 2015 https://navalny.com/p/4117/ (access 3 January 2020).

to minimize the risk of their failure. In itself, "cultivation" of institutions would seem to be a reasonably justified technological solution, and sometimes it can help overcome resistance on the path of reforms. However, this approach is a double-edged sword for institutional reforms: a failure of new institutions (often caused by inefficient implementation) threatens to bury innovations entirely.

The causes of failure of "cultivation" of institutions are mostly political rather than technological in nature. In fact, projects for creating new institutions "from scratch", let alone diffusing them beyond narrow niches, require the allocation of considerable resources, encounter resistance from rent-seekers, and additionally require public legitimation. Patronage from the top political leadership is necessary, but clearly insufficient to accomplish these tasks. This is why for "cultivation" of certain innovations, a specific governance solution, which in Latin America has become known as "pockets of efficiency", is often used.[317] The idea is that a certain limited number of projects prioritized by the top political leadership are implemented beyond the standard hierarchy of the "power vertical", and general norms and rules of governance with their routines do not apply. Due to their relative autonomy and patronage, these organizations and groups have fewer agency costs compared to their "standard" equivalents, and can allow themselves a certain amount of room to maneuver by promising results in the future. These promises may ultimately be fulfilled, but there is also a chance that they will not.

The economic growth of the 2000s, accompanied by a mass inflow of rents, gave post-Soviet leaders the chance to patronize various pet projects, with the hope of turning them into successful "pockets of efficiency". But their future depends not only on the fate of political leaders themselves, but also on the possibility of providing resources to an extent sufficient for large-scale dissemination of policy innovations. In the Russian context, an example of this approach is the Skolkovo innovation center, which was an

---

[317] See Geddes, *Politician's Dilemma; The Politics of Public Sector Performance: Pockets of Effectiveness in Developing Countries*, Michael Roll (ed.), (London: Routledge, 2014).

important focus of Dmitry Medvedev's attention during his presidency, and received priority financing from the state and business, despite the skepticism of a number of key actors.[318] After the end of Medvedev's presidential term, the level of financing for Skolkovo dropped drastically, and its planned role as an engine of development for high technology and economic growth has been swiftly forgotten. It is difficult to say how a possible decline in financing may affect yet another Russian "pocket of efficiency" – the large-scale program to place five Russian universities in the international top-100 list. The contraction of a planning horizon invariably stimulates the "power vertical" to demand that "pockets of efficiency" should deliver advancements "here and now", to the detriment of long-term plans for dissemination of policy innovations.

The lifespan of "pockets of efficiency" proves to be short, because patronage from political leaders (like the leaders themselves) is not eternal, and the potential for their long-term large-scale financing is limited. After implementing the initial task and achieving the first of their original goals, "pockets of efficiency" have difficulty coping with routinization, which is often accompanied by a loss of their exclusive status. Also, in many ways "pockets of efficiency" are efficient because of their small scale. They sometimes begin to grow rapidly based on the expectations of their leadership: organizations that are too large in scale cannot be closed down or destroyed from the outside ("too big to fail"). But at the same time, there is a risk that they may mutate internally, becoming a new version of the informal "core" of bad governance, with all its negative effects. As a result, efforts to disseminate the cutting-edge experience of "pockets of efficiency" beyond its limits may result in the opposite effect: the logic of "institutional isomorphism"[319] tells us that the informal "core" has every chance

---

[318] See Katri Pynnöniemi, 'Science Fiction: President Medvedev's Campaign for Russia's "Technological Modernization"', *Demokratizatsiya: The Journal of Post-Soviet Democratization*, 22, no.4 (2014), 605–625.

[319] See Paul Di Maggio, Walter Powell, 'The "Iron Cage" Revisited: Institutional Isomorphism and Collective Rationality in Organizational Analysis', *American Sociological Review*, 48, no.2 (1983), 147–160.

of remaking "pockets of efficiency" in its own likeness. Rent seeking and the "power vertical" may become the attributes of the new institutions and mechanisms of governance to just as great an extent as the previous ones.

To conclude, although the parallel presence of an informal institutional "core" and new norms, rules and mechanisms of governance makes it possible to at least partially fulfill certain tasks of "narrow" modernization, this coexistence does not solve the fundamental problems and contradictions of reforms. Policy changes in many areas of socio-economic development have only a partial effect at best, often encountering insurmountable barriers and restrictions due to the politico-economic order of bad governance, resulting in eternal illusions of the possibility for successful development. Under conditions of economic growth, the inflow of resources would make it possible to compensate, at least partially, for the unavoidable defects of "narrow" modernization, but the end of this period casts the possibility of implementing the program of "narrow" modernization into doubt. Neither "borrowing" nor "cultivation" of institutions in themselves raise these chances very much. Rather, policy reforms may either be sacrificed to the current tasks of preservation of the regime and the politico-economic order, or after a certain time they may be launched again, but with the same contradictory consequences. In any case, the experience of a number of African nations[320] gives no grounds to expect that new norms, rules and mechanisms of governance will in themselves limit the pernicious influence of the existing politico-economic order: its principles may be reproduced in the long term.

Thus, technocratic reformers who operate within the framework of the (imperfect) technocratic model find themselves in the crossfire. If they attempt to satisfy strong interest groups, and make compromises, this approach may be ineffective: reforms simply will not achieve their goals.[321] Even if reformers are able to

---

[320] See Easterly, *The Tyranny of Experts*.

[321] See Anna Dekalchuk, 'Choosing between Bureaucracy and the Reformers: The Russian Pension Reform of 2001 as a Compromise Squared', in *Authoritarian*

outmaneuver their opponents in adopting and implementing the decisions they propose, and achieve their goals, these reforms will not be irreversible. They may soon be replaced by counter-reforms initiated by the same or other interest groups, which will return the situation to the former "point of departure" or even aggravate it. This is why technocratic reformers are often unable to limit themselves to policy: they are forced to seek support from politics – but less from political parties and/or public opinion than from political leaders. Indeed, political leaders may be interested in successful conduct of policy reforms, which strengthen their power and/or consolidate their public support. But support from political leaders does not mean unquestionable success for the policies which technocratic reformers advocate: even if this condition is necessary, it is not sufficient. A change in leadership primarily threatens policies implemented with its active support – as was the case with "modernization", which was announced as a priority in Russia during the presidency of Dmitry Medvedev. Furthermore, if the priorities of political leaders change, reforms may be shifted in a completely different direction than initially planned. The Russian authorities' shift from goals of economic development to geopolitics after the annexation of Crimea in 2014 left the Russian technocratic reformers on the sidelines as Putin so drastically changed priorities. But even if political leaders sincerely adhere to changes in policy and remain interested in reforms for a relatively lengthy period, the number of their priorities cannot be too great by definition. In supporting reforms in two or three key directions, they are forced to leave other policy areas on the periphery of their attention. The reverse side of the "success story" of the tax reform of the early 2000s in Russia, actively supported by Putin,[322] was the failure of a number of other changes.

The support of the political leader is vital to reformers in order to overcome or at least weaken resistance to changes from in-

---

*Modernization in Russia: Ideas, Institutions, and Policies*, Vladimir Gel'man (ed.) (Abingdon: Routledge, 2017): 166–182.

[322] See Appel, *Tax Politics in Eastern Europe*; Gel'man, Starodubtsev, 'Opportunities and Constraints'.

terest groups. Sometimes even this support may prove insufficient: strong and established interest groups are capable of redirecting changes in the direction they prefer; this was the case with the police reform in Russia in the early 2010s, which despite broad public discussion (or even because of it), was essentially a matter of changing labels and reshuffling personnel.[323] But even if political leaders overcome the resistance of interest groups, technocrats are rarely capable of taking control of at least the section of the bureaucracy on which the implementation of their proposed policy depends, which often requires cooperation and coordination by different agencies. It is no coincidence that while finance ministries and heads of central banks in a number of post-Soviet nations successfully pursued a macro-economic policy, targeted inflation and conducted tax reforms (with political support),[324] social policy reforms in Russia were stalled and/or followed the path of primitive redistribution of funds.[325] Among other reasons, the difference was connected with the fact that governance of state finances and policy reforms in this area ultimately depended on decisions taken by a small group of people, and their formal and informal coordination made it possible to pursue reasonable policies. But successful social policy required coordination not only of individuals, but of different segments of the bureaucracy at national and sub-national levels. To achieve this coordination given a low quality of bureaucracy was impossible not only for technocrats, but for political leaders as well.

To conclude, one might say that within the imperfect technocratic model, many policy changes may be implemented only partially even in the most favorable conditions, their essence is diminished in the process, and their nature and direction are distorted. For technocratic reformers, whose credibility depends on their

---

[323] See Brian Taylor, 'The Police Reform in Russia: Policy Process in a Hybrid Regime', *Post-Soviet Affairs*, 30, no.2–3 (2014), 226–255.

[324] See Johnson, *Priests of Prosperity*.

[325] See Wengle, Rasell, 'The Monetisation of L'goty'; Meri Kulmala, Markus Kainu, Jouko Nikula, Markku Kivinen, 'Paradoxes of Agency: Democracy and Welfare in Russia', *Demokratizatsiya: The Journal of Post-Soviet Democratization*, 22, no.4 (2014), 523–552.

reputation in the eyes of the politicians who hired them, there may be no second chance to conduct reforms. This factor stimulates technocrats to prioritize launching policy changes that can provide rapid positive effects within the "window of opportunity" when it opens for them, while reforms with a long-term perspective may either be postponed or accompanied by compromises that often emasculate their essence. By contrast, with the "success story" of tax reform of the early 2000s in Russia,[326] a vivid example is the failure of the pension reform, which was also begun in the same period.[327] Where tax reform provided positive results almost immediately after it was introduced, pension reform was initially proposed with a long-term process of implementation, and significant expenses for citizens and companies, with a transition to a fully funded system and an increase in the pension age. As technocratic reformers and the political leaders who initially supported them had no incentive to implement measures, which could provide a positive effect only decades later, and the bureaucracy, which acted as a veto player, was interested in maintaining the status quo, the result of numerous discussions was a "compromise squared". The partial and contradictory reform of 2002 not only did not solve the country's pension problems, but postponed these problems into the future, when conditions for implementing the necessary changes would be much less favorable (as indeed happened in Russia in 2018). However, in a more general sense, the preference for short-term priorities reflected the fact that the time horizon of political leaders rarely went beyond one electoral cycle.

In other words, the imperfect technocratic model of policy-making in Russia and beyond faces major constraints, some of which seem insurmountable. Technocratic reformers and their patrons among political leaders are forced to give priority to policy reforms focused on short-term results, to the detriment of long-term goals. The low quality of the bureaucracy and the influence of interest groups distort the goals and means of policy changes,

---

[326] See Appel, *Tax Politics in Eastern Europe*; Gel'man, Starodubtsev, 'Opportunities and Constraints'.

[327] See Dekalchuk, 'Choosing between Bureaucracy and the Reformers'.

and leave a negative imprint on their results. Even if the technocrats' various stratagems (quasi-experimenting, creating special conditions for reforms with patronage from political leaders, cooptation and compromises accompanied by rejection of certain measures etc.) are successful, their cost is high from the viewpoint of their public support and likelihood of irreversibility. However, having recognized all of these flaws and defects of the technocratic model of policy-making in Russia, the possible alternatives to it often appear even less desirable and realistic "here and now", and their expected results and consequences are far from obvious.

## Alternatives to Technocracy: from Bad to Worse?

What will happen in Russia if for whatever reason policy reforms are not conducted at all, in any fields, and all the activity of technocrats in government agencies is reduced simply to maintaining an acceptable status quo in areas that are vital for political leaders? In the short term, it is likely that neither the leaders themselves nor their fellow citizens will notice anything new. They may even breathe a sigh of relief, as they are weary of the numerous reforms (both successful and unsuccessful) over the last three decades. With this approach (which looks quite probable), the negative effects of the status-quo bias will only become noticeable after a certain time, which may also coincide with a change in political leaders.[328] But in any case, issues of policy reforms and mechanisms for their implementation will sooner or later become an important part of the agenda for Russia, making it a priority to find an alternative to the imperfect technocratic model.

According to a number of analysts, and reformers themselves, the technocratic model is in urgent need of a reconfiguration, which will enable it to overcome its defects and bypass obstacles on the path of policy implementation. Specifically, this concerns incentives for increasing the effectiveness of bureaucracy

---

[328] See Travin, *Prosuchestvuet li putinskaya sistema do 2042 goda?*

through competition between agents,[329] limiting the powers of various agencies and their functions, and in the extreme case, replacing "bad" political leaders, whose "winning coalitions" consist mainly of rent-seekers, with "good" leaders, who are eager for reform, and serve as "benevolent dictators".[330] The problem is that this does not only involve the personal qualities of political leaders. Their incentives are such[331] that they leave little potential to overcome the defects inherent in the imperfect technocratic model through improvement of the model itself. It would be foolish to deny that personnel reshuffles and changes in certain "rules of the game" in various policy areas may be useful for solving a number of problems. Without denying the importance of the role of personalities in the post-Soviet transformations, even a hypothetical recruitment of "best and brightest" reformers for key positions in the government will not in itself guarantee that the fundamental problems of the post-Soviet technocratic model of policy-making will be solved. On the contrary, attempts to improve this model amidst a low quality of bureaucracy and dominance of special interest groups of rent-seekers often leads to the opposite outcome. Amplifying the crushing weight of over-regulation, toughening its density and further increasing the considerable discretion of supervisory and law enforcement state agencies[332] may result in the creation of new obstacles to policy reforms.

But how likely is it that a hypothetical move from the imperfect technocratic model of policy-making to a political model will bring positive effects? At the very least, in the short-term prospect, this is more than dubious. The experience of such countries as Moldova and Ukraine does not show that cabinets of ministers that are politically accountable to parliaments, and formed as a re-

---

[329] See Andrey Yakovlev, 'Stimuly v sisteme gosudarstvennogo upravleniya i ekonomicheskii rost (opyt SSSR, Kitaya i Rossii', *Obshchestvennye nauki i sovremennost'*, no.2 (2015), 5–19.

[330] See Ronald Wintrobe, *The Political Economy of Dictatorship* (Cambridge: Cambridge University Press, 1998).

[331] See Olson, 'Dictatorship, Democracy, and Development'; Bueno de Mesquita, Smith, *The Dictator's Handbook*; Svolik, *The Politics of Authoritarian Rule*.

[332] See Paneyakh, Titaev, Shklyaruk, *Traektoriya ugolovnogo dela*.

sult of free and fair elections, cope with policy reforms better than technocratic governments – rather, the opposite is true. In these cases, one might talk of "state capture"[333] from the outside, i.e. by oligarchic interest groups competing with each other for rents. Policy reforms, even when they are declared a priority by political leaders, may be blocked for the foreseeable future. A succession of weak and corrupt governments torn by conflicts is hardly an attractive alternative to the technocratic model. The risk in this scenario is the exacerbation of principal-agent problems within the state apparatus[334] against a background of decentralized corruption (which is even more dangerous than the centralized kind).[335] The other risk of moving to a political model is that new governments may be "captured" by economic populists who are prepared to use the mandate of mass support to pursue an intentionally ineffective policy. Anti-authoritarian populism, which is often seen in Third World countries as a reaction to the numerous defects and failures of the technocratic model,[336] is capable of causing a turn from bad to worse from the viewpoint of policy-making, and temptations of this kind only increase with time.

However, in present-day Russia, neither a transition from the imperfect technocratic policy-making model to a perfect version nor a transition to a political model seem at all likely. The political regime[337] is in no danger of a full-scale crisis, and the incentives do not encourage changes, but preservation of the status quo. As such, a realistic alternative in Russia's case will not be attempts to improve the quality of policy-making, but adjustment of policies to meet the interests of rent-seekers, who will grow increasingly avaricious under conditions of economic stagnation. We can see an example of this in the lamentable story of the ideologist of post-Soviet technocracy who was quoted at the beginning of this chap-

---

[333] See Hellman, 'Winners Take All'.

[334] See Markus, *Property, Predation, and Protection*.

[335] See Andrei Shleifer, Robert Vishny, 'Corruption', *Quarterly Journal of Economics*, 108, no.3 (1993), 599–617.

[336] See Easterly, *The Tyranny of Experts*.

[337] See Gel'man, *Authoritarian Russia*.

ter. In November 2016, Alexei Ulyukaev, who at that point was the minister of economic development of Russia, was detained, fired, and later jailed with a long sentence on charges of bribery during the process of privatization of oil company Bashneft. According to the media, Ulyukaev, who had opposed the proposed scheme for the privatization of Bashneft, was probably not guilty of the crimes with which he had been charged.[338] But after Ulyukaev was removed from his position (and replaced by another technocrat, Maxim Oreshkin), this privatization was conducted according to an extremely non-transparent and suspect scheme.[339] The beneficiaries of the deal were the top management of state-owned company Rosneft, headed by Igor Sechin, a member of Putin's inner circle, one of the most voracious rent-seekers even in an environment saturated with rent-seeking by CEOs of Russian state and quasi-state companies.[340] Ulyukaev, who for many years had remained a supporter of other policy priorities, not only could not oppose Sechin in any way, but was practically sacrificed to the interests of rent-seekers with the consent of the political leaders. There was no question of any policy reforms in this case.

Ironically, Ulyukaev's own statement, made over two decades before these events, in many ways proved prophetic. Decision-makers connected to privatizing Bashneft stakes were, as in many other cases, "competent, and depended on knowledge and experience, and not on the results of voting". The problem was that the competence, knowledge and experience of rent-seekers were much more significant for decision-making than the competence, knowledge and experience of Ulyukaev himself and other Russian technocratic reformers. By striving to avoid the negative

---

[338]   See Ilya Zhegulev, Ivan Golunov, Evgeny Berg, Alexander Gorbachev, 'Chelovek Gaidara, sporivshii s Putinym', *meduza.io*, 15 November 2016. https://meduza.io/feature/2016/11/15/chelovek-gaydara-sporivshiy-s-putinym (access 3 January 2020).

[339]   See 'Spetsoperatsiya "privatizatsiya": kogo perekhitril Igor Sechin', *finanz.ru*, 15 December 2016 http://www.finanz.ru/novosti/aktsii/specoperaciya-privatizaciya-kogo-perekhitril-igor-sechin-1001608380 (access 3 January 2020).

[340]   See Vladimir Gel'man, 'The Vicious Circle of Post-Soviet Neopatrimonialism in Russia', *Post-Soviet Affairs*, 32, no.5 (2016), 455–473.

influence of politics on policy-making and ensure a "regime of non-intervention" by the political sphere on other spheres of public life, the technocratic reformers found themselves in a trap. Policy-making was subjected to numerous negative influences, while politics not only made it impossible to suppress these influences, but aggravated them further. The technocratic cure proved worse than the disease, and only the future will show whether Russia is capable of finding other, more effective means of treatment.

# Conclusion

The results of our analysis demonstrated that the "Russian path" is not some country-specific trajectory of development that completely differs from the paths of development of other European countries. There are no fundamentally insurmountable obstacles on this path. Russia launched its modernization approximately in the era of the Great Reforms of Alexander II (1860s–1870s), but lags greatly behind the majority of its Western neighbors, both in terms of building a market economy and in the formation of democracy. This lag is connected with two important factors. On the one hand, each nation's historical path has a certain distinct nature: it may accelerate or slow economic and political development. On the other hand, there are special interest groups, which strive to exploit difficulties in development for the sake of rent seeking; these play a major role in present-day Russia.

To understand how modern authoritarian Russia has emerged, we began our analysis by focusing on the issue of what Soviet people wanted in the final decades of the Soviet Union. By the beginning of perestroika, four sets of ideas competed within their minds, but their appeal was unequal. Hardly anyone stood for orthodox-Communist views by that point, despite the fact that, in principle, they should have dominated. In practice, these views could only be used to manipulate the perceptions of the most unenlightened groups of the Soviet people, but even the manipulators who exploited these ideas could not achieve noticeable success. Reformist-socialist views dominated in the minds of elite members belonging to the generation of Sixtiers; these views had the best conditions for realization during the perestroika period, when the Sixtiers came to power. But international experience demonstrated that on this ideological basis, it would be difficult to achieve positive results in economic reform. Market-capitalist views dominated primarily in the minds of those who belonged to the generation of Seventiers. These views had not coalesced when perestroika began because of the existing taboo, but their importance increased as the Seventiers grew up, gained experience and began to hold positions in the higher ranks of power and business. National-patriotic and imperialist views had a long period of gestation within the Soviet system, barely meeting with any resistance. By the time perestroika began, they were influential in elite circles. But Soviet and Russian society, concerned with its material problems, could not rely on an ideology in which the economy was practically ignored. This entire set of ideas was transformed drastically during perestroika (in the second half of the 1980s), and the reforms conducted during the presidency of Boris Yeltsin (the 1990s). These major changes took place under the influence of various interest groups that had formed in Russia.

It was utterly impossible to implement a reformist-socialist agenda, as it was based on the illusion that it was possible to build "socialism with a human face". When this socialism began to be built during the perestroika years, it emerged that no one was actually interested in it. Even groups, which could benefit from spontaneous privatization (enterprise directors, cooperative heads, bankers) were interested in private ownership and were not satisfied with half-hearted changes. Market-capitalist ideas triumphed, and it was on this basis that the Russian economy ultimately moved from recession to growth. The significance of these changes, launched by Yegor Gaidar, is great, but the outcomes of the reforms were imperfect. Dominant interest groups were opposed to financial stabilization, which the reformers attempted to achieve. As a result, Russia was gripped by high inflation, which was essentially a compromise that preserved the market economy and satisfied (at least temporarily) the interest groups that strove to lobby for financial support. It was possible to target inflation for a while via a pyramid of state debt, which collapsed in August 1998. Dominant interest groups not only affected financial policy, but also privatization, which benefited labor collectives and the directorate of enterprises. But in the end, those companies that were of interest to investors did receive capital and played an important role in the economic development of Russia in the 2000s.

An important aspect of our analysis was clarifying how Russia's historical path affected the formation of interest groups. They did not form arbitrarily. The dominance of opponents of financial stabilization in many ways determined the economic structure that present-day Russia inherited from the Soviet Union. The Soviet economy gave rise to key enterprises that were incapable of performing under market conditions without major support from the state. Primarily, these were enterprises of the MIC. The same was true of enterprises of a range of sectors of heavy industry (mining, metallurgy, machine-tool building, transportation, agricultural machine-building etc.), which the Soviet regime attempted to develop in volumes well beyond the actual needs of the economy. Employees of these enterprises found it difficult to enter the market, demanded financial support from the state, and accordingly enabled a transition from a reform-oriented to a pro-inflationist policy under pressure from various interest groups. However, the dominance of the MIC and heavy industry in the Soviet economy was not accidental, nor a result of voluntarism on the part of the party leadership. The militarization of the economic system in the Stalin era was in many ways a consequence of the Bolshevik foreign policy aimed at world revolution. Accordingly, this foreign policy was based on the Marxist theory of the proletarian revolution, according to which this revolution needed to be victorious in the entire world (or rather, in the majority of developed countries) at the same time. The Soviet leaders were convinced that they would have to battle international imperialism, which would strive to suppress the revolution in Russia, and so militarization of the economy and development of the MIC and heavy industry sectors was much more important than satisfying the need for food, clothing, housing, and the like.

Thus, Bolshevik ideology had a major impact on how the Soviet economy was organized. It was impossible to reform this economy painlessly. A large number of Russian citizens heavily lost out in the transition to the market economy in the short term, and demanded support from the state. The financial support they were given caused the high inflation of the first half of the 1990s, which in its turn slowed the move from economic recession to economic growth. In Russian society, this period has come to be seen as "the wild 1990s" (*likhie devyanostye*), i.e. the era of market reforms and democratic changes in Russia is widely regarded as an era of chaos and major hardships.

With the rejection of democracy, which was a consequence of the difficulties endured in the "wild 1990s", an authoritarian regime was established and consolidated in Russia in the 2000s. The consolidation of the autocracy was enabled by the economic success of the early 2000s and the rise in standards of living connected with the economic recovery. This success mainly resulted from the devaluation of the ruble, which took place after the 1998 crisis and helped to reduce imports and develop local production in Russia. Furthermore, high global oil and gas prices provided large revenues to the economy and increased tax returns, which also resulted in an increase in standards of living in various ways: pensions were raised, along with salaries of workers in the public sector and social welfare of certain groups. Russian society was happy with the rise in income and the increase in standards of living, and supported the current political regime despite the establishment of institutions, which blatantly hindered the further development of the country and were mainly aimed at supporting rent seeking by ruling groups and various interest groups connected with them.

From 2009 onwards, the Russian economy entered a state of stagnation. Economic growth over the past ten years has been slightly above 1% per year on average. Russia annually loses a large amount of capital because of capital flight abroad. More recently, the real incomes of the population have begun to fall. The cause of all this stems from institutions under which property rights are not protected, and private assets may be seized in any given moment. Business faces difficulties because criminals, who are often connected with the state and are just as often themselves members of certain state agencies (primarily law enforcement), are able to confiscate others' property. The law enforcement agencies do not truly protect business, and many entrepreneurs have been imprisoned when they did not surrender their assets to those who have the support of the regime. Despite the stagnation in the economy and a certain decrease in standards of living, Russian society continues to support the status-quo political regime – although, judging by public opinion surveys, this support is gradually decreasing. This support is driven by an entire set of illusions, which on the one hand fulfills Russian citizens' need to hope for the best, and on the other is a result of Russia's powerful system of state propaganda.

Mass support for the regime had fallen by 2013, but it increased again drastically after Russia annexed Crimea in March 2014. Russian society considered this move to be a restoration of justice, as many Russian citizens believe that for historical reasons, Crimea should not have belonged to Ukraine. Supporters of the annexation of Crimea feel proud of Russia as a result of this action. It is not surprising that a feeling of pride, whatever its source, helps many people to endure recent economic hardships and overcome the disappointment connected with Russia's shift from successful development to stagnation. The annexation of Crimea contributed to illusions that Russia is continuing to develop successfully, not in socio-economic terms, but in terms of foreign policy. Some even believe that the annexation of Crimea will help to restore the Soviet Union, and Russia's former status as a global superpower which competed with the United States in the military arena.

However, illusions of this kind are not permanent. They helped Vladimir Putin win the presidential election in 2018, but soon many Russian citizens felt new waves of disappointment, especially after Putin raised the retirement age soon after his re-election. It is difficult to say now whether the Kremlin will find new ways to produce new illusions, which will facilitate continuing public support for the regime and its policies. Nevertheless, sooner or later, these illusions will vanish, and Russia will continue the drive towards modernization that began back in the second half of the nineteenth century.

# SOVIET AND POST-SOVIET POLITICS AND SOCIETY

Edited by Dr. Andreas Umland | ISSN 1614-3515

121 *Mykhaylo Banakh* | Die Relevanz der Zivilgesellschaft bei den postkommunistischen Transformationsprozessen in mittel- und osteuropäischen Ländern. Das Beispiel der spät- und postsowjetischen Ukraine 1986-2009 | Mit einem Vorwort von Gerhard Simon | ISBN 978-3-8382-0499-4

122 *Michael Moser* | Language Policy and the Discourse on Languages in Ukraine under President Viktor Yanukovych (25 February 2010–28 October 2012) | ISBN 978-3-8382-0497-0 (Paperback edition) | ISBN 978-3-8382-0507-6 (Hardcover edition)

123 *Nicole Krome* | Russischer Netzwerkkapitalismus Restrukturierungsprozesse in der Russischen Föderation am Beispiel des Luftfahrtunternehmens „Aviastar" | Mit einem Vorwort von Petra Stykow | ISBN 978-3-8382-0534-2

124 *David R. Marples* | 'Our Glorious Past'. Lukashenka's Belarus and the Great Patriotic War | ISBN 978-3-8382-0574-8 (Paperback edition) | ISBN 978-3-8382-0675-2 (Hardcover edition)

125 *Ulf Walther* | Russlands „neuer Adel". Die Macht des Geheimdienstes von Gorbatschow bis Putin | Mit einem Vorwort von Hans-Georg Wieck | ISBN 978-3-8382-0584-7

126 *Simon Geissbühler (Hrsg.)* | Kiew – Revolution 3.0. Der Euromaidan 2013/14 und die Zukunftsperspektiven der Ukraine | ISBN 978-3-8382-0581-6 (Paperback edition) | ISBN 978-3-8382-0681-3 (Hardcover edition)

127 *Andrey Makarychev* | Russia and the EU in a Multipolar World. Discourses, Identities, Norms | With a foreword by Klaus Segbers | ISBN 978-3-8382-0629-5

128 *Roland Scharff* | Kasachstan als postsowjetischer Wohlfahrtsstaat. Die Transformation des sozialen Schutzsystems | Mit einem Vorwort von Joachim Ahrens | ISBN 978-3-8382-0622-6

129 *Katja Grupp* | Bild Lücke Deutschland. Kaliningrader Studierende sprechen über Deutschland | Mit einem Vorwort von Martin Schulz | ISBN 978-3-8382-0552-6

130 *Konstantin Sheiko, Stephen Brown* | History as Therapy. Alternative History and Nationalist Imaginings in Russia, 1991-2014 | ISBN 978-3-8382-0665-3

131 *Elisa Kriza* | Alexander Solzhenitsyn: Cold War Icon, Gulag Author, Russian Nationalist? A Study of the Western Reception of his Literary Writings, Historical Interpretations, and Political Ideas | With a foreword by Andrei Rogatchevski | ISBN 978-3-8382-0589-2 (Paperback edition) | ISBN 978-3-8382-0690-5 (Hardcover edition)

132 *Serghei Golunov* | The Elephant in the Room. Corruption and Cheating in Russian Universities | ISBN 978-3-8382-0570-0

133 *Manja Hussner, Rainer Arnold (Hgg.)* | Verfassungsgerichtsbarkeit in Zentralasien I. Sammlung von Verfassungstexten | ISBN 978-3-8382-0595-3

134 *Nikolay Mitrokhin* | Die „Russische Partei". Die Bewegung der russischen Nationalisten in der UdSSR 1953-1985 | Aus dem Russischen übertragen von einem Übersetzerteam unter der Leitung von Larisa Schippel | ISBN 978-3-8382-0024-8

135 *Manja Hussner, Rainer Arnold (Hgg.)* | Verfassungsgerichtsbarkeit in Zentralasien II. Sammlung von Verfassungstexten | ISBN 978-3-8382-0597-7

136 *Manfred Zeller* | Das sowjetische Fieber. Fußballfans im poststalinistischen Vielvölkerreich | Mit einem Vorwort von Nikolaus Katzer | ISBN 978-3-8382-0757-5

137 *Kristin Schreiter* | Stellung und Entwicklungspotential zivilgesellschaftlicher Gruppen in Russland. Menschenrechtsorganisationen im Vergleich | ISBN 978-3-8382-0673-8

138 *David R. Marples, Frederick V. Mills (Eds.)* | Ukraine's Euromaidan. Analyses of a Civil Revolution | ISBN 978-3-8382-0660-8

139 *Bernd Kappenberg* | Setting Signs for Europe. Why Diacritics Matter for European Integration | With a foreword by Peter Schlobinski | ISBN 978-3-8382-0663-9

140 *René Lenz* | Internationalisierung, Kooperation und Transfer. Externe bildungspolitische Akteure in der Russischen Föderation | Mit einem Vorwort von Frank Ettrich | ISBN 978-3-8382-0751-3

141 *Juri Plusnin, Yana Zausaeva, Natalia Zhidkevich, Artemy Pozanenko* | Wandering Workers. Mores, Behavior, Way of Life, and Political Status of Domestic Russian Labor Migrants | Translated by Julia Kazantseva | ISBN 978-3-8382-0653-0

142 *David J. Smith (Eds.)* | Latvia – A Work in Progress? 100 Years of State- and Nation-Building | ISBN 978-3-8382-0648-6

143 *Инна Чувычкина (ред.)* | Экспортные нефте- и газопроводы на постсоветском пространстве. Анализ трубопроводной политики в свете теории международных отношений | ISBN 978-3-8382-0822-0